THE AMERICAN PRESIDENCY

AN ANALYTICAL APPROACH

Presidential scholars increasingly turn to science to address the fundamental issues in the field, but undergraduates are rarely taught the skills to do the same. *The American Presidency* introduces students to new insights produced by the scientific study of the presidency and the scientific endeavor itself. After chapters on the scientific study of the presidency and background information on the presidency, the text discusses prominent theories of presidential power. Chapters on presidential elections, the president's relationship with other political actors (such as Congress and the Supreme Court), the president's roles in foreign policy and economic policy, and presidential greatness include guided research exercises that provide students with the opportunity to apply the scientific method to empirical questions with significant theoretical content. *The American Presidency* provides students with the opportunity to learn about the presidency and enables them to draw their own reasoned conclusions about the nature of presidential power.

Irwin L. Morris is Professor and Director of Graduate Studies at the University of Maryland, College Park. His research has appeared in a number of journals, including the *American Journal of Political Science*, *American Politics Research*, *Political Research Quarterly*, *Social Science Quarterly*, *Legislative Studies Quarterly*, *Public Choice*, and the *Journal of Macroeconomics*. Professor Morris's research spans the fields of American politics (from the presidency to public opinion to Southern politics), public policy (from monetary policy to immigration policy), and political economy.

D1452784

The American Presidency
An Analytical Approach

IRWIN L. MORRIS

University of Maryland, College Park

CAMBRIDGE UNIVERSITY PRESS
Cambridge, New York, Melbourne, Madrid, Cape Town, Singapore,
São Paulo, Delhi, Dubai, Tokyo, Mexico City

Cambridge University Press
32 Avenue of the Americas, New York, NY 10013-2473, USA

www.cambridge.org
Information on this title: www.cambridge.org/9780521720434

First published 2010

Printed in the United States of America

A catalog record for this publication is available from the British Library.

Library of Congress Cataloging in Publication data
Morris, Irwin L. (Irwin Lester), 1967–
    The American presidency : an analytical approach / Irwin L. Morris.
        p.   cm.
    ISBN 978-0-521-89592-7 (hardback) – ISBN 978-0-521-72043-4 (pbk)
    1. Presidents – United States.   I. Title.
    JK516.M67 2010
    352.230973–dc22   2010021651

ISBN 978-0-521-89592-7 Hardback
ISBN 978-0-521-72043-4 Paperback

For Chris, Maddie, and Cameron

Contents

☆ ☆ ☆

Introduction

Think for a second: without Googling the question, how many American presidents can you name? 25? 35? All of them? Now think about how many Chief Justices of the Supreme Court you can name? 5? 10? Current Chief Justice John Roberts is number 17. If you were asked to write down all of the Speakers of the House, could you? Could you name half of them? Could you name 5? Speaker Nancy Pelosi (D-CA) is the 60th Speaker. Except for scholars who study Congress and the Supreme Court (and even some among them) most Americans know the names of far more presidents than they do Chief Justices or Speakers of the House. We Americans simply have an attachment to our presidents wholly unlike our association with any other individual in government.

We have a national holiday for presidents. Their homes and birthplaces become museums – think of Washington's Mount Vernon or Andrew Jackson's home, the Hermitage – and we build monuments to their honor. It is no accident that all of the monuments on the Mall in Washington named for people are named for presidents. For particularly popular presidents, the efforts to honor and remember can become quite extensive – consider the wide array of books and events honoring the recent bicentennial of Lincoln's birth.

There is no question that Americans have a unique attachment to their presidents. But what is the source of this fascination? It is not a fascination that we share with the Founders. With no more than a handful of exceptions, the Founders plainly considered Congress the more important – and more powerful – branch of government. For example, in *Federalist Paper* #73, Alexander Hamilton, an admitted supporter of a strong executive, speaks of "The superior weight and influence of the legislative body in a free government, and the hazard to the Executive in a trial of strength with that body" (Hamilton et al. 2001). The perspective of legislative dominance is, even today, common among students of American institutions. As Whittington and Carpenter argue, "Many contemporary scholars ... adhere to a narrative of legislative dominance in American politics, in which Congress is the preeminent branch of government and controls policy outcomes" (2003: 495).

This fascination with presidents has led to a wide array of scholarship on presidents and the presidency. Journalists, biographers, historians, psychologists, and political scientists continue to build on a vast literature directly relating to individual presidents, the presidency, or the executive branch. The ever-growing body of work on Abraham Lincoln alone is striking. One of the most popular subjects for biographers, a recent Amazon search for books on Abraham Lincoln generated over 13,000 entries. For comparison, a search for books on Robert E. Lee – arguably the most famous nonpresident from the same time period – generated fewer than 2,000 entries. At least a dozen journals and periodicals are dedicated solely to Lincoln studies, including the *Journal of the Abraham Lincoln Association.*[1] And Lincoln is not the only president that has generated significant interest. An Amazon search for books on Ronald Reagan generated over 2,400 entries, and a similar search for George Washington generated a list of more than 15,000 entries.

But even with all of this research, there is still a great deal we do not know about the presidency. Consider the following open questions:

1. How much does campaigning influence the outcome of presidential elections? Political scientists have become adept at predicting presidential election outcomes before the beginning of the general election campaign. How is this possible if the electoral outcomes depend upon the particulars of the most expensive campaigns in the world?

2. Is Congress more productive – that is, does it pass more important legislation (including legislation the president supports) – during periods of divided government or during periods of united government? While no one argues that legislative productivity is *enhanced* during divided government, some scholars argue (relatively convincingly) that legislative productivity is unaffected by the partisan relationship between Congress and the president.

3. Can presidents manipulate the Supreme Court through "judicious" use of the appointment power? Supreme Court justices serve life

[1] For a list of these publications, see Abraham Lincoln Online at http://showcase. netins.net/web/creative/lincoln/resource/publish.htm. Last viewed on December 20, 2009.

terms, and only Washington had the opportunity to fill all of the seats on the Court.[2] Yet some scholars contend that Presidents George W. Bush's appointments to the Court will be his most significant political legacy. How is this possible given the separation of powers and the system of checks and balances established by the U.S. Constitution (and, ironically, historic Court rulings)?

4. Is the president in a position to control the executive branch or are the departments and agencies populated primarily by career civil servants beyond presidential influence?

5. Does the president exercise significantly more authority in the foreign policy arena than the domestic policy arena? If yes, why and how?

6. How much influence does the president have over the national economy? In desperate times, is the president actually in a position to make a difference and stem the tide of financial devastation?

7. What makes a president great?

And finally, what is the source of presidential power? Is power mainly determined by the president's own personal skills and characteristics? Is it a function of public opinion or partisan dynamics, or does power flow most directly from the institutional prerogatives provided by the Constitution? These broader theoretical questions that underlie many of those above also lack adequate answers.

Why do these important questions remain? An important reason for this is the general absence of a *scientific* orientation to the study of the presidency until very recently.[3] Only a small portion of research on the presidency was written from a scientific perspective. Nonscientific presidency research often focuses on one or two presidencies, and when scholars do generalize – draw conclusions about a whole group of presidents (if not all presidents) from information about only one or two – there is little effort to evaluate or justify these claims beyond a reexamination and reiteration of the details of the one or two presidencies on which the conclusions were originally based.

As the scientific perspective toward the study of the presidency began to take shape, it also became increasingly apparent that the more traditional research on the presidency – while valuable in its own

---

[2] Two other presidents came relatively close to appointing the entire Supreme Court. Franklin Roosevelt filled eight seats on the Court during more than a dozen years as president, and Andrew Jackson filled five seats on the Court at a time when the Court had only seven justices.

[3] I will define and describe a *scientific* orientation – what I will refer to as the *scientific study of the presidency* – in far more detail in the next Chapter. This book is, at least in part, an introduction to the scientific study of the presidency.

right – suffered from serious limitations. Traditional research on the presidency focused on historical analysis, legal analysis, or biography. There are hundreds of histories of the presidency (or some set of presidents), and a few are justifiably famous.[4] The best of these works provide interesting analyses of past presidents and presidential history; what this research does not provide are clear answers to questions related to the presidential *present*. Similarly, presidential research focusing on questions of constitutional law can help us understand the formal position of the president within the federal government, but this research does not address questions related to the practical exercise of presidential power, nor does it provide a compelling explanation for actual presidential behavior. And biographies – especially those on a single president – often tell us little about the broader institution of the presidency or, frankly, other presidents. Even Richard Neustadt, in *Presidential Power* – widely considered the most important book ever written on the American presidency – based his original conclusions about the nature of the presidency and presidential power on only three presidencies – one of which, Franklin Roosevelt's presidency, was arguably unique. As one of political science's most prominent methodologists concluded over two decades ago:

> The traditional presidency literature has accomplished an enormous amount in the area of history and contextual description. However, progress in a social science of the American presidency is far less advanced.
>
> ... We need to insist absolutely that any prediction or explanation must come with a fair assessment of its uncertainty. My example of research based on the president as the unit of analysis demonstrates just how uncertain some of our best work is likely to be even in the foreseeable future. (King 1993: 409)

What exactly is the scientific study of the presidency? A scientific study of the presidency is a *theoretically oriented, empirically disciplined* effort to answer the broadest and most significant questions about the presidency, the executive branch, and their role in the national government. "Theoretically oriented" refers to an effort to understand the general relationship between presidential behavior and the most important influences on presidential behavior. Scholars

---

[4] *The American Presidency: An Intellectual History* (McDonald 1995), the multivolume *A Ferocious Engine of Democracy* (Riccards various years), and Leonard White's volumes (1954 and 1959) on the first century of the administrative state are just a few examples.

with a theoretical orientation seek general answers to questions such as the following: What is the relationship between public approval and presidential power? How and when do presidents negotiate with members of Congress? Can the president control the federal bureaucracy? "Empirically disciplined" refers to a comprehensive effort to test our guesses about the answers to these questions with data – and a willingness to use the information from these tests to reject those guesses that are wrong.

With ever greater frequency, students of the presidency apply the tenets of social science to their research on the presidency. What brought about this change in the study of the presidency? Partly, it was the general development of political science. The growth and diffusion of new perspectives and new intellectual tools caught the attention of presidency scholars (and, at least as significantly, their students). The presidency also caught the attention of scientifically oriented scholars, scholars whose research in other areas of American politics – voting, legislative studies, or public policy – fostered an interest in one or more literatures related to the presidency.

In the time since King (1990) criticized the state of the research on the presidency, the scope and significance of scientific research on the presidency has grown dramatically.[5] Research published in *Presidential Studies Quarterly*, the primary subfield journal for the study of the presidency, has seen a significant increase in the number of articles incorporating complex statistical analysis, formal models of various aspects of presidential politics, or both. This increasing emphasis on statistical analysis and formal models is a manifestation of the growth of the scientific study of the presidency.

As we study these and other questions related to the presidency, I will demonstrate how a scientific approach to these specific issues opens the door to a more complete and integrated understanding of the politics of the presidency. This scientific approach presumes that our understanding of the general nature of presidential power should inform our specific understanding of the relationship between

---

[5] The earliest significant quantitative literature – meaning more than just an isolated article or two – focused on presidential elections. More specifically, it focused on (1) the economic determinants of aggregate electoral outcomes or (2) individual-level vote choice and turnout studies. In the first case, much of the research was conducted by economists rather than political scientists (see Nordhaus 1975, for example). The second literature was an important component of what is known as the "Michigan school," a name for psychologically oriented research initiated by political scientists at the University of Michigan. This research on presidential elections did not translate quickly into similarly scientific research on the institutional aspects of the presidency.

Congress and the president, or the Supreme Court and the president, or the cabinet-level departments and the president – even presidents' own relationships with their parties. So, for example, a theory of presidential power that focuses on institutions should inform our understanding of the relationship between the institutional structure of the appointment and confirmation process and the relationship between the ideological orientations of Supreme Court justices and the presidents who appointed them. Likewise, if presidential power depends upon the level of public support of the president, then that conjecture should provide insight into the roles the president plays in domestic and foreign policy and the extent to which they are distinctive. In short, useful theories of presidential power provide a wide range of insights about various aspects of presidential politics. A scientific orientation to presidential politics requires that we identify, examine, and evaluate these theoretical connections.

This sort of comprehensive, integrated understanding of presidential politics is quite rare. Just as it is in this text, Neustadt's seminal work on the American presidency, *Presidential Power* (1960), is often the starting point for chapters on presidential power. What is uncommon is an explicit connection between other aspects of the presidency and the original coverage of Neustadt's perspective. In this text, these connections will be explicit. Our discussion of the nature of presidential power will inform our analysis of other dimensions of presidential politics and policy making, from the president's relationship with Congress to the president's role in foreign policy making.

This effort to generate theoretically meaningful and empirically justifiable connections is not costless. It can complicate matters somewhat because these connections are often undeveloped, and we rarely conceive of various aspects of the presidency as a seamless extension of a clear, well established, and fully specified theory. What we actually have is a small number of incomplete theories of the source and use of presidential power. What I intend to elucidate is the way in which our current understanding of the various dimensions and aspects of the presidency depend upon one (or more) broad conceptualization of presidential power. The four primary theories of presidential power are the *bargaining*, *public opinion/bully pulpit*, *partisan*, and *institutionalist* perspectives. Though these perspectives are not perfectly distinct, their foci and emphases are sufficiently different (and different in ways that have important implications for the role the president can play in the American political system) that it is useful and appropriate to treat them as conceptually distinct. At the least, they emphasize distinct sources of presidential power.

The substance of our discussion of the American presidency will be focused on these theoretical perspectives toward presidential power. Evaluating the usefulness of each of these perspectives in helping us understand the various aspects and dimensions of the presidency will be our goal. We will discuss the ways in which the current understanding of the details of presidential politics depends upon these theories of presidential power, and then we will examine and evaluate the extent to which the enhancements or developments of these foundational theories – explicit or not – are consistent with our data (the empirical information we have about presidential politics).

This text describes and communicates not only the new insights produced by the scientific study of the presidency but also the character of the scientific endeavor itself. The nature of the scientific enterprise is inherently methodological, and the distinguishing characteristic of scientific research is its *method*. The definitive aspect of scientists – what makes them different – is what they do and how they do it, not what they study. Social scientists share this same methodological orientation. It is not enough to know what political scientists think about the presidency; it is also important to understand *why* political scientists think the way they do about the presidency. What evidence, for example, convinces scholars that the presidency is a more powerful office today than a century ago? And why do researchers accept the presence of a relationship between national economic conditions and the reelection prospects of an incumbent president? These are just the sorts of questions that concern political scientists who study the presidency, and so they are also the sorts of questions that will concern us.

This is not a conventional presidency textbook. The core of most presidency textbooks is *facts* and *explanations*. By facts, I mean all of the empirical details relating to the presidency, such as tables of historical election results or lists of regulatory agencies, sets of brief presidential biographies or charts of the system of checks and balances. This factual material is important, but it is not the primary focus of this text. Nor is the main focus of this text a detailed description of the various theories and concepts used to understand who becomes president, what powers the president may exercise, what presidents do, and the like. This sort of explanation is an important secondary focus, but it is not the primary focus. While more traditional textbooks tend to focus on information related to the presidency, this text focuses on the process used to generate knowledge. Ideally, this book will help you do the following:

1. Understand what you are learning in other texts (or readings).
2. Evaluate what you are learning from other texts (or readings).

3. Conduct your own evaluations of the answers and explanations given by others.
4. Evaluate the (often unjustified) claims about the presidency and presidential power made by others.
5. Develop your own answers to the question related to the presidency that you consider most important.

Each chapter will have an explicit theoretical focal point. The study of the presidency has produced a vast and interesting literature. Each chapter topic – for example. presidential elections or the president's role in foreign policy making – is the focus of a substantial body of scholarship. Whole books have been written and are still being written on each of these topics. To avoid becoming lost in these massive literatures, I focus on one or two particular aspects of each literature – a recent theoretical innovation, an important empirical controversy, or both – in each of these topic areas. By focusing the discussion and analysis, it will be possible to examine the topic in sufficient depth while still remaining within the space constraints of a single, conventionally sized book chapter. By focusing on a "prominent" or significant aspect of each literature, I will be able to discuss the broader literatures because of the important connections between the primary focus and other aspects of the broader literature.

For example, the focal point of the chapter on the president's role in foreign and defense policy making is Aaron Wildavsky's decades-old "Two Presidencies" (1966) thesis. The foundation of Wildavsky's contention that presidents effectively exercise significantly more power in foreign policy making than domestic policy making include institutional, organizational, and situational assumptions that may or may not have been true when he was writing (in the early to mid-1960s) and may or may not be true today. Examining the extent to which the nature of the institutional, organizational, and situational context of foreign and defense policy making has changed since the 1960s provides us with an opportunity to examine the validity of the most recent claims regarding an increasingly *imperial* presidency in foreign policy making (and, some argue, in domestic policy making as well). In effect, Wildavsky's decades-old argument provides the launching pad for a wide-ranging examination of the nature of presidential power in the realm of foreign policy making.

Each of the chapters following the introductory section has this sort of analytical "launching pad." In the chapter on presidential elections, we look at campaign effects. Do they exist? If yes, are they significant? The chapter on the relationship between Congress and the president begins with a discussion of the impact of divided government, and the chapter on the president and the executive branch examines the way in which multi-institutional models provide us with a means for evaluating if and when the presidential control, congressional dominance, and independent agency models are appropriate. In the last chapter, the chapter on presidential greatness, we have an empirical springboard – the results from a collection of various presidential "greatness" surveys over more than half a century. These chapter-specific focal points provide (1) an *entrée* to the depth and breadth of the modern literature in each of these topic areas and (2) a fulcrum for the subsequent evaluation of the theoretical and empirical foundations of that literature. At the very least, these focal points give us a place to start – ideally, an especially useful place to start in each and every case.

Each chapter following the introductory chapters is also designed to provide an understanding of the logic of the scientific study of the presidency. As we will discuss below, a scientific orientation is inherently *methodological*. Science is much more a process and logic of inquiry than it is a body of knowledge. In this case, we will not only discuss what scholars think about various aspects of presidential politics; we will also discuss why they think the way they do. We will discuss the relationship between theory and evidence, the limitations of both, and what is to be done in those all-too-common situations in which our theoretical expectations are not borne out by the data used to test them.

Finally, each chapter following the introductory chapters includes a short set of *guided research exercises*. In some chapters, the exercises focus on the analysis of a large number of cases. In other chapters, the analysis focuses on a more detailed examination of a significantly smaller number of specific cases. Both types of exercise provide you with the opportunity to "get your hands dirty" by (1) collecting data relevant to the topic of the chapter, (2) analyzing that data, and (3) drawing specific inferences from that analysis.

Each set of guided research exercises includes *bivariate* exercises and *multivariate* exercises. Bivariate exercises involve the analysis of the relationship between two variables (one independent variable and one dependent variable) at a time. Multivariate exercises involve the analysis of the relationship between a dependent variable and multiple independent variables simultaneously. In most cases, the multivariate analyses include no more than two independent variables.

Both bivariate and multivariate sections include *descriptive* exercises and *inferential* exercises. The descriptive exercises will provide information about relationships in the sample of data that is analyzed. So, if I want to evaluate the contention that there is a positive relationship between income growth and the percentage of the vote received by the incumbent president (or the candidate from the incumbent president's party) during the 1932–2008 time period, I can examine a scatter plot, calculate a correlation coefficient, or calculate a regression coefficient. If, however, I want to make a more general claim about a relationship between income growth and the percentage of the vote received by the incumbent president (or the candidate from the incumbent president's party), then I would need to consider my data (say, from the time period 1932–2008) as a sample of the larger population of past, present, and future economic circumstances and presidential elections, and to provide a specific test of the likelihood that my result for the 1932–2008 time period occurred by chance. *Inferential statistics* provide these types of tests. The descriptive exercises may be done with little preliminary instruction (and certainly would not require a prior class in statistics), but the same cannot be said for the inferential analyses.[6] By providing both sets of exercises, all readers have a chance to participate in scientific examinations of various aspects of the presidency at a level of statistical sophistication that is appropriate for their own prior training.[7]

The bivariate descriptive analyses will focus on the relationship between one independent and one dependent variable at a time. There will be no need to estimate any inferential statistics to complete the descriptive component of the bivariate analyses exercises. The inferential bivariate analyses will involve the calculation of one or more inferential statistic. These statistics might include a difference of means test or a bivariate regression.

The multivariate descriptive analyses will focus on the relationship between an independent variable and a dependent variable while *controlling* for an additional independent variable. So, in the case of

---

[6] All of the bivariate exercises may be completed with pencil and paper, but it will be much easier (and more efficient) in most cases to use spreadsheet software (such as Excel) or statistical software (such as SPSS or STATA). The multivariate exercises require, at least practically speaking, familiarity with a statistical software package. Students who have completed a standard undergraduate research methods course in political science should have no trouble with the technical demands of any of the multivariate exercises. The technical demands of the descriptive bivariate exercises require no statistical background.

[7] *The Fundamentals of Political Science Research* (Kellstedt and Whitten 2008) is an excellent methodological reference book for the guided research exercises.

presidential elections, we might be interested in determining whether or not the relationship between economic conditions and the vote percentage of the incumbent (or incumbent party's candidate) varies by party. What if Republican presidents are punished for a bad economy in a way that Democratic presidents are not? For the multivariate descriptive exercises, we might divide elections by the party of the incumbent president, plot the data points for each set of elections (with the value of a particular economic variable – such as inflation, GDP growth, or unemployment – on the y-axis and percentage of the overall two-party vote on the x-axis), and then we could visually compare the scatter plots. We might even calculate regression lines for each scatter plot and compare the lines (or, more precisely, the slopes). The inferential exercises in the multivariate section will tend to involve the estimation of one or more relatively simply regression model with a dependent variable and multiple (though rarely more than 2 or 3) independent variables. The same statistics calculated for the inferential analyses in the bivariate section would be calculated for the inferential analyses in the multivariate section.

The exercise descriptions below – and the assignment descriptions in the subsequent chapters – include the following:

1. one or more research questions or hypotheses
2. a list of potential data and data sources to be used for the research
3. a description of the types of analyses to be conducted

Note that these research assignments also allow for some flexibility in the data used to conduct the analyses, the particular tests used to evaluate the research hypotheses or answer the research questions, and in the specific hypotheses and research questions themselves. Among other things, these assignments are meant to foster an appreciation for and provide hands-on experience with scientific research on the presidency in particular and social scientific research more generally. These assignments are starting points; the ending points depend only on your own interest in and enthusiasm for the topic.

In Chapter 2, I introduce the idea of a scientific orientation to the study of the presidency. This idea will not be foreign to many scholars who study the presidency, but it is an unusual focal point for a textbook. Arguably, and this is especially true for the study of the presidency, what we do as scholars is divorced from how we present our subject matter as teachers. Though we are comfortable thinking of our own work as contributing to a rigorous, scientifically oriented analysis of the presidency, we do not – at least I have not until recently – explain to our students what that means, how to understand the pursuit of a rigorous analysis of the presidency, and, most importantly, how to contribute to this endeavor. In Chapter 2, I briefly explain the theoretical underpinnings of a scientific orientation to the study of the presidency. I discuss important concepts such as falsification, hypotheses, operationalization, dependent variables, independent variables, theory, and research programs (a term that may be new to many of you). It is important to emphasize from the very beginning that this is not the standard positivist approach to science or scientific inquiry. We will not talk in terms of "disproving" in a general or universal manner any of the theoretical perspectives briefly referenced above. What we will do is discuss the ways in which the empirical applicability of each of the theories referenced above may be evaluated and, over time, how we should think about scenarios in which one (or two) of these primary theories are shown to have increasingly broad applicability to real political situations and dynamics, while the others appear (perhaps) increasingly limited (and restricted to particular phenomena or individuals). I also identify exemplary research within the realm of a science of the presidency and I explain why it is important for us to develop a rigorous, analytical understanding of the presidency.

Chapter 3 is a discussion of the "nuts and bolts" of the founding and development of the presidency. The first section of the chapter is a historical description of the Founders' experiences with executive power (or its absence) and the variability of the implications they drew from those experiences. The following section provides a description of the institutional structure of the presidency and the development of the office since the Founding. Subsequent sections provide the necessary background information for each of the following chapters.

In the next chapter, we examine the four primary theoretical perspectives toward the presidency and the sources of presidential power. In the presidency literature, there are four primary sources of presidential power: skill at bargaining and negotiation, public opinion, formal institutions, and party alliances. In each of the four sections of this chapter, I discuss a prominent example of a theory focused on one of these sources of presidential power. These theories certainly do not exhaust the perspectives on presidential power, but they provide useful examples of the way in which scholars think about each of the primary sources of presidential power. Included in each of these sections is a discussion of the character of the power that we are trying to understand. So, for example, we see that Neustadt's "bargaining" theory of presidential power presumes that the goal of the exercise of power is policy – most frequently manifest as the enactment of new laws, the development of new programs, and the creation of new agencies. This is power exercised to create.

The institutionalist orientation of the proponents of the "imperial presidency" perspective takes a different view of power. At the extreme, the goal of power, at least from the imperial presidency perspective, would be *control*. In this case, power might manifest, as it did during the Nixon administration, in illegal efforts to silence critics, defeat political opponents, and so on. Using some measure of legislative productivity in the context of the imperial presidency might then grossly underestimate the actual power wielded by the president. These distinctions between the various conceptualizations of power – nearly always implicit – are a recurring theme throughout these chapters.

The first section of Chapter 4 identifies and discusses the sources of presidential power. Beginning with the concept of "self-enforcing orders" – made famous by Neustadt in his seminal work *Presidential Power* – I note how rarely presidents are in a position to give these orders, and when they do give these sorts of orders, it is often as a last resort. Prior to Neustadt's (1960) seminal work on presidential power, scholars tended to focus on institutional capacity (the appointment power, treaty-making power, war powers, and so on) when examining presidential power. Neustadt's contention that presidential power was based on the president's ability to *bargain* altered the study of the executive branch permanently.

In the next section, I consider the most prominent *direct* response to Neustadt's theory, Samuel Kernell's conceptualization of "going public." Kernell argues that as political times changed during the mid- to late 1960s and early 1970s, the political world so accurately described by Neustadt ceased to exist, and the changes wrought by various social and political forces precluded the continued use of "bargaining" to achieve presidential objectives. Instead, presidents were forced to build legislative coalitions for their pet projects through direct appeals to public opinion, or "going public." Recent work suggests that the effectiveness of presidential bargaining and efforts to "go public" must be appropriately contextualized, and I discuss this work as well.

The third section of Chapter 4 is an introduction and discussion of the *institutionalist* perspective toward presidential power and authority. A widely shared understanding in the pre–Neustadt era, it was resurrected in the post–Watergate and post–Vietnam 1970s and has recently been reinvigorated in the post–9/11 era. Proponents of the institutionalist perspective attribute presidential power to the institutional resources associated with the office – the staff and bureaucracy, war powers granted by the constitution, and so on. For institutionalists, the president is often viewed as the dominant player in the national political game, and the extent of presidential dominance, as well as the range of presidential power and authority, is viewed as having grown considerably over the course of American history. Recent research has reinvigorated the institutionalist perspective (particularly with regard to the veto power and the president's use of executive orders, executive agreements, and signing statements), and I discuss these new insights as well.

Finally, the last section in this chapter focuses on a partisan theory of presidential power and authority. In *The Politics Presidents Make*, Stephen Skowronek argues that presidential power and authority have tended to ebb and flow in a more or less predictable cycle since the start of Thomas Jefferson's administration. This cycle results from the birth, maturation, and death of partisan regimes, and a president's power is a function of his (historical) attachment to the dominant partisan regime (Is he a member or not?) and at what point in the cycle he becomes president. (Is his administration during the creation and growth of the regime or does his administration begin as the regime is disintegrating?) Skowronek argues that the nature of this cycle has changed somewhat over the course of American history, and we will consider these alterations as well. I conclude this chapter (and section) with a discussion of the extent to which various formal institutional powers, bargaining opportunities, the "bully pulpit" (for "going public"), and partisan allies provide the president with strategic advantages that vary across political contexts. To understand presidential power we must take these variations into account.

Chapter 5 focuses on the presidential selection process. Moving from the early nomination process through the November election, the focus of this chapter is the strategic forces that push candidates to campaign in certain areas and in certain ways and the increasing importance of financial resources for electoral success at the primary and – increasingly – at the general election level. The selection process has changed dramatically since the 1950s, let alone the beginning of the modern presidency in the 1930s, and these changes have implications for the types of candidates that are likely to win sufficient support to be president. I discuss the caucus and primary season, the theoretical conflict between pocketbook voting and sociotropic voting, general election predictions, and problems with the Electoral College. The specific theoretical focus of this chapter is the controversy over the effect of general election campaigns. Are presidential elections predictable? And if we can predict outcomes before the beginning of the campaign, how can campaigns matter? That our selection process is not ideal is hardly news; that research increasingly suggests that it would not be easy to improve is something of a surprise. We will also discuss the 2008 election in some detail, evaluate the extent to which this new "case" met (or did not meet) our theoretical expectations, and discuss why (or why not) that is the case. Finally, we will transition to the chapter on various theories of presidential power by highlighting two important (and related) insights from the study of presidential elections and their "meaning" (and subsequent significance for the exercise of presidential power).

In Chapter 6, I review and elaborate on the nature of the interinstitutional relationship between Congress and the president. The jumping-off point for the discussion of the relationship between Congress and the president in this chapter is a short discussion of David Mayhew's relatively recent work on divided government and its impact on legislative policy making, and the fact that he found no relationship between divided government and the prevalence of landmark legislation. This result – which is not uncontroversial – suggests that presidents may achieve their legislative policy objectives even in relatively unpropitious times. Focusing on the two ends of the legislative policymaking process – agenda setting and vetoes – I describe the ways in which presidents relate to members of Congress and participate, either directly or indirectly, in the legislative policy-making process.

In the next chapter, the examination of the relationship between the president and the Supreme Court focuses on the appointment power. Is the appointment power all it is cracked up to be? This chapter begins with two brief case studies, the appointment of Earl Warren and the failed appointment of Robert Bork. In both cases, presidential objectives were thwarted. Such is the nature of the appointments process, particularly when successful appointees have life tenures. The focus of this chapter will be an examination of the president's ability to mold Supreme Court decision making through the appointment power. The appointment process has been something of a cottage industry for Court scholars with a rational choice orientation for nearly two decades, and this research has produced several novel and important insights. In particular, it is increasingly clear that the ability of the president to influence the Court's policy-making behavior is not only a function of the types of appointees that the Senate will confirm, but also a function of the types of appointees that are being replaced. The recent spate of (and controversy over) Court appointments provides an ideal context in which to highlight and discuss these new insights.

Chapter 8 focuses on the relationship between the president and the other individuals and organizations in the executive branch. I begin with a brief discussion of the tremendous growth in the executive branch since the early days of the Republic (focusing on growth since the 1930s) and the transformation from a spoils-based partisan bureaucracy to a civil service bureaucracy. Though the president is the titular head of the executive branch, his or her capacity to direct its activities varies across time and across agencies. In this chapter I describe the various types of federal agencies and highlight the distinctive character of the president's relationship to cabinet-level departments and independent regulatory agencies. Basing my discussion on insights from a recent wave of rational choice models of bureaucratic policy making, I examine the tools presidents use to influence bureaucratic policy making and the contextual dynamics that tend to enhance or mitigate the effectiveness of these institutional prerogatives.

Chapter 9 is an analysis of the president's role(s) in the arena of foreign policy making. I begin with a discussion of Wildavsky's (1966) controversial "two presidencies" thesis. According to Wildavsky, the distinctive characters of domestic and foreign policy making – including differences in formal presidential powers across the policy areas – provide for the more effective exercise of presidential authority in foreign policy making than in domestic policy making. I track research on the "two presidencies" – focusing primarily on the contextual dynamics that foster and mitigate distinctions in presidential authority in the foreign and domestic policy realms, and I highlight the recent renewal of interest in the *institutional* advantages that may provide a firm foundation for the continuation of the two presidencies.

The president's role in the economic policy arena is the subject of Chapter 10. This chapter outlines the various types of economic policy making. Chapter 10 includes a detailed description of fiscal policy and monetary policy and a discussion of the ways in which presidents might manipulate economic policy to boost their electoral fortunes or to provide macroeconomic benefits to their fellow partisans.

In the final chapter, I tackle the topic of describing, estimating, and predicting presidential greatness. It begins with the results of a recent survey of historians on presidential "greatness." In discussing presidential greatness and disagreements over relative "greatness," there is a natural (perhaps unavoidable) focus on the individual (and individual skills, aptitudes, and talents). In this chapter, I examine recent research on the determination of presidential greatness and highlight an important gap in the literature: the absence of performance-based measures in explanatory models of presidential greatness. The final set of guided research exercises provides you with the opportunity to examine the impact of macroeconomic policy success and foreign policy (military) success on evaluations (those of average citizens and professional historians) of presidential greatness and draw your own conclusions about the long-term relationship between performance in office and presidential greatness.

2

☆ ☆ ☆

Science and the Study of the Presidency

WHAT DO SCIENTISTS DO?

What images come to mind when you hear the word "scientist"? A person in a lab coat surrounded by chemicals and hi-tech machinery? A disheveled physicist standing at a whiteboard filled with equations? What about the scientists on CSI? My father is a chemistry professor, and I understand those reactions. During college, I satisfied physical and life science requirements with courses entitled (literally) "Chemistry for Non-Science Majors" and "Biology for Non-Science Majors." I saw no irony in the fact that I, a political science major, had found my way into these courses. But scientists do much more than study chemistry or physics or biology. They study markets (economists), groups (sociologists), and politics (political scientists). The practice of science does not depend upon a particular subject matter. Science is a process; it is a *method*. The definitive characteristic of a scientist is not what they study but what they do. So what do scientists do?

Scientists build theories and test theories so that they can describe, explain, and predict. These activities are clearly interrelated, but understanding their distinctiveness is important. *Description* is the process of determining – that is, measuring – the relevant properties of the object of inquiry. For a chemist, this might include the mass, color, and boiling point of a particular substance. For an astronomer, it might be the size of a planet and the planet's distance from a particular star. For a political scientist interested in the presidency, it might be the number of Electoral votes received by a presidential candidate or the number of vetoes cast by a particular president. Both explanation and prediction depend upon accurate description.

Explanation is the process of identifying the underlying causes of a particular phenomenon. Explanation answers the "why" question. Why do some presidential candidates win and some lose? Why are some presidents more popular than others? Why do some presidents win re-election and others do not? Why are some presidents considered "great" and others are not? Explaining all of these political phenomena is difficult enough, but political scientists hope to be able to make predictions as well, and making justifiable predictions is no easy task.

Prediction is the process of applying existing knowledge to the estimation of future behaviors or outcomes. Basically, we make inferences – based on our descriptions and explanations – about the future. Effective political prognostication is a tall order – far more difficult than describing or explaining politics. Still, if our descriptions and explanations are accurate, we should be able to make meaningful and relatively accurate predictions. If we cannot make accurate predictions, then how do we use our knowledge of presidential politics to choose better presidents, make choices about the proper relationship between the president and other federal institutions, or decide whether or not to support presidential policy initiatives? We should not overlook the practical usefulness of accurate predictions; if we can make good predictions, we can improve our government.

What sort of information do scientists use to describe, explain, and predict? They use *concepts* and *theories*. A concept is an idea that captures the inherent traits of a set of items or objects. Now, for political scientists, a list of these items or objects would include interest groups, citizens, bureaucracies, and governments. Scientists create concepts to help them group together those things that are alike and distinguish between those things that are different. Concepts are never set in stone, and concepts can be more or less useful.

What tends to interest scientists is variation among concepts – how does the change in the magnitude or character of one concept alter the magnitude or character of another, potentially related, concept? To describe, explain, and predict, scientists use a language focused on *variables*. Objects of study always exhibit some variation. Scientists find constants relatively uninteresting. When we are trying to explain the variation of a concept, we refer to that concept as the *dependent variable*. We refer to concepts that may cause changes in the dependent variable as *independent variables*. Theories are (1) collections of interrelated statements of relationships between independent variables and dependent variables and (2) explanations for why these relationships exist. Scientists refer to specific statements of relationships between variables (or concepts that vary) as *hypotheses.*

Consider the following example. Political scientists have long wondered about the relationship between the state of the national economy (in terms of unemployment, inflation, and income growth) and presidential election outcomes. The conventional expectation – or hypothesis – is that there is a positive relationship between the state of the national economy and the percentage of the national vote received by an incumbent president. While the percentage of the national vote is easily observed, there is no data source for "state of the national economy." How do we overcome this problem? We must decide how to operationalize the theoretical concept of the state of the national economy.

Scientists operationalize a concept when they define it in mea-sureable terms. For example, an important component of the state of the national economy is the rate of income growth. One way to opera-tionalize the state of the national economy would be the growth rate of the gross domestic product (GDP) for the last complete quarter prior to the November election. We could find this data in several places, and with this data and the percentage of the popular vote for the incum-bent president for several elections, we could compare the variation in income growth with the variation in the percentage of the popular vote. If income growth is relatively high, is the incumbent's vote per-centage also high? If income growth is relatively low, does the incum-bent struggle at the polls? If we are correct about the presence of a positive relationship between the state of the national economy and an incumbent president's electoral success, this is the sort of covaria-tion we should expect to see.

But we do not always see what we expect to see. What if a robust economy fails to prevent the loss of an incumbent president? How do we understand this *observation* – a single piece of data – in the context of our theory and the other observations (election results) in our *sam-ple* – a collection of observations?[1] Sometimes our expectations about the relationship between variables are not borne out by the data. A persistent inconsistency between what our theories tell us we should expect to see and what we actually see becomes a *puzzle.* Scientists spend a lot of time trying to solve puzzles. Thomas Kuhn, a student of the history of science, who we will discuss shortly, claimed that puz-zle solving is what scientists do more of than anything else. In a recent article in a widely read (at least among political scientists) political

---

[1] The full set of all possible observations is the *population.*

science journal, Robert Keohane (2009) argued that *puzzle solving* is one of the primary activities of political scientists.[2] How scientists go about solving puzzles is what much of the rest of this chapter is about. How political scientists go about solving puzzles related to the presidency is what much of the rest of this book is about.

THE CONJECTURAL NATURE OF SCIENCE

Not all that long ago, scientists conducted experiments in an effort to confirm their hypotheses and prove their theories. Scholars who study the history and philosophy of science refer to this perspective on data and experimentation as *positivism*. Positivists rejected nonempirical claims to knowledge. They demanded that knowledge claims be based on physical evidence, and they accepted the presumption that positive knowledge claims – hypotheses – could be proven with sufficient evidence.

Philosophers and historians who study science now widely reject this presumption. One simply cannot prove any general hypothesis or prove any theory regardless of the number of experiments scientists conduct or the amount of data they gather. Over two centuries ago, Scottish philosopher David Hume raised the first serious objection to the feasibility of positive scientific proof by highlighting the fact that *induction* – the process of drawing general conclusions from specific data – is inherently limited. In Hume's famous example, the effort to prove the hypothesis that "all swans are white" through observation alone is impossible. Regardless the number of white swans you are able to find, you can *never* be totally sure that the next swan you see *won't* be black.

But the full implications of Hume's insight were not apparent until the breakdown of Newtonian physics in the late nineteenth and early twentieth century. For two full centuries, Newton's understanding of the physical universe – both from terrestrial and astronomical standpoints – dominated the fields of physics and astronomy. Widely considered the most important scientist in history, he also made pathbreaking contributions to the study of optics and mathematics. And yet, the relativism revolution spearheaded by Albert Einstein posed several serious criticisms of Newtonian mechanics – criticisms that Newton's supporters could not answer.

---

[2] The other activities that occupy the attention of political scientists are analogous to the primary activities of other scientists: (1) creating concepts (a crucial aspect of theory building), (2) describing and interpreting, and (3) making (and testing) causal inferences (Keohane 2009).

Because Newton's work had stood the test of time in a uniquely dramatic fashion, its failures were particularly difficult to comprehend, and the orientation toward science (and the foundations of knowledge, more generally) that had for so long reinforced the Newtonian perspective came under scrutiny. The self-conscious confidence with which scientists had promulgated Newtonian physics as the "truth" evaporated, and it became far more difficult for scientists to hold traditional opinions of science and the pursuit of truth. In particular, verificationist perspectives were largely discredited. It became clear – at least to a significant number of scientists (and philosophers and historians of science) that Hume's critique of *inductionism* – basing the assessment of foundational positive truth on verification through empirical analysis – was more damning (and more problematic) than had been previously realized.

As the hopes of finding a way to resurrect verificationism waned, Karl Popper proposed a novel solution to the "problem of induction." In simplest terms, the problem of induction is the logical inconsistency of the following three generally-accepted contentions:

1. *First, positive proof of scientific laws and theories is impossible.* Hume clearly explains, during the eighteenth century, how laws and theories go well beyond even the theoretical limits of the data that might *potentially* be gathered in support of a law or theory. In his terms, the terms of swans, he quite simply noted that you cannot *prove* the statement that "all swans are white" simply because you have never seen a black swan. A black swan might be just around the corner, and philosophically, there is always another corner up ahead.

2. *Science is full of laws and theories.* Kepler's laws of planetary motion, Einstein's theory of relativity, and so on. We have no shortage of scientific laws and theories.

3. *Empirical observation and experiment are the only criteria for evaluating the accuracy of a law or theory.* We do experiments to test our hypotheses. Hypothetical predictions borne out in experiment after experiment tend to be taken increasingly seriously, and the most important (and fundamental) of these hypotheses tend to become laws.

Popper reinterprets the problem of induction. First, while it is impossible to prove a law or theory (remember about that black swan around the corner), he argues that it is not impossible to disprove or refute a law or theory. A single black swan is sufficient to refute the contention that "all swans are white" permanently.[3] In this way, we use data from experiments and observation to evaluate scientific laws and theories. But we do not use the data to prove; we use the data to try to disprove, refute, or *falsify*. Given this understanding of the use of empirical evidence – for falsification rather than proof – the problem of induction evaporates. What is important to remember is that we still cannot *prove* a hypothesis or theory. All hypotheses and theories – even those that have stood the test of time and repeated empirical testing the best – are still, inherently, conjectures; they are sophisticated guesses.

Consider the following practical example taken from the world of sports – baseball, specifically. Suppose a prominent major leaguer, maybe a potential Hall of Famer, claimed that he had never used steroids or another other illegal performance-enhancing substance. How would you prove that? How would he prove that? Would you accept a series of negative results from periodic drug tests? Probably not. You might say that the tests were flawed – that the tests were inaccurate or that they were not properly designed to effectively determine whether or not the banned substance was present in the sample. You might also criticize the timing or frequency of the drug tests. Maybe he wasn't subject to testing during the offseason. Or maybe restrictions on the number of tests in any season would leave open a period after the final test in which he could take whatever performance-enhancing drugs (PEDs) he wished without fear of punishment.

If the player's early years – years in which he clearly became significantly larger and significantly stronger – were so long ago that there was no significant drug testing at all, then you'd have no chance of proving his statistics (and his career) were "clean." Because scientific laws deal with whole classes of phenomena – not single ballplayers – and because scientific laws are not limited to the past – we want to be able to say something about how things work, in general, not just in the past – then positive proofs are even harder to come by in the scientific world.

Today, the concept of *falsification* provides the cornerstone for the practice of science (and social science). Scholars accept the conjectural nature of empirical assertions, and Popper's conception of falsification is a cornerstone of the scientific method. We assess the consistency of our theoretical conjectures (or hypotheses) not in an effort to prove them right (which is impossible) but in an effort to determine whether or not they are wrong.

---

[3] Certainly it isn't this simple. We'll discuss a more subtle and nuanced approach to falsification later in this chapter.

However, falsification is not a simple process, because there is no perfect hypothesis test. In practice, does it make sense to reject a thoughtful and proper hypothesis and (potentially, at least) the theory upon which it is based, on the negative results of a *single* experiment? Experiments produce errant results for a variety of reasons unrelated to the empirical content of the tested hypothesis. The scientist conducting the experiment might make an error, or the instruments used to conduct the experiment might be flawed. Even if there is no error or flaw, the proper use of the instruments themselves also depends on theories that are subject to falsification.[4]

To get a firmer grasp on the difficulties associated with "falsification," let us return to our baseball example. Suppose we have some evidence that a particular baseball player used a banned performance-enhancing substance. Apart from a direct admission of guilt, what would we accept as unassailable evidence of a "falsification" of a claim of innocence? A single positive test? Labs make mistakes sometimes. Could a mistake have been made in this case? Several positive test results then? What if the test is flawed? What if the positive test result is a function of the presence of a prescription drug similar to, but not the same as, the banned substance? What if the sample is from another athlete? Falsification simply is not as simple as it might look.

The issue of falsifiability poses particular problems for political scientists. Theories of politics (including theories of presidential power) tend to have significant contextual components. For example, presidency scholars generally presume the presidency changed in a number of significant ways shortly after the election of Franklin Roosevelt in 1932; this is what most scholars refer to as the beginning of the *modern* presidency. We will discuss the modern presidency in more detail in the following Chapter, but what matters to us now is the distinction between modern and *premodern*, and scholars' general acceptance that this shift to a modern presidency was theoretically consequential. Theories of presidential power consistently reflect this *contextual* transformation, so how we explain presidential politics in the modern era is different from how we explain presidential politics

---

[4] The traditional example is Galileo's use of his crude telescope to gather data to evaluate his astronomical theories. How he interpreted what he saw through the lens of his telescope depended on at least an implicit theory of optics. With any particular data that was inconsistent with his astronomical theory, how could he tell whether this inconsistency resulted from a problem with his astronomical theory or a flawed theory of optics? Logically, he couldn't. For a more detailed description of this case, see Feyerabend (1993).

in the premodern era. To the extent context is important, tests of falsification must incorporate contextual effects. Thus, a test of a theory of presidential power based on data from the Wilson administration provides no insight into the validity of our hypotheses and theories about the modern presidency. Let's consider this issue in the case of a particular example relevant to the study of the presidency.

In the chapter on the presidential selection process (Chapter 5), we discuss the relationship between aggregate economic circumstances and partisan shares of the presidential vote. Extensive research on the relationship between national economic circumstances and presidential election results indicates that incumbent presidents are significantly more likely to be reelected during good economic times than during bad economic times. Some limited evidence suggests the relationship is somewhat weaker if the sitting president is not running for reelection, but even then, presidential candidates from the party currently holding office tend to do better (from an electoral standpoint) if the economy is good than if the economy is poor. A formalized hypothesis relating to this relationship would be.

> For candidates of the party holding the White House, there is a positive relationship between the quality of national economic conditions prior to the election and their share of the popular vote in presidential elections.[5]

So, in general, we would expect positive economic circumstances to generate electoral success for the incumbent party. But what if a good economy does not always produce electoral victory? Is the hypothesis then falsified?

Consider the presidential election of 1952. In the four years prior to the election, income had grown at an annual rate of approximately 2.5% – above average for the modern era (1932 to the present). Still,

---

[5] Technically, at this point we should include a *ceteris paribus* condition. The *ceteris paribus* condition indicates that we expect the relationship described in the hypothesis to hold as long as all other conditions *remain constant*. In any empirical setting, the manifestation of any particular hypothetical relationship depends – to some extent – on the behavior of other variables. For example, would an excellent economy be sufficient to ensure victory of an incumbent president who became embroiled in a serious scandal in the fall of the election year? Probably not. Does this mean that economic circumstances don't matter? No, but it does mean that unusual events or circumstances can prevent the manifestation of the expected result. The *ceteris paribus* assumption precludes this possibility. This is a standard assumption and is so common that it is often not explicitly applied. To avoid the awkward clumsiness of repeated references to *ceteris paribus* assumptions, I will not make explicit reference to this assumption – but will assume it implicitly – throughout the remainder of the text.

Democrat Adlai Stevenson won less than 45% of the popular vote against Republican victor Dwight Eisenhower. It still stands as the largest loss by an incumbent party that realized an income growth rate in excess of a single point.[6] A falsified hypothesis? Probably not. First, the incumbent president, Harry Truman, was not a candidate, and we know the relationship between economics and vote shares tends to be weaker if the incumbent is not in the race. Second, the Democrats had held the presidency since 1933 – what is still the longest period of single-party control since the nineteenth century, and in Chapter 5 we will discover that the longer a party remains in power, the more difficult it becomes for it to win subsequent elections. Finally, Eisenhower was a popular war hero, so it could be argued that he garnered additional support because of an unusual (i.e., unique – at least in the twentieth century) professional background. Given all of these circumstances, Eisenhower's good showing (and Stevenson's poor showing) is somewhat easier to understand – even if we accept that there is a relationship between economic circumstances and presidential election results.

But that still leaves us in a difficult spot as far as falsification is concerned. We have a straightforward hypothesis and results that are inconsistent with it. If we are to take falsification seriously, what are we to do? More generally, what can be done about these fundamental problems associated with *verification* and *falsification*? Philosophers and historians who study the intellectual foundations of "science" over time have suggested three answers to this question:

1. *Nothing* **can** *be done. Neither falsification nor verification is possible.*

According to this perspective, most prominently associated with Thomas Kuhn, a philosopher and historian of science, science and scientists are always and inherently bound within a conceptual framework that is constructed, not discovered.[7] This conceptual framework, what Kuhn referred to as a "paradigm," encompasses the theory, concepts, and methods used to study and understand a particular set of phenomena. The regular work of scientists – what Kuhn called "normal science" – revolves around the enhancement, elaboration, and empirical examination of the paradigm.

---

[6] See Gregory Mankiw's analysis of the relationship between economics and presidential election for a more detailed treatment of these issues at http://gregmankiw.blogspot.com/2007/12/forecasting-presidential-elections.html (last accessed on December 17, 2009.)

[7] For more details on Kuhn's perspective, see his *The Structure of Scientific Revolutions* (1996). This is by far his most famous book, and it is one of the most oft-cited works in the social sciences.

Powerful paradigms – such as the one associated with Newtonian physics – tend to be quite long lasting, produce important insights (i.e., explanations for phenomena not previously understood), and are practically useful (consider engineers' exhaustive use of Newton's physics). But no paradigm is perfect. Every paradigm has flaws and inconsistencies – in Kuhn's terms, "puzzles" that require further work. For powerful paradigms, this further work often effectively addresses many of these puzzles. Eventually, however, the gaps and inconsistencies become too important (or too numerous) to ignore. At this "crisis" point, a scientific revolution may occur.[8] The process of developing a new paradigm during this crisis period – a crisis leading to revolution – is known as "revolutionary science."

If a revolution occurs, there is a conflict between the proponents of a new paradigm and the supporters of the old paradigm. Normally, there is a significant generational dimension to this conflict: younger scholars tend to champion the new paradigm, while older scholars tend to champion the existing paradigm. Given the stark differences in the relative level of investment in the existing paradigm – senior scholars tend to have built their careers on the basis of the existing paradigm while junior scholars have not – the generational divide is understandable. Eventually, a crisis develops into a full-scale revolution, and the existing paradigm is replaced by a new paradigm. Note that paradigms are *never* replaced by anything but another paradigm. Scientists do not toss off something, no matter how flawed, for nothing.

Once an old paradigm is replaced by a new paradigm, can we say that the new paradigm is necessarily *better* than the old paradigm? Does it tell us more about our subject of inquiry? Does it get us closer to the truth? Kuhn is relatively clear on each of these issues. No, a new paradigm is not demonstrably superior to the paradigm that it replaces. In fact, for Kuhn, it is not even technically or conceptually comparable. For Kuhn, paradigms are sufficiently comprehensive to be analogous to scientific world views, and the nature of these vast and detailed conceptual structures is such that it is impossible to directly compare concepts across paradigms. Kuhn describes this incommensurability in the following terms:

> ... the proponents of competing paradigms practice their trades in *different* worlds .... the two groups of scientists see different things

---

[8] A successful revolution at any particular crisis point is not a foregone conclusion. Sometimes, powerful paradigms are able to beat back significant challenges. In the end, however, all paradigms are destined to be replaced (at least according to Kuhn).

when they look from the same point in the same direction. Again, that is not to say that they can see anything they please.... But in some areas they see different things, and they see them in different relations one to the other .... because it is a transition between incommensurables, the transition between competing paradigms cannot be made a step at a time, forced by logic and neutral experience. Like the gestalt switch, it must occur all at once (though not necessarily in an instant) or not at all. (1996: 150, emphasis in the original)

On the second issue, new paradigms do address previously unanswered questions. New paradigms also incorporate new tools and methods of empirical analysis that enhance analytical precision. The new paradigm is not, however, demonstrably superior to the old paradigm in all respects. For example, a new paradigm might defeat an old paradigm even if it does not effectively answer all of the questions answered by the old paradigm. And no paradigm, regardless how new, is without its gaps, flaws, and inconsistencies.[9] As far as the final question is concerned, Kuhn completely rejects the idea that a shift from an older paradigm to a newer paradigm brings us any closer to the "Truth." To the extent we view *scientific progress* as a process of moving ever closer to the truth, then, Kuhn would say, we are mistaken. If by scientific progress we mean the development and leveraging of the improvements referenced earlier, then we are correct. For Kuhn, the trajectory of science is not toward anything; for Kuhn, the trajectory of science is an evolutionary process of moving away from the starting point. Kuhn's conclusion along these lines is quite clear:

> I do not doubt, for example, that Newton's mechanics improves on Aristotle's and that Einstein's improves on Newton's as instruments for puzzle-solving. But I can see in their succession no coherent direction of ontological development. On the contrary, in some important respects, though by no means all, Einstein's general theory of relativity is closer to Aristotle's than either of them is to Newton's. (1996: 206–207)

So, from Kuhn's perspective, neither verification nor falsification is technically possible. Nevertheless, the scientific endeavor is valuable for a variety of reasons. These include the following:

a.   Over time, problem solving, the core activity of *normal* science, results in progress *within* the paradigm. While falsification may be

---

[9] If it were, what would there be for scientists to do?

intellectually unavailable – Kuhn argues against the perspective that characterizes the result of a revolutionary shift in paradigms as progress – the value of progress within a paradigm is considerable.[10]

b. We are able to model the phenomena of inquiry ("nature," let's say) with increasing precision and accuracy. This increased precision and accuracy has many potential *instrumental* benefits. For students of the natural sciences, those benefits may range from understanding (and subsequently predicting) the weather to curing disease, constructing buildings and bridges, and developing new energy sources.

c. Although we can't expect science to bring us closer to any fixed and ultimate "truth," science is "a process of evolution *from* primitive beginnings – a process whose successive stages are characterized by an increasingly detailed and refined understanding of nature" (Kuhn 1996: 170). Kuhn does, however, conclude by highlighting the fact that "nothing that has been or will be said makes it a process of evolution *toward* anything" (1996: 170, emphasis in the original).

Kuhn rejects the possibility that *science* will bring us first-hand knowledge of *Truth*. For Kuhn, the search for a transcendent, unchanging truth is tantamount to the quest for the Holy Grail – it is an endeavor doomed to failure. For Kuhn, this fundamental theoretical hopelessness did not obscure the pragmatic value of science.

2. *Nothing should be done. "Science" is no more likely to uncover truthful insights than any other intellectual endeavor.*

For some students of the philosophy of science, Paul Feyerabend's work is a natural extension of Kuhn's work. If science is an endeavor fundamentally driven by sociological concerns and dynamics, then its claims to be a pathway to the truth are flawed or indefensible. Feyerabend's perspective is most clearly delineated in a work entitled *Against Method* (1993), an extended argument against Popper's concept of falsification and Popper's privileging of the "scientific method."

For Popper, the scientific endeavor depended upon the capacity to falsify hypotheses and theories. Likewise, science was a practice or "method" more than a particular substantive knowledge. So

[10] Kuhn is clear about both of these points. On the nature of progress *within* a paradigm, he writes, "In its normal state ... a scientific community is an immensely efficient instrument for solving the problems or puzzles that its paradigms define. Furthermore, the result of solving these problems must inevitably be progress" (1996: 166). As far as the extent to which scientific revolutions may be viewed as progressive, he notes that "there are losses as well as gains in scientific revolutions, and scientists tend to be peculiarly blind to the former" (1996: 167).

the title of Feyerabend's *Against Method* is a direct attack on (and critique of) Popper's perspective. It is also a critique of Popper's privileging of the scientific endeavor. For Popper, the practice of science was uniquely suited for the development and acquisition of knowledge.

Feyerabend argues that Popper's perspective is flawed for a variety of reasons. First, he argues that nonfalsification is an impossibly high bar for a theory to maintain over any significant number of tests (or period of testing). He notes that "[a]ccording to our present results, hardly any theory is *consistent with the facts*" (1993: 50, emphasis in the original). Feyerabend observes that all extant theories have empirical "gaps," specific contexts in which the theories have no clear implications (and thus cannot generate falsifiable hypotheses) or the theories have clear implications, can generate falsifiable hypotheses, but the hypotheses are rejected. He flatly states that "*no single theory ever agrees with all of the known facts in its domain*" (1993: 39, emphasis in the original). While Popper discusses the practical issues associated with the determination of a "true" falsification – a falsifying experiment that is incorrectly implemented or flawed in some nontrivial manner cannot be the sole referent on falsification of a theory (or even of that individual hypothesis) – Feyerabend's criticism gets at the more widely accepted results that are inconsistent with a particular theory. From Feyerabend's perspective, "[t]he right method must not contain any rules that make us choose between theories *on the basis of falsification*. Rather its rules must enable us to choose between theories which we have already tested *and which are falsified*" (1993: 51, emphasis in the original). For Feyerabend, there is no such rule or set of rules; therefore, he rejects the privileging of *any* particular method – even science.

Feyerabend also criticizes Popper's methodologically oriented conceptualization of the history of science – namely that falsification is not only flawed, it is also *not* what scientists (even the greatest scientists) have done throughout history. A significant portion of Feyerabend's *Against Method* is a detailed historical discussion of the role of Galileo in the development of the study of astronomy and physics. Today, Galileo's contributions to science are widely viewed as placing him among the greatest scientists of all time. Yet during his life, his views were often controversial. His support for the Copernican heliocentric (as opposed to geocentric) solar system was particularly controversial and resulted in a long and bitter battle with the leadership of the Catholic Church. He was finally forced to recant his support for heliocentrism, and he died while under house arrest.

Feyerabend argues that Galileo's scientific practice was inconsistent with the standard procedures of science as enumerated by Popper and his supporters. According to Feyerabend, Galileo ignored evidence that was apparently inconsistent with the heliocentric theory (thus, he refused to allow for falsification of the theory). Galileo also readily accepted data generated through procedures and instruments (including the telescope) that were not yet well understood.[11] And Galileo is also criticized for playing somewhat fast and loose with the conceptual language of physics current in his day. From Feyerabend's perspective, he simply altered – in a dramatic and significant fashion – the meaning of a set of important concepts so that they would more easily fit within his theoretical framework. All of these behaviors suggest that the greatest scientist of his day, and one of the greatest scientists of all time, did not play by the rules of the standard procedures of science. In fact, Feyerabend goes on to argue that if anyone was playing by the rules of standard science during Galileo's time, it was the Catholic Church. From a procedural standpoint, the Church criticized Galileo on grounds that are consistent with the scientific method. Feyerabend's counterintuitive conclusion is not that Galileo should have followed the proper method but that Galileo was merely doing what scientists normally do. Feyerabend argues that scientists *do not* follow the textbook procedures associated with falsification, nor should they. He argues that science is no different from any other social endeavor, and efforts to associate the distinctiveness of science with its method are inaccurate and pernicious.

Ironically, there is a way in which Feyerabend's critique of Popper could be viewed as the logical result of the full development of Popper's conception of "critical rationalism." Popper argues that all theoretical statements are inherently conjectural, and that the essence of critical rationalism is criticism and continual effort to reject these theoretical statements. In terms of science, critical rationalism implies an acceptance of the conjectural nature of scientific theories and an acceptance of the definitive characteristic of science – the process of falsification. Given Popper's understanding of critical rationalism (and the crucial role of falsification in science), one can view Feyerabend's critique of Popper's critical rationalism as a logical intellectual response – a response that fully and easily fits within the context of

[11] Newton, who was born the year (1643) after Galileo died (1642) would not publish his major work on optics – the first comprehensive treatment of the subject – until the early eighteenth century, over 60 years after Galileo's death. Arguably, no one had a rigorous explanation for how telescopes actually worked until years after Galileo's death.

critical rationalism itself. So, as much as Feyerabend's perspective can be viewed as a rejection of Popper's orientation toward critical rationalism and science, it might also be reasonably viewed as the perfect manifestation (and clear evidence) of Popper's theory at work (even if Feyerabend is "correct").

3. *Science is salvageable, but we must rethink our understanding of falsification. If we think rightly about falsification, we can put forth justifiable claims about the way the world works.*

A student of Popper and a friend of Feyerabend, mathematician and philosopher of science Imre Lakatos, rejected both Kuhn's and Feyerabend's critiques of Popper's falsificationism. He argued that their understanding of falsification was too simplistic – that they were actually criticizing what he referred to as "strict falsificationism" (Lakatos 1970). This strict falsificationism was overly restrictive and failed to capture the full extent of Popper's own thoughts on the subject.

Lakatos argues that Popper never intended for "falsification" to be understood in such limiting and simplistic terms. From Lakatos' perspective, Popper was plainly cognizant of the problems associated with strict falsificationism. On one hand, there is the problem that a simplistic understanding of falsification will result in the "Feyerabend" scenario: All theories are more or less immediately falsified. Not only are no theories perfect (as Popper himself notes), but theories are so quickly and convincingly falsified that there is no way to distinguish the relative quality of the available theories. Not only are all "falsified"; all are viewed as equally valid.

The "Kuhn" scenario – though beginning at what would seem to be a significantly different starting point – ends in much the same place as the Feyerabend scenario. Kuhn, like Feyerabend, admits that all theories start out with gaps and inconsistencies – clear opportunities for strict falsificationists to discard any theory *quickly* and with little effort. For Kuhn, however, scientists work to fill these gaps and correct these inconsistencies, and these efforts are the bread and butter of the practice of science, what Kuhn refers to as "normal science." So the quick and superficial efforts to falsify a theory preclude the full development of the theory and the potentially dramatic and important insights the theory might produce. The practice of normal science, however, has no obvious end point, no theoretical conclusion. At some point, scientists simply replace it with an alternative theory that is deemed preferable by a sufficiently large portion of the scientific community – the aftermath of the scientific "revolutions" to which

Kuhn refers. Kuhn, then, concludes that falsification, in any but the most trivial and superficial sense, is not only *not* what scientists do; it simply isn't possible. Scientists do decide to switch from one theory to another, but never for the simple and straightforward reason that one is fully and fundamentally discredited (falsified) and another is not. Whether we side with Kuhn or Feyerabend, we come to much the same place. We are without an effective mechanism for assessing the relative quality of distinct scientific theories.

At this point, Lakatos throws us a lifeline. First, he admits that falsification in its strictest sense – the empirical evaluation of the implications of a theory, the clear inconsistency of the theory's implications with the data, and the fundamental and final rejection of the theory in toto – is impossible. Lakatos argues that it will always be possible to protect theories from falsification through post hoc restrictions on the applicability of the theory to a particular empirical setting.[12] Scientists make choices about the way in which they test theories and they make choices about how they interpret the results of these tests. What might appear to be a falsifying case or test can be addressed in a variety of ways that save or protect the crucial components of the theory, what Lakatos refers to as the "hard core."[13] Hints and suggestions about possible explanations for why a particular case or test might have appeared inconsistent with the implications of the theory are referred to as the "*positive heuristic*."

If scientists choose what parts of a theory to test, how to derive testable implications from the theory, and then how the results from any particular test should be evaluated, how does meaningful falsification survive? Lakatos resurrects falsification by introducing the concept of a "research program" (1970: 132). Rather than thinking of theories in isolation, we should think in terms of families of theories. A family of theories is a "research program." For Lakatos, what matters is the content of the whole series of theories or research programs, and he refers to this perspective as "sophisticated methodological falsificationism" (1970: 132).[14] Rather than evaluating individual theories, we should concentrate on the evaluation of research programs (or families of theories).

[12] He notes that "Kuhn is right in rejecting naïve falsification, and also in the *continuity* of scientific growth, the *tenacity* of some scientific theories" (1970: 177).

[13] Lakatos uses the term "*negative heuristic*" (1970: 135) to indicate those methodological decisions that preclude the direct testing of the hard core.

[14] As Lakatos writes, "one of the crucial features of sophisticated falsificationism is that it replaces the concept of *theory* as the basic concept of the logic of discovery by the concept of *series of theories*. It is the succession of theories and not one given theory which is appraised as scientific or pseudoscientific. But the members

Lakatos distinguishes between two types of research programs: *progressive* and *degenerating* (or *degenerative*). Progressive research programs share the following characteristics:

1. They produce consistently progressive theoretical "problemshifts." This means that Theory 1b in a particular research program has greater empirical content – predicts and explains more novel facts – than Theory 1a (the previous theory). In simple terms, Theory 1b predicts new (more) facts. According to Lakatos, research programs that lack progressive theoretical problemshifts are fake theories, or "pseudoscientific" (1970: 118).

2. They produce intermittent (at least) progressive empirical "problemshifts." This means that Theory 1b's additional theoretical content is corroborated by empirical evidence. Not only do we have new explanations and predictions, but we also have empirical support for the new explanation or prediction.[15] Individual theories may be viewed as "falsified" when they are "superseded by a theory with higher corroborated content" (Lakatos 1970: 118).

Theories in progressive research programs are useful and productive; theories in degenerating research programs are not.

In some respects, Lakatos's perspective is similar to that of Kuhn. The iterative process of theory development within research programs is similar to what Kuhn refers to as "normal science." The rejection of degenerating research programs in favor of progressive research programs is at least superficially similar to the shift to a new paradigm following a scientific revolution. But the fundamental difference between Kuhn's and Lakatos' perspective is crucial. Lakatos correctly concludes that "[f]or Kuhn scientific change – from one 'paradigm' to another – is a mystical conversion which is not and cannot be governed by rules of reason and which falls totally within the realm of the *(social) psychology of discovery*. Scientific change is a kind of religious change" (1970: 93, emphasis in original). Lakatos, on the other hand, finally agrees with Popper that "scientific change is rational or at least rationally reconstructible and falls in the realm

---

of such series of theories are usually connected by a remarkable *continuity* which welds them into a *research program*" (1970: 132, emphasis in original).

15 Again, in Lakatos' terms, "a series of theories is *theoretically progressive (or 'constitutes a theoretically progressive problemshift')* if each new theory has some excess empirical content over its predecessor, that is if it predicts some novel, hitherto unexpected fact. Let us say that a theoretically progressive series of theories is also *empirically progressive (or 'constitutes an empirically progressive problemshift')* if some of this excess empirical content is also corroborated, that is, if each new theory leads us to the actual discovery of some *new fact*" (1970: 118).

of the *logic of discovery*" (1970: 93).[16] What we learn here is the importance of clearly stating our theoretical perspective, deriving testable propositions from our theory in a straightforward manner, testing these propositions, and then returning to the theory to extend the area of corroboration or address the need for increased restrictiveness in our theoretical projections. We also learn the importance of an honest evaluation of the theoretical and empirical limitations of our perspective. As Lakatos notes, "Intellectual honesty does not consist in trying to entrench, or establish one's position by proving (or 'probabilifying') – intellectual honesty consists rather in specifying precisely the conditions under which one is willing to give up one's position" (1970: 92).[17]

Finally, an important distinction between naïve falsification and sophisticated methodological falsification is that one is based on an absolute choice (naïve falsification) and the other is based on a relative choice. Naïve falsification presumes the rejection of a theory is a simple and direct response to a verifiable empirical result that is inconsistent with the theory being tested. There is no requirement that an alternative theory be available. So, naïve falsification might result in the rejection of the only available theory. Sophisticated falsificationists do not reject a research program without an alternative to replace it. Again, Lakatos' sophisticated falsificationism reflects Kuhn's perspective; regardless of the problems with a paradigm, it is only rejected when it is replaced by an alternative paradigm. In science, nothing never beats something.

Given these options, what should scientists do? Among scientifically oriented students of the presidency, the third response, that

---

[16]   The distinction between Kuhn and Popper is crucial, especially for Lakatos, who writes, "The clash between Popper and Kuhn is not about a mere technical point in epistemology. It concerns our central intellectual values, and has implications not only for theoretical physics but also for the underdeveloped social sciences and even for moral and political philosophy. If even in science there is no other way of judging a theory but by assessing the number, faith and vocal energy of its supporters, then this must be even more so in the social sciences: truth lies in power. ... But Kuhn does not understand a more sophisticated position the rationality of which is not based on 'naïve' falsificationism. I shall try to explain – and further strengthen – this stronger Popperian position which, I think, may escape Kuhn's strictures and present scientific revolutions as constituting rational progress rather than as religious conversions" (1970: 93).

[17]   This is so important for Lakatos that he goes on to conclude that "[c]ommitted Marxists and Freudians [targets of disparagement for Popper] refuse to specify such conditions: this is the hallmark of their intellectual dishonesty. *Belief* may be a regrettably unavoidable biological weakness to be kept under the control of criticism: but *commitment* is for Popper an outright crime" (1970: 92, emphasis in original).

delineated by Lakatos, is becoming increasingly popular. Presidency scholars are increasingly focused on the following:

1. the developing theories that generate testable hypotheses
2. testing the hypotheses with data (most often, quantitative data)
3. evaluating the results of the hypotheses tests and their implications for the *applicability* of the theory to the phenomena to be explained

Positive test results indicate evidence that the theory *is* applicable to the particular range of phenomena sampled for the empirical test. A series of positive test results indicates broad applicability, and this suggests that the research program based on this theory (and subsequent iterations of the theory) is *progressive*. Negative tests results suggest just the opposite; the negative results imply that the theory is actually more limited than previously realized. A series of negative results leads to an ever-decreasing area of applicability for the theory (and subsequent iterations of the theory in response to these new results). The research program based on this series of theories is degenerating. Over time, scientists gravitate toward progressive research programs. In mature fields, a degenerating research program might be fully eclipsed by a progressive research program.

Progressive research programs offer more than puzzle-solving power; they also generate important practical benefits. Progressive research programs can aid in the solution of social problems. Most of us who study the presidency are not solely interested in knowledge for its own sake. We want to be able to leverage our knowledge of the presidency to improve our institutions of government, to aid in the selection of the best chief executives, and to generally enhance the quality of national policy making. Progressive research programs provide a frequent and consistent mechanism for self-evaluation and correction. The definitive characteristic of a progressive research program is the ability to make novel predictions that are subsequently supported by real-world data. Advice or counsel based on a flawed theory will lead to predictions that are not supported by new data. And without continued success, a progressive research program becomes a degenerative, regressive research program. And degenerative research programs are not appropriate foundations for advice and counsel.

As political scientists trying to "speak truth to power" (Wildavsky 1979) to improve our government, we need progressive research programs. But progressive research programs don't grow on trees. Partly because of the relative youth of the scientific study of the presidency, we have several – I will identify four in subsequent chapters – theories that could form the bases for research programs. At present, we are just beginning to set the boundary parameters for these research programs. There is evidence that each has empirical content. The extent to which each can be effectively applied to a wide range of increasingly diverse phenomena in a wide range of contexts remains to be seen. I will discuss these theories in more detail in subsequent chapters. But before we move to more substantive issues related to the presidency, it is important that we understand just what makes a theory a "good" theory. I turn to that next.

What is a good theory?

If we take sophisticated falsification seriously – or, more generally, if we take the scientific endeavor seriously – then our theories must have certain structural characteristics. Besides being about some aspect of the presidency (a substantive criterion for students of the presidency), a theory should satisfy the following criteria:[18]

1. *It is falsifiable.* Theories are inherently conjectural. To be meaningful, they must make one or more claims that can be evaluated against a current or future empirical record for consistency. While it is always possible to modify a hypothesis (after the fact) to avoid falsification, this practice effectively precludes falsification. To the extent this is done, the theory or hypothesis is protected from falsification (or falsification is prevented). In these cases, we can have no confidence that the hypothesis (and underlying theory) have any empirical content at all. Basically, we have no way of determining the accuracy of the hypothesis or the theory on which it is based. We must realize that falsification is not a simple standard (as Lakatos makes clear), but theories that are inherently unfalsifiable are beyond empirical evaluation. Theories that are beyond empirical evaluation are inherently flawed because we have no way to evaluate the extent to which they are consistent with the real world. The following is an example of a falsifiable hypothesis derived from a partisan theory of presidential power: *Legislative productivity is higher during periods of united government than periods of divided government.* Once we decide how to operationalize "legislative productivity," "united government," and "divided government," we can test this hypothesis with historical data. The data may support the hypothesis or not, but this clear statement of a straightforward relationship between two variables is clearly subject to falsification.

---

[18] King et al. (1994) provide the standard (and significantly more detailed) discussion of each of these criteria in *Designing Social Inquiry*. For students with an

2. *It is logically consistent.* In the absence of logical consistency, we cannot determine the interrelation between the various components of the theory, nor can we derive testable hypotheses from the theory. Without testable hypotheses, we cannot evaluate the theory. If we cannot test the theory, it's of no value. To continue on with the legislative productivity example above, what if the theory on which the divided government/united government example was based were multifaceted (or had multiple components), and what if one aspect or component of the theory suggested that legislative productivity were greater during periods of divided government and another component of the theory suggested that legislative productivity were greater during united government? This would be a logical inconsistency and would be problematic because it would produce inconsistent hypotheses that would prevent the empirical evaluation (or falsification) of the broader theory.

3. *It is concrete.* The conceptual building blocks of the theory must have clear empirical referents, and the relationships between the concepts must be specific and transparent. Good theories may be complex. Good theories are not, however, a manifestation of confusion. C. Wright Mills, a prominent twentieth-century sociologist, made a famous critique of an equally (if not more) prominent twentieth-century sociologist, Talcott Parsons, that centered on this issue of concreteness. Mills (1959) argued that the "grand theory" Parsons presents in *The Social System* (1951) was all *syntax* and no *semantics*. Mills contended that Parsons' theory was a complex web of interrelationships between concepts that had neither practical definitions nor any empirical referents. This was a significant critique that Mills generalized with the following: "Grand theory [of which Parson's was only a very prominent example] is drunk on syntax, blind to semantics. Its practitioners do not truly understand that when we define a word we are merely inviting others to use it as we would like it to be used; that the purpose of the definition is to focus argument upon *fact*, and that the proper result of good definition is to transform argument over terms into disagreements about fact, and thus open arguments to further inquiry" (1959: 34).[19] According to Mills' critique, Parsons' theory was beyond falsification – it was unscientific – because without empirical referents for the core concepts in the theory, there was no way to conduct empirical tests of

interest in learning more about the social scientific endeavor – especially those interested in graduate education – this is an excellent resource.

[19] By "grand theory," Mills meant "the associating and dissociating of concepts" (1959: 26).

the theory's implications. The relationship between divided/united government and legislative productivity is a particularly good example of concrete theorizing. The differences between divided and united government are not difficult to identify, and while "legislative productivity" is a somewhat more complex term, there are also obvious (and meaningfully appropriate) operationalizations for this concept.

4. *It produces a variety of novel, testable hypotheses.* To be interesting, a theory must tell us something that we did not already know. Good theories make a significant contribution to our body of knowledge. In particular, they make new claims about the relationship between variables of substantive significance. Good theories provide new explanations of phenomena for which we lack compelling explanations. If these explanations are especially surprising and if they lead directly to additional explanations, that is even better. Ideally, a theory accurately captures the interrelationships of the most fundamental forces in the empirical context of interest. Let us continue with the divided government example begun earlier. If our general premise that the nature of partisan control of Congress and the Presidency is accurate and our theory is internally consistent and sufficiently detailed and concrete, then we should be able to derive a variety of hypotheses about the relationship between different types of divided government (one party controls both chambers of Congress, but not the presidency; one party controls the House and the other controls the Senate and the Presidency, etc.) and legislative productivity. Our theory might also provide us with the means to derive the impact of differing levels of partisanship on the impact of divided government.[20]

5. *It effectively incorporates new data and can be readily applied to new political contexts.* Theories should be based on conceptual building blocks that allow the relatively seamless extension to new contexts. Theories of presidential policy making developed in the twentieth century that are not transferable to the twenty-first century are not particularly useful and cannot form the basis for a progressive research program. Theories applicable only to the past may be interesting from a historical standpoint, but they are not useful for the broader study of the presidency.

[20] It may be that divided government (or, conversely, united government) simply matters more – meaning the difference between the two produces a greater effect on legislative productivity – if the overall level of partisanship is higher. That might not be the case, but it is a possibility. Hopefully, our theory would lead to some expectation about the specific character of that relationship.

What is a good hypothesis?

Just as good theories share a set of attributes, good hypotheses also share certain characteristics or attributes. A good hypothesis clearly states the relationship between an independent variable and a dependent variable. Remember, the independent variable is the factor to which we attribute the effect realized in the dependent variable.

Hypotheses may characterize the relationship between these two variables in several ways, and we endeavor to incorporate the full level of detail provided by the theory. So, a hypothesis might indicate simply the presence of a relationship between the independent and dependent variable without specifying the direction (positive or negative) of the relationship. For example, we might hypothesize that presidential support will be affected by international conflicts or wars. It's relatively easy to see that a war could potentially push public support higher than it might otherwise have been (see, for example, Roosevelt in 1944) or potentially weaken what might otherwise have been relatively strong public support (probably true for Johnson in 1968). But hypotheses with so little detail are not especially interesting. At the very least, they tend to beg the question – in our case, what sorts of wars will tend to boost presidential support and what sorts of wars will tend to depress presidential support?

A more detailed – and interesting – hypothesis would indicate the direction of the relationship. So, we might hypothesize that there is a positive relationship between the percentage of the popular vote received by an incumbent president running for reelection and the percentage growth in aggregate income (say, GDP) over the year immediately preceding the election. Finally, our hypothesis might not only indicate the direction of the relationship, but it might also indicate the magnitude of the relationship. For example, we might hypothesize that for each percentage point increase in GDP growth, the incumbent president wins another 2% of the popular vote.[21]

Good hypotheses also clearly state the limiting "conditions" under which the relationship is expected to manifest. The *ceteris paribus* – or "all else equal" – assumption is common. It is one thing to hypothesize that legislative productivity is greater during unified government than during divided government. It is something different to hypothesize that legislative productivity is higher during periods of unified government

---

[21] This level of detail might be suggested by previous empirical tests, but theories in political science, certainly theories of the presidency, are rarely sufficiently precise to allow this level of detail – a level of detail that is common in the natural sciences (and in some areas of economics).

than during periods of divided government *when the level of partisan- ship is high.* Ideally, the theory upon which the hypothesis is based provides us with the means to determine the specificity of the hypothesis.

Now that we know what a hypothesis is – and we know the difference between good hypotheses and bad hypotheses – how do we go about testing our hypothesis? Since this is not a textbook on data analysis, we aren't going to go into great detail on the available tools for statistical hypothesis testing. There are many other texts that describe and explain these tools in detail. Still, the logic behind hypothesis testing is important for students of the presidency to understand. So, let us start with the *formal experiment* – the process that provides the foundational logical for hypothesis testing.

How do we test hypotheses?

We test theories by testing hypotheses. We test hypotheses with data. Where does this data come from? It depends on the theory, the research question, and the hypothesis. In the hard sciences – and, increasingly, in some areas of social science – the formal *experiment* is the mechanism for testing hypotheses. A *formal* experiment has the following components:

1. *A sample of observations that is representative of the population of interest.*

   A "sample" is simply a subset of the population, and the "population" is the full set of observations that satisfy the characteristics of our stated object of analysis. For example, suppose we wished to evaluate the effect of a new drug on women between the ages of 18 and 25. The population would be all women between the ages of 18 and 25. A sample would be a subset of women between the ages of 18 and 25. Note that at this point, we are making no claims about the "randomness" of this sample. The sample need not be selected randomly from the population. In fact, in real-world experiments, the participants (the overall sample) are rarely selected randomly. While there is normally an effort to assure that the members of the sample group are representative of the population being analyzed, the overall sample is not necessarily (and not likely to be) chosen at random.

2. *Random selection of each sample member into one of the two groups: a treatment group and a control group.*

   The members of the overall sample are randomly assigned to one of two groups: a treatment group and a control group. Random

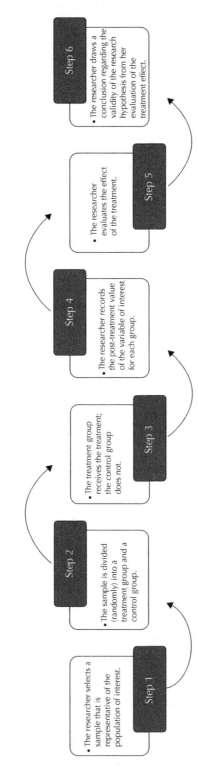

Figure 2-1: Stages of the experimental process.

assignment at this point is crucial because the scientist conducting the experiment wishes to be able to argue that the two groups – the treatment group and the control group – are comparable in all important respects. Why is this comparability important? I discuss that later in the Chapter.

3. *One group receives a treatment, the other group receives a placebo (or simply no treatment).*

One of the groups is chosen to receive some treatment or stimulus, and this group is referred to as the treatment group. The other group – the control group – does not receive the stimulus.

4. *The effect on each observation – both in the treatment sample and the control sample – is recorded.*
5. *The scientist evaluates the extent to which the "effects" in the treatment sample are significantly different from the "effects" in the control sample. If there are significant differences in effects (or responses), the scientist concludes that the stimulus is responsible for the differences in effects.*

Figure 2-1 provides an illustration of the steps delineated above.

Why is the scientist able to conclude that the poststimulus "effects" realized in the treatment group are a function of the stimulus? Because of the random assignment of the participants into the treatment group and the control group, the scientist may reasonably argue that these groups are only different in one significant respect – the stimulus itself. Thus, any significant difference between the two groups following the stimulus can be attributed to the stimulus.

Obviously, students of the presidency face several significant obstacles to the use of formal experiments in their work. First, at any particular point in time, there is only one president, so it is not possible to gather together a set of fully "comparable" presidents or presidencies into a sample in anything like the way common in experiments. There are certainly important commonalities between presidents and presidencies, but the level of comparability is significantly less than that would be expected for the purposes of a formal experiment. Second, it is obviously impossible to randomly assign presidents to a treatment sample or a control sample. Scholars certainly can't (and shouldn't) have the power to manipulate the political dynamics of a presidency, so what happens during a presidency is never the function of an artificial stimulus in the manner of a conventional experimental stimulus. Finally, even with random selection, the ability to determine the statistical significance of the effect of a particular stimulus – the likelihood that the difference between the control and the stimulus groups is truly attributable to the stimulus and did not occur simply by chance – depends to some extent on the size of the stimulus and the control samples. Experiments are rarely done with less than two or three dozen subjects. While we have had 43 presidents, the changes in the nature of the office, the size and significance of the national government, the nature of partisan politics, and other factors[22] make it very difficult to include many of the earlier presidents in analyses focusing on current (or modern) presidential political dynamics. If we limit our analysis to the modern presidents, our sample is only 12[23] – a number that makes the determination of the statistical significance of any stimulus "results" quite difficult.

As the formal experiment is largely unavailable to students of the presidency,[24] scientifically oriented research on the presidency depends almost exclusively on the use of observational studies. In these observational studies, which are standard components of the literature in political science more generally, scholars must make the case for the comparability of their observations (presidencies, presidential decisions, presidential elections, etc.), utilize an analytical technique that effectively provides for the evaluation of alternative hypotheses ("control variables" in the parlance of multivariate quantitative analyses), and report the extent to which their results are sufficiently significant (both statistically and substantively) to allow them to draw a conclusion regarding the hypothesis (or hypotheses) being tested. In the following section, I provide a more substantively meaningful discussion of this type of research in political science (in general) and as it relates to the presidency (more specifically). We start, however, with a brief discussion of the nature of the scientific endeavor as it relates specifically to politics.

What is a science of politics?

A *science of politics* is the effort to develop theories of interrelated causal hypotheses about political phenomena and the subsequent empirical evaluation of those causal hypotheses. As with other social

---

[22] More on this in Chapter 3.

[23] The list includes Franklin Roosevelt, Harry Truman, Dwight Eisenhower, Lyndon Johnson, Richard Nixon, Gerald Ford, Jimmy Carter, Ronald Reagan, George H. W. Bush, Bill Clinton, and George W. Bush.

[24] One area of research related to the presidency – vote choice and turnout – does include a significant number of formal experiments, and this type of research is becoming increasingly popular. Recent examples include Gerber et al. (2008); Green and Gerber (2005); and Green et al. (2003).

sciences, a science of politics is inherently more complicated than a *hard* science (such as physics or chemistry). There are several reasons for this additional complexity.

First, human beings and human interrelationships are simply more complicated than stones or stars. Social sciences are inherently more complicated than physical or biological sciences because the subject of inquiry is itself inherently more complicated.

Second, political science (and, for that matter, economics, sociology, and psychology) is a far younger discipline than mathematics, physics, or chemistry. It is certainly possible to make an argument that the first political scientist was Aristotle,[25] but even if Aristotle were aptly characterized as a political scientist, a community of empirically oriented students of politics – a community of political scientists – did not develop until at least the latter part of the seventeenth century (certainly not until after the publication of Hobbes' writings), and the first formal association of political scientists (the American Political Science Association) is just over a century old. What this means is that mathematicians, physicists, chemists, and biologists have an enormous head start on political scientists. We have a lot of work to do just to catch up.

Third, humans are strategic beings that learn and respond accordingly. Why would that be important? Well, suppose we think we know why some presidential candidates tend to be more successful than other presidential candidates. It might mean better fundraising skills (at least during the primary campaign), or policy stances that are more attractive to a larger portion of the voting population (Downs' median voter theorem, for example), or it might be oratorical style or professional background. Once this knowledge is disseminated, what is there to stop candidates from using this information to modify their campaigns – enhance their campaigns – in ways that they hadn't before. These enhancements might then make the original understanding of why some candidates tend to do better than others obsolete. It wouldn't necessarily result in the obsolescence of the theory, but the potential for this type of learning and strategic activity is certainly something that physicists, astronomers, and chemists don't need to worry about. Again, the social sciences are no walk in the park.

THINKING LIKE SCIENTISTS: RESPONDING TO PUZZLES

If scientists spend much of their time dealing with puzzles, we should think about why we have scientific "puzzles" in the first place. We

---

[25] Though he was a uniquely important political philosopher, few scholars consider Plato a political "scientist."

have puzzles because our perception of the empirical world is often inconsistent with our theoretical expectations; our theory tells us we should see one thing, and we end up seeing something else. What, then, is a scientist to do? A scientist tries to figure out the source of the inconsistency. The most obvious possibility is that the theory is flawed, and so it would seem that every time there is a puzzle, there is a need for a new theory. But theories don't grow on trees, and so scientists have learned to look for other options, other possibilities that don't require the wholesale rejection of the way we think things are. So, short of needing a whole new theory, puzzles may also flow from the following:

1. *Problems with the data.* We may not be seeing what we think we see. For example, the data used to conduct the analysis might be corrupted in some way, or the way in which a concept is operationalized might be faulty. A case must often be made for the choice of a particular operationalization, and the case may not be compelling.
2. *Problems with the methods used to analyze the data.* Our results are only as good as the methods (and data) used to produce them. While no method is perfect, significant methodological shortcomings are often the focal point for criticism.
3. *Problems with the interpretation of the results.* Even when scholars agree about the appropriateness of the data and method, they may not agree about the interpretation of the results. In some cases, what one scholar might consider a significant result another might consider trivial. Not infrequently, the disagreement over significance centers on the distinction between *statistical* significance and *substantive* significance. A result may achieve a conventional level of statistical significance – indicating that it is quite unlikely to have occurred simply by chance – while the magnitude of the result is so small that its substantive significance comes into question.

These sets of problems are highlighted in Figure 2-2.

The proper response to the first case is obviously an effort to correct the issue with the data. In some cases, this is relatively easy; in other cases, particularly in those of a historical nature, it may be impossible. If the problem with the data cannot be effectively addressed, scholars may be forced to discard the data and move on to other tests (and other data) to evaluate their hypotheses.

Responses to the second case normally involve an improvement in the methods used to evaluate the data. Over time, as new and improved methods become available, this occurs on a regular basis. In some cases, disagreements over certain aspects of the methodology are not

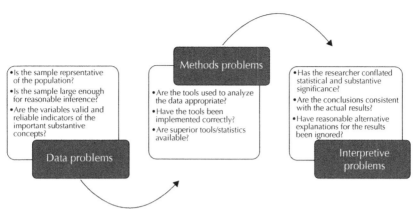

Figure 2-2: Research and potential problems.

amenable to resolution through the application of a new and improved methodology. In these cases, methodological disagreements tend to be resolved over time by the accumulation of additional results from other types of substantively related analyses. The original issue – say, a disagreement over the operationalization of a concept – may well become less important as alternative operationalizations prove useful in subsequent empirical tests.

Responses to the third option are somewhat more complicated. In this case, there is no easy resolution without further study. If further analysis suggests that the original result overstated the magnitude of the effect, then the contention of substantive significance will be increasingly difficult to maintain. By the same token, if further analysis suggests that the original result actually understated the magnitude of the substantive effect, then the presence of a substantive effect will become more widely accepted. Again, there is no easy response that avoids the need for further analysis.

A second general possibility related to the relationship between the original hypothesis and the evidence is that the evidence suggests that the validity of the hypothesis is contextually dependent. For example, suppose we hypothesize that presidents are much more successful in securing favorable policy from Congress on issues related to foreign and defense policy than they are on domestic policy issues.[26] We then set up our test of this hypothesis. One way to do this would be to

---

[26] This is a statement of the "two presidencies" thesis (made famous by Aaron Wildavsky) that we will discuss in more detail in Chapter 9.

collect data on the success of each of the pieces of legislation on which the president took a public position (either supporting or opposing it). After dividing the legislation (or votes on the legislation) into the two primary categories (foreign and defense policy and domestic policy), we could then create a score that reflects the percentage of pieces of legislation (or roll call votes) on which the president was victorious. If the percentage is higher for the set of foreign and defense policy issues than it is for the domestic policy issues, the evidence is consistent with our hypothesis.

But what if we are unsure of the robustness of this result across time? Conducting a test on data that groups a set of administrations together might hide or obscure important administration-specific variation. Well, we could separate the data into discreet administrations and run the test again. If we have the same result for each administration, then we have even stronger support for our initial hypothesis. But suppose there is some variation in the strength of the effect across administrations. What if we notice that the effect only manifests during the administrations of Democratic presidents, and during Republican administrations we see no difference between presidential success on foreign and defense policy issues and domestic policy initiatives?[27]

We have several options. First, we could question the results as suggested above. Is there a problem with the data? With the method? Have we interpreted the results in a reasonable manner? Alternatively, we may choose to revise our theory in light of the new data. As we are modifying the old theory in response to the analysis, that analysis cannot be viewed as a test of the new theory. If we take this route, we must understand that the new theory is still *untested*. The old theory, found wanting, was revised. To test the new theory, we will need to collect additional data and begin the analytical process again. Or someone else might gather new data and conduct their own independent analysis. This is the nature of the scientific endeavor; it is a communal operation, and good science depends upon a community of scholars doing just this type of work.

WHY A SCIENTIFIC STUDY OF THE PRESIDENCY?

One of the strengths of traditional research on the presidency is the consistently detailed descriptions of particular events and particular people related to presidential history. This description might be

---

[27] There is some evidence of just this type of partisan difference in the literature related to the "two presidencies" hypothesis. More on this in Chapter 9.

based on memories of one's own personal experience in the executive branch (as is a small portion of Neustadt's *Presidential Power*), interviews with current or former public figures, passages from the diaries and memoires of former executive branch officials, or on data from cabinet-level agencies. If we are interested in the sequence or content of meetings between a particular president and congressional leaders during a specific time period, for example, or if we are interested in the growth in the size of the federal workforce since the onset of the New Deal, traditional presidency research is quite helpful.

Traditional presidency research is less helpful when we try to answer more general questions about presidential politics. These questions might include one or more of the following:

1. Why are presidents much more likely to win reelection than lose?
2. Must a president be popular to be powerful?
3. Does the president have control over the executive branch?

The strength of traditional research – painstakingly detailed descriptions – is not especially helpful here. Why? Because no matter how careful the analysis of any particular aspect of a single presidency or a single event during a presidency, case-specific information doesn't necessarily tell us anything about other aspects of that presidency (or other presidencies). Without a scientific orientation, we cannot draw justifiable general conclusions from the detailed, descriptive analyses that are so prevalent.

We could always simply assume that presidents and presidencies are so similar that a comprehensive understanding of any single president or presidency is the same as a comprehensive understanding of all presidents and presidencies. But we cannot justify this assumption. So, claims about Franklin Roosevelt's political strategy during the first 100 days of his administration based on extensive data on his political strategy from the first 100 days of his administration is not an effort at generalization – nor is it an effort to build theory. This is not a criticism of these claims, it is just to say that they are limited – more history than political science. However, if a scholar were to make some claims about the nature of Roosevelt's political strategy over his entire administration based only on information from the first 100 days, this would be an effort to generalize a result from an analysis of an explicitly limited set of data to a broader empirical context. The same could be said for claims about the nature of presidential power – in general – based only on the historical record of the Roosevelt administration. A scholar making these sorts of claims is attempting to generalize from a limited set of data to a much larger empirical context.

As traditional research on the presidency moved beyond historical studies, scholars made just these sorts of empirical claims. Arguably the most famous book on the American presidency – Richard Neustadt's *Presidential Power* (1960) – is a study of presidential power based on three case studies, the Roosevelt, Truman, and Eisenhower administrations. How can we tell which of Neustadt's claims – all based on the Roosevelt, Truman, and Eisenhower administrations – are true for the Clinton administration, or the (second) Bush administration, or the Obama administration? One way to evaluate Neustadt's initial claims is to study each subsequent administration. This is what he did in subsequent editions of *Presidential Power* (through the George H. W. Bush administration). Is it reasonable to conclude that every president worked with his cabinet like Washington or Lincoln? Do all presidents lead like Roosevelt? Do all presidents scheme like Nixon? Or falter like Clinton?

Consider a more recent example – the presidential election of 2008. Would you be willing to draw conclusions about other presidential elections from 2008 alone? The 2008 election would appear to be relatively distinctive. First, you have the most successful female candidate for the president (and wife of a former president) locked in a brutal pitched battle for delegates with the most successful African American candidate for president in American history. Second, the battle for one party's nomination nearly goes to the party convention without resolution for the first time in decades. Third, had the Republican candidate, John McCain, won the presidency he would have become (1) the oldest person ever elected president of the United States and (2) the only American president born outside the United States.[28] Finally, we elected the first African American president, Barack Obama, in American history. Even if you had the most comprehensive and detailed knowledge of the 2008 election, could you use it as the "standard" election from which conclusions about presidential elections *in general* could be drawn? If not the 2008 election, what about the election in 2000 – an election in which the votes in the Electoral College (finalized by an eleventh-hour Supreme Court ruling) conflicted with the popular vote for the first time in over a century? Or what about the election of 1992, an election that included the most popular third-party candidate since former president Theodore Roosevelt ran under the Bull Moose banner? Would any of these elections be sufficiently "standard" for the purposes of generalization?

---

[28] Or colonies that would become states.

Unfortunately, this piecemeal evaluation scheme is unsatisfactory. Inevitably, circumstances vary and the desire to modify the original claims or shift the emphases of the original arguments, however slightly, to fit the new data is difficult to avoid. And it is these shifts and modifications that make it so difficult to evaluate the *general accuracy and applicability* of the original argument. The original claims may be accurate and widely applicable, but in the absence of a more rigorous means of evaluating these claims, we simply don't know. In fact, no single election could possibly be sufficiently "standard" to form the sole basis for general conclusions about presidential elections. Significantly, individual cases do provide insight into what conclusions are *not* always true – for example, the winner of the Electoral College vote wins the popular vote – but individual elections (or individual presidencies) do not provide sufficient information to draw general conclusions about what *is* true for presidential elections (or presidencies or individual presidents).

This tendency to misuse information we receive from a single case or example is widespread, and it's something scientists must be particularly careful about. In his book *Why We Make Mistakes*, Joseph Hallinan (2009) states that we tend to overestimate the significance of especially colorful, surprising, or striking stories; people have a perverse but natural tendency to generalize from exceptional cases. Hallinan describes this behavior as follows:

> … beware the anecdote. … we often give vivid information – like diet testimonials – more credence than it deserves. As a consequence, we frequently make a bad decision. Indeed the power of anecdotes to lead us astray is so strong that an influential CIA study advises intelligence analysts to avoid them. Analysts, it concluded, "should give little weight to anecdotal and personal case histories," unless they are known to be typical, "and perhaps no weight at all if aggregate data based on a more valid sample can be obtained." That's good advice. So, ask for averages, not testimonials. (Hallinan 2009: 215)

Similarly, our efforts to understand presidents and their behavior can too easily fall victim to what social psychologists refer to as the "fundamental attribution error" – the tendency to attribute behavior to personal skills and traits (see Jones and Harris 1967). Social psychologists find that people are far more likely to explain behavior in terms of internal characteristics than in terms of external opportunities or constraints. In the context of the study of the presidency, this cognitive flaw manifests in a preoccupation with inherently idiosyncratic descriptions and explanations of presidential behavior, descriptions and explanations that change from term to term, from president to president. The scientific study of the presidency can help us avoid inferential mistakes resulting from the fundamental attribution error.

But what if your only concern is a single election or a single presidency? Intensive study of one election or one presidency may produce important insights about *that* election or *that* presidency, but your research will be unavoidably incomplete. No amount of time and energy can provide the means with which even a trained scholar can fully replicate reality. Descriptions, regardless of the detail, are inherently incomplete. No description – even if we ignore issues of bias – adequately captures "reality." Due to the infinite complexity of reality, even the most skilled and careful scholars overlook or ignore important details. In *Designing Social Inquiry*, King, Keohane, and Verba cogently describe the crux of the problem:

> ... the most comprehensive description done by the best cultural interpreters[29] will drastically simplify, reify, and reduce the reality that has been observed. Indeed, *the difference between the amount of complexity in the world and that in the thickest of descriptions is still vastly larger than the difference between the thickest of descriptions and the most abstract quantitative or formal analysis.* (1994: 43)

If our very best efforts to describe, analyze, and explain a single phenomenon (e.g., a presidential election result) by focusing solely on that phenomenon are unavoidably limited and incomplete – if our best efforts to include *everything* are hopeless – what are we to do? We can study other phenomena as well. If we cannot avoid missing or excluding details, then we want to make every effort to avoid missing the most *important* details. But if we only study a single case, then we have no idea, a priori, which details are important and which are not. What we need is a way to differentiate between *important* details and *trivial* details. Helping us make just these sorts of distinctions is one of the great benefits of the scientific approach to the presidency.

Scholars who take a scientific approach focus on the systematic similarities and differences between presidents. If they were to focus instead on the individuality of each president, their analyses would be severely limited. Suppose we attribute presidential success in the policy-making arena or presidential "greatness" (more on this in Chapter 11) to a set of idiosyncratic individual characteristics. Descriptively

---

[29] King, Keohane, and Verba are commenting specifically on a type of data gathering referred to by anthropologists as "thick description." However, the gist of the conclusion is true for all descriptive efforts.

and historically speaking, we may then discuss how certain particular presidents were able to achieve particular policy goals, or exercise influence, or achieve greatness; but we are not in a position to determine *why* they were able to do these things (and other presidents were not) – unless we are willing to consider some personalistic, idiosyncratic answer sufficient.

Viewing presidents solely from an individualistic perspective (what some scholars would refer to as the president-centered approach) prevents us from drawing any *general* conclusions about presidential power or presidential policy making. If we hope to use the research on the presidency to predict the behavior of a failure, then the individualistic approach cannot help us. If we hope to use research on the presidency to inform our choice of future presidents, the individualistic approach is equally ineffective. The individualistic approach may be invaluable if our interests are exclusively historical. It is, however, important to realize that the individualistic approach has very different goals – and provides quite different insights – than the scientific approach.

The distinction between the president-centered approach and the scientific approach does not imply that inherently personal aspects of the presidency may not be studied in a scientific manner. For example, there is a considerable amount of self-consciously scientific research on presidential psychology. James David Barber's most famous work, *Presidential Character* (originally published in 1972 and now in its fifth edition), is an attempt to analyze presidential psychology – and its impact on presidential success – from a scientific perspective. Now, the extent to which Barber is successful is an admittedly open to question; nevertheless, he makes a concerted effort to rigorously and scientifically deal with a topic that is traditionally treated in a descriptive, historical manner. Similarly, the bargaining and negotiation theory associated with Neustadt has also generated a considerable amount of work in the scientific vein – research that is arguably more scientific than the work which spawned it, *Presidential Power.*

Just as the scientific study of the presidency does not revolve around presidential individualism, neither is it "institutionally" focused. The institutions of the presidency do not exist in a vacuum, nor are they necessarily impervious to the skills and abilities of the particular president who holds the office. Institutionally oriented research (what some scholars would refer to as "presidency-centered" research) directs our attention away from the other factors (such as public support or the strength of political parties) that might well play a role in presidential politics.

A scientific orientation to the study of the presidency has grown in some areas of the literature much more quickly than in others. For example, presidential election studies have long been analytically rigorous, and distinctive theories and research programs developed in this subfield relatively quickly. Individual-level quantitative analysis of vote choices and turnout in presidential elections goes back at least to the 1940s (see, for example, Berelson, et al's [1954] *Voting*, a study of voting patterns in Elmira, New York, during the 1948 presidential elections). Some of the most prominent research in political science focuses on presidential elections, and it is often based on the most rigorous empirical methods and theoretical tools available.[30]

The early rigor and scientific orientation of the presidential election literature is not, however, characteristic of the great bulk of the scholarly literature on the American presidency – even that part of the literature that is often included in courses on the presidency in political science departments. This has changed in the past 20 years, but there is still a long way to go.

In the following chapters, you will be introduced to the scientific study of the American presidency. Each chapter starts with a specific puzzle, followed up by a discussion of the most important recent research on that puzzle. Then, through a set of guided research assignments, you will have a chance to examine some data and investigate this puzzle yourself. Along the way, you will learn about the presidency, the relationships presidents have with their peers and subordinates, the roles they play in policy-making environments, and what makes them great. And you will also learn something about how to learn.

IMPORTANT TERMS

control
deduction
degenerating research program
dependent variable
description
experiment
explanation
falsification
hypothesis

---

[30] *The American Voter* (Campbell et al. 1960) is only the most famous example.

independent variable
induction
logic of discovery
naïve falsification
normal science
observation
operationalize
population
positive heuristic
positivism
prediction
progressive research program
psychology of discovery
puzzle
sample
science
sophisticated methodological falsification
theory
treatment
verification

3

☆ ☆ ☆

The Presidency

Background and Foundations

Throughout this text, I presume a basic knowledge of American politics. Political science majors who have taken an introductory course in American government should have this basic knowledge. Most readers will have taken other courses in American government – courses on Congress, interest groups, voting, parties, the Court, public policy – and the information and insight you have gained in these other courses will serve you well as you study the presidency. However, a scientific study of the presidency requires a substantive background rarely taught outside of courses specifically focused on the presidency and the executive branch. I present some of the more detailed background information in the chapters that follow; this chapter includes the most fundamental aspects of that background knowledge – the "nuts and bolts" of the presidency.

The organization of this chapter largely mirrors the overall organization of the book. After an introductory section focusing on the Founding era – especially the Founders disagreements over the character and scope of presidential power – there are relatively brief informational sections on each of the following:

1. the historical development of the office of the presidency including a discussion of presidential powers (both formal and informal)
2. the selection process
3. presidential relations with Congress
4. presidential relations with the Supreme Court
5. the broader Executive branch
6. the president's role in foreign policy making
7. the president's role in economic policy making

Each of these sections includes information that will support your mastery of the related material included in subsequent chapters. We now begin with a brief discussion of the founding of the American presidency.

THE FOUNDING AND THE HISTORICAL DEVELOPMENT OF THE PRESIDENCY

Most students of the presidency would argue that the modern institution (usually viewed as having been established during Franklin Delano Roosevelt's administration) is dramatically different from the presidency of earlier time periods (even 10–20 years earlier, let alone a century earlier). If that's the case, why would we (as political scientists rather than historians) actually care (except from the standpoint of historical interest) about the presidents and the presidency before 1932?

First, we care because of the uniquely insightful and important debates about the presidency and presidential power during the Constitutional Convention. Neither before nor since has a group of political figures had such a vested interest in getting the structure of the American government correct. In the mid-1780s, the threat of reprisal from the English and the growing French threat were real dangers. Failure to design and establish a government significantly more efficient and effective than the government under the Articles of Confederation posed significant costs and, frankly, grave dangers. As the absence of a meaningful executive (to say nothing of an executive branch) was one of the more or less widely accepted shortcomings of the Articles, the design of the new and improved executive branch was of primary concern during the constitutional debates. As it happens, these debates highlighted and elaborated on a set of crucial issues surrounding the construction of an effective executive branch, and these issues – though often in a somewhat different form – remain today.

Second, one of the ways we learn is from comparison; to fully comprehend the modern presidency, we must understand how and why it is different (and how and why it is the same) as the earlier presidency. I certainly will not argue that the twenty-first-century presidency is but a subtle revision of the presidency of the nineteenth or early twentieth century. But I will argue that the difference is one of degree; the categorical or qualitative differences are to be found in other institutions or in the relationship of the national and state governments more generally. Arguably, of the three branches of the national government, the presidency has changed the least. We'll discuss why that contention is so controversial.

Third, and consistent with the point above, the strategic dynamics of presidential politics may vary in certain ways (or along certain dimensions), but in other ways they are constant across time periods. To the extent there is this presumed consistency, understanding the behaviors of the historical presidents in earlier institutional presidencies provides direct insight into the behaviors of the modern presidents. The reason why we have tended to view the modern presidency as so different from the presidency of earlier eras actually has more to do with our perspective than it does with any specific or inherent characteristic of the institution or those who have inhabited it. If we do not know where we have come from, it is difficult, if not impossible, to have any confidence in our expectations about where we are going.

VIEWING THE PRESIDENCY AS A RESPONSE TO FAILURE

The first constitution of the American states was the Articles of Confederation. Approved by the Second Continental Congress in the fall of 1777, the Articles were not formally ratified by the states until March of 1781, two years from the end of the American Revolution. The shortcomings of the Articles of Confederation are a common topic of discussion in introductory courses in American politics (and in grade school social studies classes, if my daughter's experience is any indication). We have neither the space nor time to deal with these issues in a comprehensive manner, but it is important to discuss in some detail the shortcomings of the Articles that directly or indirectly related to the Founders' understandings of the need for and proper structure of executive power under a new constitutional order.

First, the Articles failed to establish a distinct national executive. Arguably, the Articles provided for no significant executive authority at all, but this is probably going slightly too far. The executive authority provided by the Articles was vested in the president of the legislature (the early Congress), so in some ways, the legislative authority under the Articles (the only significant authority under the Articles) encompassed the executive authority in much the way the legislative authority dominates parliamentary systems today.[1] There was no sense in which the executive and legislative authorities were separate under the Articles, and there was certainly no thought of any system of checks and balances – a crucially important structural component of the Constitution.

The Founders were generally frustrated with the performance of the Articles of Confederation. Though the primary criticisms of the

---

[1] There was no meaningful judicial authority at all.

Articles did not revolve around executive power explicitly, nearly all criticisms went directly to the absence of what Hamilton would refer to as sufficient "energy" in government (for Hamilton, "energy in the executive") in the *Federalist Papers* published during the ratification period for the U.S. Constitution. The structure of the Articles posed several obstacles to effective national coordination, and these obstacles to coordination made it difficult for the national legislature to act at all. First, the national government was given no taxing power (even for defense expenditures). While the legislature could request payments of various kinds from the states, the legislature had no mechanism for enforcing these fees or levies. Without an effective taxing authority, it was difficult for the national government to provide for its armed forces, and it became impossible to service the national debt following the war. The Articles also failed to provide a legislative mechanism for constructing a reasonably open national economy. At the end of the Revolutionary War, state borders were still significant barriers to trade, and the inability to coordinate an effective and meaningful compromise on these internal barriers generated significant economic costs.

It would not be fair to say that the Founders were of the same mind on the necessary improvements to the Articles. In fact, the two most important postrevolutionary political groups (not quite yet political "parties" in the sense that we mean the term – or even in the sense that the term would have been used in the early nineteenth century), the Federalists and the Anti-Federalists, were of quite distinct opinions on the proper revisions of the Articles. Ultimately, the Anti-Federalists wished to revise the existing Articles (and maintain the confederational structure of the national government) and the Federalists wished to replace the Articles with a new document. In the end, the Federalists won. What is important to note at this point is that *no one* was satisfied with the Articles themselves. Regardless of their preferences regarding solutions to the flaws of the Articles, there was a general consensus that the document was insufficient for the purposes of founding a new nation.

In the context of the Founders' experience with various types of executive authority, the weakness of the Articles does not seem so unreasonable. The primary experiential referents for executive power for the Founders were the British crown and the colonial governors. Significantly, the Founders rarely included the English prime minister in their discussions of examples of executive authority. Since the United Kingdom had a prime minister a full half-century before the Revolutionary War, the failure to reference the prime minister as an example of executive authority is not from lack of experience. The Founders simply did not think of the prime minister as a significant executive authority.

To the extent that the Founders' practical appreciation for and understanding of executive authority is based on their experience with the British crown and the colonial governors, their fear of a significant executive authority was nearly universal. And these fears were far from unwarranted. Though the British crown in the late eighteenth century was not the all-powerful monarch of the Middle Ages, King George's powers were extraordinary. In the American colonies, they were often (rightly) perceived as tyrannical. That King George was the face and the leading figure of a growing empire that would shortly make Great Britain the most powerful nation in the world did nothing to diminish colonial fears. Colonial governors as the local representatives of this perceived tyranny were, if possible, even more reviled.

Deviations from the general aversion to executive authority were rare – at least until the widely recognized failure of the government under the Articles of Confederation. While it would not be fair to say that there was a groundswell of support for a powerful new national executive authority, a significant segment of the Founding generation (and the politically active Founders themselves) began to view a *meaningful* executive authority as a prerequisite for a sufficiently strong and successful national government.

While the Legislature is discussed in its own titled article, there is no article for the executive branch in the Articles of Confederation. In fact, in every instance of the use of the words "executive power" (or simply "executive"), the Articles refer solely to that power vested in the governors of the individual states. The closest approximation to an executive power or authority is the *president* of the "Committee of the States" – a body to be appointed by the "United States in Congress assembled" to deal with the business of the national government – including the appointment of necessary officers of government – during times of congressional recess. Committee decisions required a supermajority of nine of the thirteen signatory states. Consistent with the parliamentary nature of the legislature under the Confederation, the legislature appointed the Committee members (one from each state). The Committee then appointed the president, and the president must, himself, have been a member of the Committee. Presidents could hold the office for no more than a year at a time. Aside from the implicit responsibility of presiding over the debates and discussions of the Committee, the president under the Articles had no formal or explicit responsibilities.

CONSTRUCTING THE PRESIDENCY

The available records of the debates of the Constitutional Convention – primarily from the notes of James Madison – indicate that the construction of the executive branch was a topic of considerable importance for the representatives at the convention. It was not, however, the primary issue addressed at the convention. Neither was it the issue of second-most importance. In fact, apart from the controversy surrounding the (1) number of executives (whether or not the president would be singular or plural) and (2) the mechanism to be used to select the president(s), the discussion of the president's actual powers was relatively limited. When one makes a direct comparison between the powers of Congress (in the longest constitutional article, Article I) and the powers of the president, this may not come as such a surprise.

The debate over whether or not there would be more than one executive – probably a surprising topic of discussion for those not especially familiar with the convention debates – was addressed, almost as an afterthought, through the negotiations for the "great compromise" – the agreement to establish two chambers of Congress, one (the Senate) in which representation of the states would be based on equality and one (the House) in which representation of the states would be based on population. The choice of the singular executive was a component of this compromise.

The disagreement over the selection process – which we discuss in considerably more depth in the next section – was multifaceted. First, there was the issue of whether or not the executive should be chosen by the members of the legislature. While the Virginia plan – which was, in game theoretic terms, the agenda setter for the constitutional convention – specified the creation of three branches of the federal government (legislative, executive, and judicial), it also left the choice of president to the legislative branch. Alternatives included some manner of popular vote and/or state nominating conventions. The final choice, the Electoral College, was arguably an odd amalgam of the various proposals. Another structural issue raised with regard to the selection of the president was the proper term of office and the possibility of reelection. Proposed term lengths ranged from two to six years, and there was considerable disagreement over whether or not a president should be able to run for reelection (and if able to run for reelection, how many times a sitting president might stand for reelection). Again, in the end, the decisions of the conventioneers on these matters were largely a function of compromise. The term length was set at four years. Presidents were allowed to stand for reelection, and there was no limitation placed on the number of times a president might stand for reelection (though there was clearly a strong sentiment against standing for reelection multiple times).

The specific powers of the president engendered relatively little controversy because they follow in a seemingly straightforward fashion from the failures of the Articles of Confederation. Also, it is worth noting, they are significantly more limited (at least in number) than those granted to the legislative branch, and while the explicit powers of the legislative branch are subject to implicit constitutional extension through the interpretation and use of the "necessary and proper" clause, no such opportunity is available to the president, because the executive article includes no necessary and proper clause.

In hindsight, the structure of the executive power, such as it is under the Articles, appears strikingly insufficient for the tasks then at hand. The effective coordination of foreign policy in all its forms and guises was clearly beyond the competence or capability of Congress under the Articles or even the significantly smaller Committee – the presence of a chairman (or "president") notwithstanding. There was also no question that the foreign policy powers rightfully rested with the national government. So it is no surprise that the president is designated the "commander in chief" of the national military forces[2] or that the president is responsible for negotiations with foreign powers (indicated by the treaty-making power). In both cases, however, Congress retains a significant check on the authority of the president. In the case of the commander-in-chief power, only Congress may declare war. In the late eighteenth century – with the Founders' expectation that a standing army during peacetime would be but a skeleton force[3] – the declaration power was a significant constraint to the independent exercise of the president's authority as commander-in-chief. Likewise, the president could not enter into any treaty with a foreign power without the advice and *explicit* consent of the Senate.

The Constitution also provides for the establishment of an executive branch beyond the office of the president (and vice president, which is explicitly identified – and whose responsibilities are delineated – in the Constitution), but the document is silent on the proper size and structure of the executive branch, and given that the power of the purse resides with Congress, the president's control over the

---

[2] The president was also designated commander-in-chief of the militias of the various states once they are called into federal service.

[3] Whether or not there would be a standing navy during peacetime was at this time an open question.

extent and activities of the executive branch remains limited by another branch of the federal government. However, what appears so clearly to be a limited executive in 1789 becomes a far more powerful office in later years.[4]

PRESIDENTIAL SELECTION PROCESS: THE WASHINGTON FACTOR AND BEYOND

The constitutional structure of the executive branch – including the distinctive selection process – was developed in the context of the knowledge that George Washington would be the first president, that he would be elected without any significant opposition whatsoever, and – maybe somewhat more controversially – that he would serve as long as he wished. For all intents and purposes, issues relating to the selection process or lengths of administrations simply were not imminent problems.

Washington's own popularity obscured, at least for a time, the difficulties associated with the growing partisan conflict within his own administration. Shortly after Washington took office, it became clear that Secretary of the Treasury Alexander Hamilton and Secretary of State Thomas Jefferson had very different perspectives on the proper role, size, and power of the national government (relative to the state governments), and it also became clear that they each preferred a different side in the brewing international conflict between England and France. While Hamilton strongly favored the British, Jefferson favored the French.

The secondary nature of the structure of the executive branch is reflected in the dialogues and debates between prominent politicians during the ratification period (including the Federalist Papers and various writings that have come to be known, informally, as the Anti-Federalist Papers) and during the ratification debates in the states. Other issues were simply more prominently (and energetically) discussed and debated. The primary issues during the ratification debates centered, not surprisingly given the nature of the new federal system being discussed, on the representative structure of the legislature and the issue of slavery. Though the constitutional convention lasted less than four months (from May 29, 1787 to September 17, 1787), discussion

---

[4] How powerful, particularly in relation to Congress, is an important issue we will address in Chapter 6. That the prerogatives and practical powers of the president significantly exceed those found within the parameters established during the Constitutional convention is, however, a more or less uncontroversial assertion among students of the presidency.

of the powers of the executive branch and the appropriate procedures for selecting the president took up no more than 10 days of the
convention.[5]

The executive branch issues that did generate the most interest
(and the most extensive and intense debate) were related to the division of powers between the executive branch and the Supreme Court,
the length of office (and the allowance for reelection) of the president,
and the procedure used to select the president. Debate over the proper
position and status of the Supreme Court relative to the president was
intense even though it was also relatively brief. Some conventioneers
were of the opinion that the Court should be institutionally tied to
the president, while others sought, and eventually won, a separation
of the powers and authority of the executive and judicial branches.
One of the more interesting aspects of this debate was the more or less
general assumption that the legislative power would (at least initially)
be the greatest. Thus, one of the primary arguments for the institutional connection between the executive and judicial branches was as
a defense against the aggrandizement of the power of the legislative
branch. The same perspective also led to the support for an executive veto. Along these lines, the position Madison attributes to James
Wilson is illustrative:

> After the destruction of the King in Great Britain, a more pure and
> unmixed tyranny sprang up in the parliament than had been exer-
> cised by the monarch. He insisted that we had not guarded against
> the danger on this side by a sufficient self-defensive power either to
> the Executive or Judiciary department. (Ketcham 1986: 160)

These issues were, however, significantly less controversial – and produced much more limited debate – than the disagreements and discussions over the selection process and term length for the presidency.
None of the Founders were particularly pleased with any of the extant
options obviously available to them during the convention. Madison's
own perspective on this is illustrative:

> There are objections against every mode that has been, or perhaps
> can be proposed. The election must be made either by some existing
> authority under the National or State Constitutions – or by some spe-
> cial authority derived from the people – or by the people themselves. –
> The two Existing authorities under the National Constitution would

---

[5] This conclusion is based on the most complete set of minutes compiled by a par-
ticipant at the convention, those of James Madison. For more detail, see Ketcham
(1986).

be the Legislative and the Judiciary. The latter he presumed was out of the question.[6] The former was in his Judgment liable to insuperable objections. (Ketcham 1986: 132)

One possibility was selection by Congress, but this was problematic for several reasons. With few exceptions, the Founders were not interested in a parliamentary system modeled on the British system of government.[7] The congressional selection process also suffered from the criticism that it provided insufficient independence for the president and the executive branch. If the president were to be selected by Congress, it was argued, this would, in practice, significantly curtail the extent to which the president could act as an independent bulwark – a truly separate branch in a system of checks and balances – against the encroachment and aggrandizement of legislative authority.

The issue of presidential selection was sufficiently complicated and contentious that the first draft of the Constitution included no selection process at all. It was not until the latter part of the convention (in early September) that a committee formed to address this issue, and the question of the president's tenure in office, presented an outline of the Electoral College in more or less the form we know today. The aspect of the committee report that produced the most controversy was the suggested tie-breaking procedure to be used in the event that no candidate received a majority of the votes of the electors of the Electoral College. The original committee proposal suggested that the president be chosen by the Senate if the Electoral College process failed to produce a winner. The choice of the Senate, instead of the House, was relatively unpopular, so the committee proposal was amended so that the House would select the president if the Electoral College process failed to choose a winner. The Senate would then be responsible for selecting the Vice President.[8]

---

[6] Note that the odd construction here is a result of the fact that Madison is paraphrasing the debates – even his own comments.

[7] Of the Founders, Alexander Hamilton was the most supportive of a governing system that reflected as closely as possible the British system, but even he did not seriously suggest the establishment of a government fully based on the British model. Whether this was due to his own actual preferences or whether it was due to his political pragmatism – and the realization that a British system would not win sufficient support at the convention or at the subsequent ratifying conventions – is still unclear.

[8] Originally, there was only a single ballot for the presidency, and the candidate with the second highest number of electoral votes – the runner-up for president – was designated the vice president. In the event that two candidates were tied in the runner-up position, the Senate would select the vice president. This process was revised rather quickly (in 1804) by the passage and ratification of the Twelfth Amendment that established separate ballots for the presidency and the vice presidency.

Controversy over the term length and tenure of the president was related to the nature of the selection process. As long as selection by Congress was seriously considered, there was considerable support for a rather longer term of office than the current four years but without the possibility of reelection; so the idea of a single seven-year term had considerable support. However, with the shift to an Electoral College system, a shorter term with the possibility of reelection gained in popularity (and, in fact, was a component of the committee report identifying the Electoral College as the procedure for selecting the president). The Founders finally agreed upon a four-year term with the possibility of reelection. Prior to the ratification of the Twenty-Second Amendment in 1951, the Constitution included no restrictions on the number of times a president could run for reelection. The Twenty-Second Amendment established our current restrictions that preclude a sitting president from running for reelection more than once.[9]

The modern Electoral College is institutionally identical to the Electoral College of the early nineteenth century. Electors still cast ballots in their individual states, the ballots are still sent to Washington for counting, and the President of the Senate is still responsible for counting the ballots in a joint session of Congress. The constitutional rules for the selection of Electors have also remained the same since the ratification of the Constitution. What has changed over the course of over 200 years is the manner in which the Electors are chosen. According to the Constitution:

> Each State shall appoint, in such Manner as the Legislature thereof may direct, a Number of Electors, equal to the whole Number of Senators and Representatives to which the State may be entitled in the Congress: but no Senator or Representative, or Person holding an Office of Trust or Profit under the United States, shall be appointed an Elector. (U.S. Constitution, Article II, Section 1)

Today, states use various procedures to select slates of electors. In an overwhelming majority of states, each party's slate of electors is chosen at a party convention (a meeting of party members). In several other states, the executive committees of the state parties select the electors, and there are a couple of states that leave the decision about how to select the electors to the individual parties.[10] In the early years

---

[9] Presidents who have served more than two years of a term for which another person was originally elected (which was vacated due to death or resignation) are only eligible for a single election.

[10] The web site of the National Archives provides detailed information on the Electoral College and the way it works (included information on the selection

of the Electoral College, there were no formal state political parties, so electors were chosen by either state legislatures or state congressional delegations. Over time, as national parties organized at the state level, the state parties took over responsibility for selecting slates of electors.

All states (and the District of Columbia) now use popular elections to select the state's slate of electors for the Electoral College. Though relatively few state ballots actually include the names of the electors along with the candidate to whom they are pledged, the technical role of the ballot in the election process is that of a mechanism for selecting the electors who will actually select the president and vice president. Except for Maine and Nebraska, all states allocate electors on a winner-take-all basis. In a winner-take-all system, the electors for the presidential candidate with the largest percentage of the popular vote in the state (not necessarily a majority of the vote) are all selected and, assuming away the possibility of a *faithless elector*,[11] that candidate receives all of that state's electoral votes. In Maine and Nebraska, two electoral votes are allocated on the basis of a statewide winner-take-all system. The remaining electoral votes are allocated to candidate's electors on the basis of the popular vote in each of the congressional district. With each district receiving a single elector, the winner of the popular vote in each district receives that district's elector.

Following the certification of the vote totals in the individual states (normally by each state's Secretary of State), the selected slate of electors meets in the state capital to cast their (separate, since the Twelfth Amendment) ballots for the president and the vice president. These ballots are then sealed and transmitted to Washington to be counted during a joint session of Congress shortly after the beginning of the following calendar year. Traditionally, the presiding officer of this joint session is the President of the Senate (or the vice president). If one candidate (in the presidential and vice presidential races) receives a majority of the Electoral College votes, that candidate becomes the next president (vice president). If neither candidate (for the presidency or vice presidency)

---

processes for electors). See http://www.archives.gov/federal-register/electoral-college/faq.html#selection (last accessed on December 17, 2009).

[11] A faithless elector is one who casts an electoral vote for a candidate other than the one to whom she is committed. While the Supreme Court has upheld state efforts to require electors to pledge to particular candidates (see *Ray v. Blair* 1952), the Court has not ruled on the constitutionality of legislation actually *punishing* faithless electors after the fact. Faithless electors are quite rare, and if we consider only those situations in which an elector pledged to one major party candidate cast a ballot for the other major party candidate, there have been no instances of this type of significant "faithlessness" since the end of the nineteenth century.

receives a majority of the votes cast by the members of the Electoral College, then the House of Representatives is responsible for selecting the president and the Senate is responsible for selecting the vice president. In the House, representatives cast ballots as state delegations,[12] and so there are 50 votes.[13] A candidate must receive the support of a majority of the state delegations to become president, and additional ballots are taken until one candidate receives a majority of the vote. In the Senate, each senator casts a single ballot. As in the case of the House selection of the president, a candidate must receive a majority of the votes cast to become vice president. Additional Senate ballots are taken until one candidate receives a majority of the votes cast.

The modern selection process includes primary and general election campaigns. During the primary campaigns, candidates vie for their party's nomination for the general election campaign. In both the Democratic and Republican Parties, the nominees are formally chosen at the party convention during the summer prior to the November election. Today, because of the primary and caucus system used to select delegates, convention votes tend to be little more than the official notarization of a previously determined outcome. It was not always so, and during the heyday of party conventions – from the 1830s through the 1960s – the nomination process at the convention was often contentious and unpredictable. In some cases, it has taken dozens of ballots for a nominee to be chosen, and in other cases, "dark horse" candidates have come from far down (or off the initial ballot) to take the nomination (and, in some cases, the presidency).[14] Since the 1976 Republican convention, each party's

---

[12] This procedure has not been used since the nineteenth century, but when it was used, the practice was to allocate a state delegation's single vote to the candidate who received a majority of the votes of the representatives from that state. There are, however, no constitutional requirements relating to the choice procedure used by the individual state delegations in situations such as this.

[13] The District of Columbia does not cast a ballot as it does not have a representative with full voting privileges.

[14] The convention record for the most ballots is the 103 ballots that were necessary for the Democratic Party to select John W. Davis as its nominee in 1924. He was defeated by Calvin Coolidge in the general election. This Democratic convention was also the longest single national convention in American history. James K. Polk won the Democratic Party's nomination (and, subsequently, the White House) following eight ballots on which his name did not appear, and in 1860, the initial Democratic Party convention was so contentious that it ended without the selection of a nominee. The split party would later select two nominees, Stephen Douglas and John C. Breckinridge. Abraham Lincoln's nomination by the Republican Party was not a foregone conclusion. After running second on the first two ballots, he won on the third ballot.

eventual nominee has won a majority of *committed* or *pledged* delegates in advance of the convention, and so the actual convention ballot has been anticlimactic.[15] The parties have a distinct process for the apportionment of delegates among the states, but in both cases, the distribution is related to the size of the state and the strength of the party within the state.

Primary campaigns are composed of a series of state caucuses and primaries that begin with the Iowa caucus. Caucuses, which are somewhat less common than primaries, are composed of a set of small local party meetings, and the participants at these meetings – rather than casting formal ballots at a public polling place – indicate their preferences for the party's nominee after significant discussion with fellow partisans at the caucus. While the results – or "straw polls" – from caucuses give a strong indication of the final distribution of delegates' votes, the delegates themselves are not chosen until state party conventions weeks or months (as in the case of Iowa) later.

Primaries are party-specific elections administered by state and local election boards. Primary voting eligibility in primaries varies by state and party. *Closed* primaries are restricted to party members. *Semiclosed* primaries are limited to party members and independents (closed to registered members of the opposing party). Any registered voter may participate in an *open* primary.[16] Note that a voter may participate in no more than a single primary.

Party primaries are nearly a century old,[17] but the prominent role they play in modern presidential elections dates only to the early 1970s. In the early twentieth century, candidate participation in primaries was often viewed as a sign of electoral weakness, and primary victors had no claim to party nominations (as the Republicans' selection of William Howard Taft in 1912, after Theodore Roosevelt's set of primary victories, clearly showed). Today, strong showings in the series of presidential primaries beginning with the New Hampshire

---

[15] Convention ballots for both parties include committed and uncommitted delegates. The votes of uncommitted delegates are not tied to the primary or caucus results from their home state. In the Democratic Party, each state has a number of committed and uncommitted delegates. While the same is true for the Republican Party in most states, several states' delegates are all uncommitted.

[16] There is also a subtle variation of the open primary referred to as the *semiopen* primary. In a semiopen primary, such as in Ohio (a state that does not require a party designation during the voter registration process), a registered voter may participate in either party's primary, but she must designate her choice before casting a ballot, and if she had voted in the alternate party's primary during the previous election, she would need to sign a statement indicated her wish to vote in a different party's primary.

[17] The first presidential party primary was held in Oregon in 1910.

primary in January of the election year are crucial to a candidate's prospects for electoral success.

Both primary and general elections are expensive affairs, and the cost of both has increased dramatically over the course of the most recent elections. During the 2008 campaign – the most expensive in American history – presidential candidates raised over $1.5 billion from private and government sources.[18] Although the federal government provides funding for primary campaigns through a matching grant program, the restrictions on these funds are such that the most competitive candidates regularly eschew the funds so that they may raise and spend significantly more money without extensive regulation. The federal government also provides large general election grants to major party candidates (and significantly more limited funding to minor party candidates who receive at least 5% of the national vote). In 2008, the value of the major party general election grant was more than $84 million. However, candidates who accept the general election grant must agree to limit their expenditures to these funds (with the exception of expenditures for legal assistance and reporting requirements), so candidates in a position to raise significantly more money (such as then-senator Obama in 2008) forego these federal funds so that they may raise and spend significantly more money.

Because presidential elections are decided in the Electoral College, candidates focus campaigns on certain states, which are often referred to as "battleground" states (see Shaw 2006). Campaign visits, spending, and advertising are not evenly distributed throughout the United States. Battleground states tend to receive far more attention than states that are highly likely to go for one party or the other. The number of battleground states varies by election, but normally far fewer than half of the states fit into this category. Battleground states may range from very large (e.g., Florida) to relatively small (e.g., Iowa). Finally, remember that the distribution of electoral votes is such that victory in the largest 11 states is sufficient to win a majority of the Electoral College; this is true regardless of the vote in every other state.

CONGRESS AND THE PRESIDENT

The primary interinstitutional relationship in the national government is between Congress and the president. The relationship between the executive, legislative, and judicial branches is often characterized as a *separation of powers*. In a formal sense, this characterization is

---

[18] Specific information on the receipts and expenditures of each candidate may be accessed at the web site of the Federal Election Commission, http://www.fec.gov (last accessed on December 17, 2009).

accurate. The formal constitutional distinctions between the branches are significant, and the ability of each to check and balance the exercise of the powers by the other is significant.

In a practical sense, the powers exercised by each branch are not separate. It is more accurate to say, as presidency scholar Richard Neustadt did a half-century ago, that powers are *shared* rather than *separated* (Neustadt 1960). The Founders themselves disagreed about the true separation of powers. For example, no less an expert on the Constitution than James Madison argued that the executive power was shared by the president and the Congress.[19] Congress may check the power of the president through the Senate's constitutional right of advice and consent. While presidents may make appointments (to the Supreme Court, to direct Cabinet-level agencies such as the Department of Defense or the State Department, or run independent regulatory agencies such as the Federal Trade Commission or the Federal Communications Commission), each of these appointments is subject to Senate confirmation. And though it is now widely expected that presidential appointees serving in positions without a fixed term (such as cabinet secretaries) serve at the pleasure of the president – meaning the president may unilaterally remove them from office without the authorization of Congress – this authority was controversial until at least the latter half of the nineteenth century.

Likewise, the president shares the legislative power with Congress by dint of the fact that presidents may veto legislation. In a formal sense, the primary executive check on the power of Congress is the veto power. Technically, there are two types of presidential veto: (1) the "normal" veto and (2) the pocket veto. See Table 3-1 for a description of the two types of vetoes and the potential congressional responses. Note that if a president fails to sign a bill received more than 10 days from the end of the adjournment of the legislative session, the bill becomes a law without the president's signature.

The use of the presidential veto – and the frequency with which Congress has successfully overridden presidential vetoes – varies dramatically throughout the American history. Seven presidents issued no vetoes at all, but all of these had administrations prior to the beginning of the twentieth century.[20] Franklin Roosevelt issued more vetoes

---

[19] See Madison's side of the Pacificus–Helvidius debates during Washington's presidency (Hamilton and Madison 2007).

[20] James Garfield was the last president to complete his term without issuing a veto, and he served less than a year. Millard Fillmore was the penultimate president to complete a term without issuing a veto, and he was a pre–Civil War president. All data on presidential vetoes was gathered from the web site of the Office of the Clerk of the House of Representatives, http://clerk.house.gov/ (last accessed on December 20, 2009).

Table 3-1: Two types of vetoes

	Presidential action	Potential congressional response
"Normal" veto	Presidents rejects a legislative act.	Final passage requires a super majority (two-thirds) of both houses of Congress. Without that, the bill fails.
Pocket veto	No action on a bill received less than 10 days from the adjournment of the legislative session.	The bill fails. Following adjournment, no congressional action is possible.

than any other president (635), but he also served significantly longer than any other president. Grover Cleveland issued almost as many vetoes (614), but he only served two (discontinuous) terms. No president since Dwight Eisenhower has issued more than 78 vetoes. The 10 vetoes issued by George W. Bush is the smallest number by a two-term president since James Madison's 7 vetoes in the early nineteenth century.

Obviously, veto overrides are far less common than vetoes. Andrew Johnson, one of only two presidents to be impeached, had 15 vetoes overridden; he also had the highest percentage of regular vetoes overridden (15 of 21). No other president has ever had more than a dozen vetoes overridden, and 11 presidents who issued vetoes had no overrides at all. For more detailed information on the numbers of vetoes and veto overrides during recent administrations, see Table 3-2.

The veto power is certainly a useful tool of obstruction – and this obstruction may easily extend beyond conventional legislation to legislative efforts to punish or reorganize executive branch departments and regulatory agencies (see Morris 2000 for a more detailed discussion of these political dynamics) – but the relationship between its use and the broader exercise of presidential power is difficult to determine. One of the primary problems associated with explaining why some presidents use the veto far more than others is determining whether the increase in vetoes is a function of (1) a significant increase in "objectionable" legislation (Rohde and Simon 1985; Shields and Huang 1995 and 1997; Woolley 1991) or (2) an increase in the individual-level propensity to veto (Gilmour 2002). In essence, it is a matter of whether presidents who issue more vetoes do so because they receive more objectionable legislation or because they are more critical of the

Table 3-2: Vetoes, pocket vetoes, and overrides: from FDR to George W. Bush

President	Regular vetoes	Pocket vetoes	Vetoes overridden
Franklin D. Roosevelt	372	263	9
Harry S. Truman	180	70	12
Dwight D. Eisenhower	73	108	2
John F. Kennedy	12	9	0
Lyndon B. Johnson	16	14	0
Richard M. Nixon	26	17	7
Gerald R. Ford	48	18	12
James E. Carter	13	18	2
Ronald R. Reagan	39	39	9
George H. W. Bush	29	15	1
William J. Clinton	36	1	2
George W. Bush	10	0	3

Source: Data from the Office of the Clerk of the House of Representatives, http://clerk.house.gov/art_history/house_history/vetoes.html (last viewed October 9, 2009).

legislation they do receive. If the answer is the former, then it is not at all clear that the frequency of vetoes is in any way an indicator of presidential power. In some cases, presidents widely perceived to be powerful (such as Franklin Roosevelt) issue large numbers of vetoes; in other cases, a plethora of vetoes (at least relatively speaking) appears to be a sign of weakness (Ford and Andrew Johnson fit here).

The most authoritative recent research on the veto power suggests that there is some truth to both explanations for the variation in the use of the veto over time. In some cases, presidents find themselves in a weakened political position and so they receive significantly more objectionable legislation than presidents in a stronger political position (see Cameron 2000; Gilmour 2002). By the same token, some presidents are simply more inclined to use the veto power than others (Gilmour 2002). Thus, while the president's ability to veto legislation is an important tool for dealing with Congress and protecting the executive branch from what might be viewed as legislative interference, actual use of the veto power may be a sign of weakness or strength.

Presidents are not limited to vetoes or simple signatures in their response to legislation passed by Congress. President may also, and have with increasing frequency issued *signing statements* in response to congressional legislation. Technically, a signing statement is a formal presidential communication explicitly associated with the final approval of a specific piece of legislation. Traditionally, signing statements tended to be hortatory comments on the new law. Though rarely used until the middle of the twentieth century, signing statements have become increasingly popular policy tools. As the use of signing statements has grown, the use of signing statements to criticize legislation has also grown.[21] Counting signing statements is relatively easy,[22] but determining which include specific criticisms of the attached legislation is somewhat more difficult. Even with this difficulty, all of the standard coding strategies suggest that George W. Bush consistently used signing statements to criticize legislation and to indicate ways in which purposes and directives of the legislation would by executed (or not) to suit the policy objectives of the president.[23] The dramatic increase in the use of signing statements – especially the increase in the use of signing statements to expand presidential authority at the expense of Congress – has drawn considerable attention, and the role of signing statements in the relationship between Congress and the president is an increasingly prominent topic of research.

EXECUTIVE ORDERS

An executive order is a formal statement either (1) directing an agency or agencies within the executive branch to implement a specific policy, rule, or procedure or (2) authorizing an agency or agencies within the executive branch to implement a specific policy, rule, or procedure. Executive orders do *not* require the assent of either chamber of Congress. For this reason, their use is unilateral – only the president may issue executive orders, and Congress cannot constrain the president's use of executive orders. Executive orders are subject to the standard of constitutionality (as determined by the Supreme Court), but efforts to have an executive order struck down are rarely successful.

[21] A recent report (Halstead 2007) produced by the *Congressional Research Service*, provides a brief description and analysis of the historical and modern-day use of signing statements. Also see Kelley's (2007) recent work on this topic.

[22] A running tally of signing statements is maintained on the web site of the American Presidency Project at the University of California at Santa Barbara, http://www.presidency.ucsb.edu/signingstatements.php (last accessed on December 17, 2009).

[23] Halstead (2007) finds that nearly 80% of George W. Bush's signing statements were critical of the approved legislation.

Presidents use executive orders for a variety of important purposes. According to Mayer:

> Presidents have used executive orders to establish policy, reorganize
> executive branch agencies, alter administrative and regulatory pro-
> cesses, affect how legislation is interpreted and implemented, and
> take whatever action is permitted within the boundaries of their con-
> stitutional or statutory authority. (1999: 445)[24]

Since the parameters of both "constitutional" and "statutory" authority are broad and constantly subject to reinterpretation by the Court,
the latitude for the effective use of executive agreements is quite extensive. Presidents issue executive orders across the full range of substantive policy areas. For example, President Obama has used executive
orders to create boards and councils such as the Economic Recovery
Advisory Board and the White House Council on Women and Girls.
He also used executive orders to close the detention facilities at the
Guantanamo Bay Naval Base and to restrict interrogation procedures
for individuals in federal custody.

The frequency of the use of executive orders varies somewhat
by president, but most modern presidents have issued several hundred executive orders. Franklin Roosevelt, as in so many other areas
relating to the number of actions, issued by far the largest number of
executive orders, well over 3,000, and, at least for the presidents in
the modern era, George W. Bush issued the fewest number of executive orders (165).[25] Finally, an important difference between executive
orders and legislative acts is that executive orders are significantly
easier to reverse. While the reversal of a legislative act requires a
subsequent legislative act, countermanding an executive order simply requires a subsequent executive order, and it is far easier to issue
an executive order than to successfully shepherd a piece of legislation through Congress. Though not as prominent as executive orders,
presidents also make policy by issuing *presidential memoranda*. Once
referred to as *presidential letters*, presidential memoranda may direct
federal agencies in a manner similar to executive orders (though normally on more detailed policy issues). Presidents also use memoranda

---

[24] Also see Mayer (2001).

[25] All of the executive orders issued since the beginning of the second term of
Franklin Roosevelt's administration are catalogued by number, administration,
and subject matter in the online Federal Register at the web site of the National
Archives, http://www.archives.gov/federal-register/executive-orders/disposition.
html (last accessed on December 17, 2009).

in response to the fact-finding requirements of federal legislation (as in cases of a *presidential determination*) or to make broad proclamations.[26] The availability of these sorts of unilateral policy-making alternatives to conventional lawmaking influences not only the president's relationship with Congress but also the president's relationship with the other members of the executive branch (which we will discuss in more detail later in the chapter).

THE SUPREME COURT AND THE PRESIDENT

The Founders disagreed about the proper scope and significance of the powers of the Supreme Court, and the treatment of the Court's powers in the Constitution is sufficiently vague as to leave room for considerable variance in interpretation. Chief Justice John Marshall's opinion in *Marbury v. Madison* is widely cited as the crucial turning point in the development of the authority of the Supreme Court and judicial review, but it was not until the twentieth century that the Court fully embraced its modern role in the federal system. Today, however, there is little question that the Court is widely perceived as the final arbiter of the meaning of the Constitution.[27] Most significantly, within the context of the study of the presidency, the Court is the final arbiter of the constitutionality of acts of Congress and the president.

Because of the Court's central role in the federal system, the president's appointment power is an important policy-making prerogative. Research on the voting patterns of Supreme Court justices indicates that a justice's ideological orientation plays an important role in determining her or his decision making on the Court.[28] As the Court is in a position to restrict or enable the policy-making activities of Congress and the president, presidents have strong incentives to appoint justices with whom they are ideologically compatible. By the same token, members of the Senate have an incentive to use the confirmation prerogative to block appointees who are deemed ideologically (or professionally) unacceptable. Supreme Court nominees tend to receive significantly more media attention and public scrutiny than any other presidential nominee, and Supreme Court nominees have

[26] Examples of recent executive orders and presidential memoranda may be found on the White House web-site at http://www.whitehouse.gov/briefing-room/presidential-actions/executive-orders (last accessed on December 17, 2009).

[27] Whittington (2007) provides a compelling explanation for the development of judicial review and the tradition of presidential acquiescence to it.

[28] See Segal and Spaeth's (2002) recent work on this perspective (the "attitudinal" model of judicial decision making).

participated in some of the most famous and contentious confirmation hearings.[29] The confirmation hearings of Reagan nominee Robert Bork and George H. W. Bush nominee Clarence Thomas are two of the most infamous confirmation hearings in modern American history. Though the Senate confirms Supreme Court nominees at a very high rate, the exceptional cases – such as that of Bork – tend to be very high profile. We will discuss the politics of the nomination–confirmation process in the chapter on the president's relationship with the Court.

THE EXECUTIVE BRANCH

The modern executive branch is a twentieth-century creation. Though the executive branch beyond the offices of the president and the vice president date to the first U.S. Congress,[30] it would be only a shadow of the current executive branch until the middle of the twentieth century. Until the latter part of the nineteenth century, the executive branch was quite small (certainly in relation to today's standards) and was populated primarily by the workings of the *spoils system*. The spoils system was the process through which elected officials distributed patronage (primarily in the form of government jobs) to their political supporters. Partisan and personal attachments were cultivated through the distribution of patronage, and as the control of Congress and the White House changed from one party to the other, a set of government employees favoring one party would be replaced by a new set of employees who favored the opposing parties. Under the spoils system, organizational skill and substantive policy expertise were rare, so the expectations placed on the bureaus and agencies were far more limited.

In the latter part of the nineteenth century, the assassination of President James Garfield after little more than six months in office by a frustrated office seeker resulted in a dramatic reorganization of the executive branch by Congress. Shortly after the rise of Chester A. Arthur to the presidency in the wake of Garfield's assassination, the Pendleton Act was passed. The Pendleton Act established the

---

[29] Supreme Court nominations require Senate confirmation.

[30] The first cabinet-level departments were created in 1789. In order, the first departments were Foreign Affairs (subsequently renamed the State Department), the War Department (renamed the Department of Defense), and the Treasury Department. Thomas Jefferson was the first Secretary of State. Henry Knox, an artillery officer who served with George Washington during the Revolutionary War, was the first Secretary of War, and Alexander Hamilton became the first Secretary of the Treasury.

Civil Service Commission, effectively ending the spoils system by eventually placing a majority of federal jobs on a merit system. The shift to a merit system provided the opportunity for the development of agencies with policy-specific expertise in the executive branch.

The rise of the Progressives in the late nineteenth century and early twentieth century also played an important role in the development of the modern executive branch. In response to the widespread economic transformation (and corruption) of the post–Civil War era, Progressives such as Theodore Roosevelt pushed for government reform and a dramatic increase in the growth of the federal government's regulatory capacity. For the growth and development of the executive branch, the ratification of the Sixteenth Amendment and the creation of a set of independent regulatory agencies were two of the most important results of the rise of the Progressive movement. The Sixteenth Amendment greatly enhanced the potential scope of the use of the income tax, and this provided a significant new revenue base for the federal government, a revenue base that could be tapped to provide the necessary resources for a significantly larger executive branch. The creation of a set of new independent regulatory agencies – such as the Interstate Commerce Commission, the Federal Reserve, and the Federal Trade Commission – during the administrations of progressives Theodore Roosevelt and Woodrow Wilson institutionalized the transfer of primary regulatory authority from the states to the federal government and provided the foundation for the subsequent growth and development of the modern administrative state.[31]

The early years of FDR's New Deal solidified the foundation of the modern executive branch. During 1934 and 1935, the size of the civilian federal workforce exploded, and the overwhelming majority of new federal employees were hired by new agencies (such as the Social Security Administration, Tennessee Valley Authority, and the Federal Deposit Insurance Corporation) or by agencies with substantial new policy responsibility (see Rockof 1998). In simplest terms, "one can say that the increase in the share of the labor force working for the federal government in the twentieth century is basically the product of 1934 and 1935" (Bordo et al. 1998: 128).

The modern executive branch is a multifaceted agglomeration of sets of distinct types of agencies and offices. These types range from cabinet-level bureaucracies, such as the State Department and

---

[31] See Carpenter (2001) and Skowronek (1982) for authoritative treatments of the growth of the federal bureaucracy during the latter part of the nineteenth century and the early portion of the twentieth century.

the Department of Defense, to independent regulatory agencies (e.g., the Federal Reserve, the Federal Communications Commission, and the Federal Election Commission), nonprofit organizations (National Endowment for the Arts and the National Endowment for the Humanities), foundations (the National Science Foundation), public corporations (the United States Postal Service, the mortgage giants Freddie Mac and Fannie Mae), and the Executive Office of the President (which houses the White House Staff). President are the chief executive officers (CEOs) of the federal government, but their relationship with each of the agencies within the executive branch varies by agency type. The key distinguishing characteristics between the various agency types are: (1) the selection and removal process for agency heads; (2) the number of agency heads; and (3) the public/private character of the agency.

The president has the closest relationship with the White House Staff. The White House Staff is not subject to the advice and consent of the Senate, and as with other executive branch officials without a fixed term of office, the staff are subject to removal at the president's discretion. The president has had at least a few personal or administrative staff – Lincoln had two secretaries for much of his presidency – since the Washington administration. The modern White House Staff, though, is a twentieth-century invention and began to take its modern form only after the creation of the Executive Office of the President (EOP) by Franklin Roosevelt in 1939.[32] Like the executive branch more generally, the size of the White House Staff grew significantly over time. It also developed policy responsibilities during this time period, responsibilities that were institutionalized during and after the Kennedy administration (see Patterson 2000). Today, the hundreds of personnel on the White House Staff include the president's chief of staff, assistant chiefs of staffs, senior advisors, staff for the First lady and the vice president, and various other support staff.

Besides the White House Staff, the EOP includes a large range of agencies, boards, and councils with a variety of significant policy responsibilities. The Council of Economic Advisors provides economic advice and economic policy expertise to the president. The Office of Management and Budget coordinates the president's budget and the expenditure of federal funds. The Office of the United States Trade Representative is responsible for international trade negotiations – both bilateral and multilateral trade negotiations – and the National

---

[32] The White House Office was one of the two original components (with the Bureau of the Budget, which would become the Office of Management and Budget) of the EOP.

Security Council provides foreign policy expertise and advice to the president.[33] Thousands of federal employees work within the EOP, and the nominations of senior officials in each of the agencies, boards, and councils in the EOP are subject to the advice and consent of the Senate. This is an important distinction between the White House Staff and the senior staff in other EOP organizations.

Cabinet-level departments and independent regulatory agencies also make up important components of the executive branch. The president's cabinet includes fifteen executive branch departments.[34] The presidential appointees responsible for coordinating the activities of each of the individual agencies are referred to as "secretaries," except for the director of the Department of Justice, who is referred to as the Attorney General. Some of the cabinet agencies are quite old. The Department of State and the Treasury Department were both "original" agencies (i.e., created in 1789). Other agencies are far younger. While only the Department of Homeland Security is a twenty-first century creation, nine of the fifteen agencies were created during the twentieth century.[35]

Departments are primarily staffed by career civil service personnel, bureaucrats who are not subject to replacement at the end of a presidential administration. Only a small layer of political leadership (including the secretary) in each department are political appointees. These political appointees are subject to the advice and consent of the Senate, and they are subject to unilateral removal by the president. The distinctive employment situations of career civil servants and political appointees will play an important role in our discussion of the relationship between the president and the executive branch in a later chapter.

Cabinet departments, unlike agencies in the EOP, have significant policy-making responsibilities. The primary responsibility of EOP agencies is to provide advice and administrative support to the president. Departments are responsible for the implementation of federal policy. Because Congress and the president make federal policy

---

[33] A full list of the organizations in the EOP can be found on the White House web site at http://www.whitehouse.gov/administration/eop/ (last accessed on December 17, 2009).

[34] The Cabinet departments are Agriculture, Commerce, Defense, Education, Energy, Health and Human Services, Homeland Security, Housing and Urban Development, Interior, Labor, State, Transportation, Treasury, Veterans Affairs, and Justice.

[35] Although the Department of Defense is technically a twentieth-century creation, the agency that it replaced, the Department of War, was part of the original cabinet.

(normally through statute or executive order), Congress takes much more interest in department activities than the activities of organizations in the EOP. Congressional oversight of the boards and councils in the EOP is quite limited; congressional oversight of departments is extensive. Department secretaries are often important political actors in their own right, and department secretaries often have a substantial independent impact on policy. Consider Secretary of State (and Secretary of Defense) George C. Marshall's role in the development of the Marshall Plan. This sort of independent political influence is very rare among senior staff in the EOP.

Finally, the executive branch also includes a host of independent agencies. Independent agencies are those separate from other federal agencies or departments. Independent agencies are created by statute, and most of them are managed by a group of senior-level policy makers or commissioners. These commissioners are appointed by the president with the advice and consent of the Senate. But unlike directors of EOP boards and councils or Cabinet secretaries, commissioners have fixed terms of office and so are not subject to removal by the president.[36] Commissioners' terms are often staggered, so it is difficult (if not impossible) for presidents to appoint a full slate of commissioners, and the terms are often quite long (significantly more than a four-year presidential term).[37]

Independent agencies have a wide range of policy responsibilities, from running the space program (NASA) to managing social security (Social Security Administration). A subset of independent agencies focuses specifically on the oversight and regulation of various aspects of the economy; these independent agencies are referred to as independent regulatory agencies. Independent regulatory agencies have policy responsibilities that range from regulating the airwaves and bandwidth (Federal Communications Commission) to the stock market (Securities and Exchange Commission), federal elections (Federal Elections Commission), and the financial sector (Federal Reserve Board). As these agencies are created by statute, their policy *portfolios* are subject to revision. In some cases, policy-making responsibilities have grown dramatically over the life of certain agencies.[38]

---

[36] Technically, this would be removal without "cause." Presidents may remove commissioners but their capacity to do so is limited by statute.

[37] Governors of the Federal Reserve Board, for example, serve 14-year terms.

[38] The Federal Reserve Board would be one IRA that has grown dramatically in stature and significance since its creation in 1913.

THE PRESIDENT'S ROLE IN FOREIGN POLICY MAKING

Congress has a long list of explicit or *enumerated* powers (e.g., the power to coin money, set weights and measures, borrow money, raise an army, declare war, and regulate commerce). Since the Founding, additional powers – what are referred to as *implied* powers – have accrued to Congress through the Supreme Court's interpretation of the *necessary and proper clause* (see U.S. Constitution, Art. I, Sec. 8). In addition, Congress has also gained authority through modification of the Constitution via the amendment process (i.e., the Sixteenth Amendment that significantly broadened Congress's taxing authority).

The presidents' explicit powers are far fewer in number, and there is no necessary and proper clause in Article II of the Constitution. But the primary formal powers that the president does have revolve around the president's role in foreign and defense policy. In the second section of Article II, the president is named the "commander and chief of the Army and Navy of the United States, and of the militia of the several states, when called into the actual service of the United States" (U. S. Constitution, Art. II, Sec. 2). The Founders considered civilian control of the military an important component of popular government, and the president was the most obvious supreme commander. That George Washington was all but certain to be the first commander-in-chief was not lost on those framing the new government.

It is important to note that the powers and responsibilities of the commander-in-chief are not specifically defined, and over the course of American history, the parameters of the commander-in-chief powers have been anything but consistent and uncontroversial. Not surprisingly, support for the exercise of commander-in-chief powers is greatest during war time, but "true" wars – those conflicts that followed a congressional declaration of war – are quite rare. Congress has declared war only five times in American history (the War of 1812, Mexican–American War, Spanish–American War, World War I, and World War II), and the U.S. has not fought a "declared" war in more than 60 years. Several major U.S. conflicts (including the Civil War, the Korean War, the Vietnam War, and both Iraq Wars) and every peacekeeping operation are excluded from this list. It is during – and prior to – the conflicts that are not declared wars that the exercise of the commander-in-chief powers was most controversial.

Conflicts over the proper exercise of the president's commander-in-chief powers tend to focus on two issues: (1) the unilateral involvement of American forces in significant overseas conflicts and (2) the proper bounds of military and security actions, both domestically and internationally.[39] Historically, Congress has granted the president wide latitude to respond to specific domestic security threats. When the use of force follows ambiguous or controversial security threats (especially when the *domestic* threat is difficult to identify or demonstrate), the president's exercise of the commander-in-chief powers comes under greater *ex post* scrutiny. Presidential actions are rarely countered in their immediate aftermath – in some cases, such as the Gulf of Tonkin incident, they garner widespread congressional support – but over time, the president's involvement of significant U.S. military forces faces greater scrutiny during armed conflicts than during declared wars.

In the later stages of the Vietnam War, congressional frustration with the President Johnson and President Nixon's use of the commander-in-chief powers in the absence of a declaration of war led to the passage of the War Powers Act (in 1973), an attempt to establish statutory limits on the use of U.S. forces in the absence of explicit congressional approval. Presidents have bristled at the constraints of the War Powers Act and have consistently claimed that it is an unconstitutional constraint on the commander-in-chief power. In general, Congress has been unwilling or unable to aggressively assert the statutory prerogatives of the War Powers Act, and the conflict between the proper parameters of the commander-in-chief power and the power to declare war is ongoing. Thus, congressional acquiescence is often a crucial component in the realization of a president's foreign and defense policy objectives. This will be a particularly important issue in the subsequent chapter on the president's role in foreign policy making.[40]

Use of the commander-in-chief power to justify the authorization of military and security actions that might otherwise be deemed unconstitutional is also controversial. During the Civil War, Lincoln used his executive authority (including, but not limited to, the commander-in-chief power) to

1. suspend the writ of *habeas corpus* in the District of Columbia (an open constitutional issue, though generally thought to be within the purview of Congress rather than the president)

---

[39] This second issue might arise during declared wars as well as other armed conflicts, but historically, the greatest conflicts related to this aspect of the exercise of the commander-in-chief power have occurred during armed conflicts that were not declared wars.

[40] Fisher (2004) provides an authoritative treatment of the constitutional issues associated with the exercise of war powers. Hinckley (1994) provides a thoughtful treatment of the obstacles faced by Congress in its efforts to implement the War Powers Act.

2. authorize the use of military tribunals instead of civil courts in areas with a significant proportion of Southern sympathizers[41]
3. initiate a blockade (by international law an act of war that only Congress was empowered to implement)
4. authorize expenditures on behalf of the war effort without the prior authorization (and appropriation) by Congress
5. free the slaves in the Confederate states through the *Emancipation Proclamation*.[42]

Each of these acts was controversial. In retrospect, the legislative dominance of Lincoln's party and the magnitude of the national emergency provide an explanation for the absence of a significant congressional effort to restrain Lincoln's broad interpretation of executive authority (including the commander-in-chief prerogative). Republican majorities in the House and the Senate and the threat of terrorist attacks may also explain the delay in the development of congressional opposition to the war in Iraq.

The president's treaty-making power is also subject to varying constitutional interpretations. How broad, for example, is the term "treaty"? Is it reasonable to view Jefferson's purchase of the Louisiana territory from France as a treaty? If not, is there another constitutional interpretation of this transaction? Jefferson himself had scruples about this use of the treaty power, but in this case, he was willing to accept questionable means to achieve necessary ends.[43] Consideration of the proper use of the treaty-making powers also raises the question of the proper use of an alternative to treaties – the executive agreement. Treaties require the advice and consent of the Senate, and a supermajority (two-thirds) is required for treaties. Executive agreements, on the other hand, require no legislative approval or sanction. While they do not carry the same weight as treaties – that is, they may be modified or ended by an additional executive agreement – they are an important policy-making tool.[44]

---

[41] Consider the position of Chief Justice Roger B. Taney in *Ex parte Merriman*. According to Taney, Lincoln had neither the right to suspend the writ of *habeas corpus* nor to use military officers to imprison suspected Confederates in the border states.

[42] While the Emancipation Proclamation was an important component of the war effort, Lincoln had neither the constitutional authority nor the practical power to free the slaves in the Confederate states in 1863.

[43] See J. D. Bailey (2007) for a thoughtful treatment of Jefferson's understanding of executive power.

[44] Krutz and Peake (2009) offer a useful examination of the interplay of the politics of treaty making and executive agreements.

THE PRESIDENT'S ROLE IN ECONOMIC POLICY MAKING

Public evaluations of sitting presidents tend to primarily involve three factors: (1) major military conflicts, (2) the performance of the national economy, and (3) major scandals involving the president. Major scandals involving the president are, thankfully, rather rare, and even when they do occur, the scandals do not always have the expected negative effect on presidential approval, particularly job-related approval scores.[45] Like major scandals, major wars are relatively rare. Far less than a third of the presidents elected after the end of the Civil War have served during a major war. In the absence of major wars (which tend to lead to relatively higher approval ratings) and major scandals (which tend to lead, though not always, to relatively lower approval standings), the state of the national economy is the primary determinant of presidential approval and the incumbent president's electoral prospects (or, if the incumbent cannot run again, the incumbent president's party's future electoral prospects) (see Erikson 1989).

As a president's popularity and future electoral prospects are tied so intimately to the quality of the national economy, the president has significant incentives to work toward improving the national economy. And while presidential authority is limited, the president is in a better position to influence the state of the national economy than any other single person.[46] In the fiscal (tax and spend) policy arena, the president is the agenda setter. It is the president's budget that Congress debates, and so the president is in the best position to set the terms of the debate. In the monetary (money supply and interest rate) policy arena, the Federal Reserve and the Treasury are the primary governmental actors, but it is the president that appoints the governors to the Federal Reserve Board and the president who appoints the Secretary of the Treasury. The president is in a unique position to influence the national economy, but the president must also share policy-making responsibility (and authority) with other prominent actors (primarily members of Congress and the Federal Reserve). Unfortunately, at least for the president, the public does not spread blame for economic downturns evenly among the president, the Congress, and the Fed.

---

[45] Even in the wake of the Monica Lewinsky scandal, Clinton's job approval ratings were surprisingly high.

[46] Some would argue that the Chairman of the Federal Reserve is the person with the greatest control over the national economy (see Greider 1989). Other research suggests that the authority of the Fed chairman is quite overstated, sometimes dramatically so (see Morris 2000).

The president takes the brunt of the punishment, and this will be an important consideration in the chapter on the presidential selection process.

CONCLUSION

This chapter provides the basic background information that you will need as you work through the later chapters in the text. I have made no effort to provide an exhaustive background. Each of the topics addressed earlier is worthy of – and has received – a book-length treatment. A number of those book-length treatments are referenced in the text (or in the footnotes) of this chapter. So if you are particularly interested in any of these topics, check out the listed references. For now, you have the "nuts and bolts" information you need to move to the next chapter.

IMPORTANT TERMS

Anti-Federalist Papers
Article II
Articles of Confederation
caucus
separation of powers
checks and balances
convention
delegates
Electoral College
enumerated powers
Executive branch
Executive Office of the President
Executive Order
faithless elector
Federal Election Commission
Federalist Papers
House of Representatives
implied powers
modern presidency
primary
  • closed
  • open
  • semiclosed
Senate

spoils system
Supreme Court
veto
   • normal
   • pocket
Vice President
White House Staff

4

Theories of Presidential Power

One of the primary flaws of the Articles of Confederation was the absence of a powerful executive, and except for a small group of the very strongest opponents of the Constitution, the Founders disagreed little about the need for the creation of an executive branch. Beyond this general agreement, however, there was no consensus on the proper extent of presidential authority. This disagreement did not derail the development of the Constitution, but ratification did not end the controversy. As we know from Chapter 3, the most prominent and important leaders of the early Republic – including Alexander Hamilton, Thomas Jefferson, and James Madison – had contentious debates about the question of the proper extent of presidential power and authority. These conflicts played an important role in the disintegration of the Federalists and the growth of the first formal political party (the Democratic–Republicans).

Why did this particular issue (only one of many) engender such and conflict? One possibility is that the nature of presidential power was viewed – accurately or not – as the linchpin of the success of the federal system of government. One may reasonably argue that the success of the American political "experiment" depended most specifically on the creation of an effective executive authority. The Founders' concern for creating an executive branch with the proper power and authority certainly suggests that the role of the executive branch – and the presidency, more specifically – was deemed crucial to the efforts to forge and maintain the new government. Why this intent focus on (and conflict over) the variation in presidential power and authority?

In general, the Founders expected the legislative branch to dominate national policy making, especially national policy making on domestic issues. Congress has by far the largest number of explicit powers of any of the three branches, and it also has the benefit of a "necessary and proper" clause that historically has provided for the enhancement of legislative authority. Though there were significant disagreements about the proper set of legislative powers, there were few advocates for a dominant executive or judicial branch during the constitutional convention or the ratification conventions. There was simply greater agreement about the role of the legislative branch in the national government than the role of the executive branch in the national government.

Conversely, the Founders had significant disagreements about the role of the Supreme Court in the national government. Whether or not the Court would exercise the power of judicial review – its primary policy responsibility since the ruling (and Chief Justice John Marshall's opinion) in *Marbury v. Madison* – was an open question during the constitutional convention. The controversy over the proper role of the Court was not as contentious as the disagreement over the proper role of the executive branch during the constitutional convention because there was little sense, at least among the Federalists, that the Court would become the dominant political actor in the national policy-making arena. While the Founders disagreed (significantly) about the proper position of the Court in the national government, there was little fear that it might overwhelm the other branches.

The powers of the president were focal points of conflict due to the perceived (accurately) relationship between the role of the executive branch in the national government and the role of the national government in the federal system. The fundamental conflict between the Federalists (supporters of the Constitution) and the Anti-Federalists (opponents of the Constitution) revolved around the relative position of the state governments vis-à-vis the national government. Though not obvious at the time, a set of Federalists and a set of Anti-Federalists realized that this federal balance of power depended to a significant extent on the particular powers and responsibilities of the president. Federalists favoring a more expansive understanding of federal authority (such as Hamilton) believed that the avenue to the realization of a dominant national government was the enhancement of executive authority. States rights advocates, alternatively, feared the aggrandizement of executive authority for exactly the same reason. The conflict over the powers of the president was so significant because it was, at least indirectly, a conflict over the size and scope of the powers of the federal government. The relationship between presidential power and the power of the national government is one reason why the nature of presidential power is still such an interesting subject of inquiry for modern scholars. Development of an accurate understanding of presidential power is a crucial component to the development of an understanding of the power of the national government more generally.

A scientific orientation to the study of presidential power depends on a theory of presidential power – some sophisticated, interrelated conjectures about what presidents can and cannot do and why. There are at least four broad theoretical approaches to the study of presidential power, and each of these approaches highlights a particular independent variable to explain the shifts and movements in the dependent variable that is presidential power. In the remainder of this chapter, we will discuss these four approaches, and I will present specific examples of each approach. As you read about these theories of presidential power, consider the following:

1. What are the primary conceptual differences between these theories?
2. Which theory do you find most compelling?
3. How would you construct specific empirical tests for each theory?
4. Would it make sense to integrate one or more of these theories?
5. How would you construct specific tests for an integrated theory?

RICHARD NEUSTADT, BARGAINING, AND THE POWER TO PERSUADE

The modern study of presidential power begins in 1960 with the publication of *Presidential Power* by Richard Neustadt. In *Presidential Power*, Neustadt argues that traditional studies tended to dramatically overestimate executive power. What explains this prevalent misunderstanding of executive power? Neustadt claims it is the consistent confusion of legal authority with practical power. He criticizes the mistaken presumption that the president's legal authority – as "commander in chief" for example – may be quickly and easily translated into policy outcomes. For Neustadt, "the probabilities of power do not derive from the literary theory of the constitution" (1960).

Neustadt develops a compelling argument against the confusion of legal authority and practical power. In a chapter entitled, ironically, "Three Cases of Command," he describes three situations in which presidents Truman and Eisenhower exercised the command power of the Oval Office. In each case, Neustadt argues, Truman and Eisenhower had exhausted all other options for achieving their policy objectives before invoking command, and that neither president felt as if they had any other choice in these public settings. In each case, the exercise of command results in relatively unsatisfactory outcomes for the president. For Neustadt, use of the command prerogative indicates a position of weakness rather than strength.

An additional difficulty with the traditional view of presidential command is the infrequency with which command may be effectively invoked. The necessary preconditions for presidential command are rarely realized in practice. The criteria for the use of the command prerogative – what Neustadt defines as a "self-executing order" – are as follows:

1. *It must be clear that the president has spoken.* It must be easy to determine whether or not the president has spoken. In how many cases does the president directly transmit an order to those individuals actually in a position to execute the order? The answer – not many. In most cases, presidential orders are communicated by one or more subordinates. Often, this sort of communication is insufficient.

2. *The content of the order must be crystal clear.* Effective response to a presidential order requires clarity on the meaning of the order. Ambiguity may not prevent a subordinate from acting on an order, but it might easily preclude the achievement of the president's intended objective. Ambiguous orders are not self-executing.

3. *The order must be public.* For Neustadt, self-executing orders must be made public. But why does the *publicity* of a presidential order matter? Why would a trusted aide ignore a secret order? Neustadt's concern with publicity is a result of his focus on compliance with *unpopular* orders. It is one thing for recalcitrant subordinates to ignore secret orders; it is far more difficult to ignore a public order.

4. *The official to whom the order is directed must have the capacity to execute the order.* Obviously, if the president wants something done, he must ask someone who is in a position to do it. What is not obvious is that command may be ineffective because no one *can* execute the order. Sometimes, subordinates fail to deliver because they cannot deliver.

5. *The official to whom the order is directed must believe that the president is making a request that is within his rights (as president).* Though it is a risky response, subordinates say "no" to the president because they consider the demand unethical or unconstitutional. Presidential aides as well as cabinet secretaries are ethically (and often legally) bound to ignore or reject improper presidential orders. So, even if all of the other criteria for a self-enforcing order are satisfied, the subordinate responsible for executing the order must see it as proper and constitutional.

Neustadt realized this was a long list of criteria, and he concluded that situations in which presidents can issue "self-executing orders" are rare. Even when these opportunities present themselves, self-executing orders are not costless. He writes, "Even though the order is assured of execution, drastic action rarely comes at bargain rates. It can be costly to the aims in whose defense it is employed. It can be costly, also, to objectives far afield" (1960: 27). Neustadt takes relationships very seriously, and authoritative demands can damage relationships.

Neustadt argues that presidential power is based on the ability to *persuade*. Rarely in a position to command – or to command without paying high costs for the loss of future compliance – presidents use the resources at their disposal to curry the favor of those whose help they need. Persuasion, convincing someone that it is in their interest to do your bidding, is no easy task, and as Neustadt notes, it is not the conventional picture (at least for the 1950s) of presidential power. In Neustadt's time, traditional research on the presidency focused on the growth of the president's formal constitutional authority, but Neustadt was unconvinced that a list of explicit powers captured the president's capacity to achieve his political goals. For Neustadt, the ability to persuade, not formal authority, determined the extent of presidential power.

The power to persuade (or "bargain") depends on two resources: professional reputation and public prestige. To persuade the set of Washington insiders who make and implement policy, presidents must develop a reputation for competence and integrity. If these insiders find the president lacking in important professional qualifications, persuasion becomes more difficult. If a president is an ineffective negotiator, or if those with whom the president must deal question his word, the weakness of the president's professional reputation seriously hinders his ability to bargain effectively. In Neustadt's world, ineffective bargaining is tantamount to policy failure. Washington insiders are also sensitive to the extent to which the president has broad public support (or public prestige); the greater the president's public standing, the more likely Washington insiders are to respond affirmatively to presidential efforts at persuasion.

Presidents find it difficult to enhance either their professional reputation or their public prestige. Damaging a professional reputation or losing public prestige is far easier. For this reason, Neustadt contends presidents must weigh their options very carefully and consider both the short- and long-term implications for the future exercise of their power of each decision they make. Unfortunately, presidential advisers may not always have the president's interests at heart. After all, advisers have their own independent objectives to consider. In the end, presidents must depend upon themselves.

Neustadt wrote *Presidential Power* during the late 1950s – a full half-century ago. Much of the modern study of the presidency is far more quantitative (and formalized) than it was in the late 1950s, so it is no surprise to see that quantitative analysis and formal theory are nowhere to be found in *Presidential Power*. Though his perspective was a significant theoretical departure from the dominant perspective of his day, the nature of his argument and the types of evidence he referenced in support of the argument are completely consistent with the standard practices of his time. Neustadt had personal knowledge of the inner workings of the Truman administration and had conversations with members of the Roosevelt, Truman, and Eisenhower administrations. He was also familiar with standard histories and journalistic treatments of these administrations. He uses all of this data to support his thesis that the source of presidential power is personal persuasiveness and effective bargaining.

As noted in Chapter 2, this method is limited. First, it is inherently time-bound. Assume Neustadt's characterization of the Roosevelt, Truman, and Eisenhower administrations is fully accurate. How do we know the same perspective captures the inner workings of the Kennedy administration? Or the Reagan administration? The second Bush administration? Second, Neustadt's presentation – very much in a historical format[1] – is not conducive to falsification. It is, in fact, not easy to figure out how one would go about showing that Neustadt's theory is flawed.

Significantly, the first serious challenges to Neustadt's theory skirted the difficulties of the second problem by focusing on the limitations inherent in the first problem. In the next section, we will discuss one of the primary competitors to Neustadt's bargaining theory – Kernell's theory of "going public." In short, Kernell argues that presidents achieve policy objectives by taking their case directly to the American people who then pressure their legislators to support the president. This variant of "outsider" politics is dramatically different from Neustadt's bargaining-oriented "insider politics." According to Kernell, this shift in focus from insider politics to outsider politics was not a function of an inherent flaw in the logic of presidential bargaining; it was simply a result of the transformation of the

---

[1] Though a political scientist, his *New York Times* obituary described Neustadt as an historian. See http://www.nytimes.com/2003/11/03/us/richard-e-neustadt-historian-dies-84-studied-power-advised-three-presidents.html (last accessed on December 17, 2009).

American political landscape during the mid- to late 1960s and 1970s. While bargaining was appropriate for an earlier era, the era on which Neustadt focused, it was no longer an effective means of achieving policy goals (at least according to Kernell) by the late 1970s. We will discuss Kernell's argument in more detail in the next section, but for now it is sufficient to realize that one of the primary criticisms of Neustadt's perspective is not that it was inaccurate, but simply that its accuracy was limited to a particular (and, frankly, relatively short) period of time.

Other research suggests that the core of Neustadt's argument is a useful perspective for understanding presidential politics well beyond the time period on which Neustadt originally focused. First, Neustadt updated his discussion of his own theory through multiple revised editions of *Presidential Power* that ran through the Reagan presidency.[2] Neustadt's effort to portray the politics of each post–Eisenhower administration as varying manifestations of bargaining is somewhat uneven. Some presidents simply fit the Neustadt model more closely than others.[3] But overall, Neustadt concludes that his bargaining theory stood the test of time. He writes:

> In writing this book thirty years ago, I sought to characterize the power of a modern American President. I addressed not the office but rather the person as one among many in a set of institutions. ... Presidential weakness was the underlying theme of *Presidential Power*. That remains my theme. ... Weakness is still what I see: weakness in the sense of a great gap between what is expected of a man (or someday a woman) and assured capacity to carry through. (1990: ix)

From a scientific standpoint, this perspective is theoretically and methodologically problematic. Consistent predictions of failure or inaction are difficult to evaluate. To address this problem, scholars using Neustadt's bargaining theory tend to focus less on the overall "weakness" of the office and more on (1) the relationship between presidential "prestige" and presidential policy success, and (2) the manifestation of presidential bargaining and negotiation in policy-making

[2] The final revised edition of *Presidential Power* was published in 1991, over three decades after the publication of the original work.

[3] The case of Nixon is particularly problematic for the Neustadt model. Because of the assumed institutional weakness of the office, Neustadt (at least in the original edition) consistently lauds efforts to accumulate and maintain power as integral components of good government. In the case of the Nixon presidency, the various attempts to accumulate power were obviously disastrous, and Neustadt, even in later editions of *Presidential Power*, never fully comes to terms with the implications of the Nixon presidency for his theory. For more on this, see Cronin (1979).

contexts. Neustadt argues that presidential prestige is one of the two cornerstones of presidential power, so studies of the relationship between presidential prestige and presidential policy success would seem to bear directly on the accuracy of Neustadt's theory. Likewise, demonstrating the presence of a relationship between bargaining and the achievement of presidential policy goals also indicates support for Neustadt's perspective. Conversely, the absence of a relationship between presidential prestige and policy success or the absence of a relationship between bargaining and policy success would be a serious blow to Neustadt's theory.[4]

Finally, treatment of the web of relationships necessary for the effective exercise of presidential power highlights the individual skills and capabilities each president brings to the office. As we discussed earlier, presidential scholars tend to think in terms of *presidency-centered* perspectives and *president-centered* perspectives. Neustadt's theory arguably fits into both categories. While he introduces theoretical constructs that play a role in the exercise of presidential power regardless of the identity of the person sitting in the Oval Office, the context in which each president finds himself or herself, their own particular aptitudes for bargaining and negotiation, and the idiosyncrasies of the times in which they live strongly suggest that the power of the presidency varies by *president*. Some relatively recent research suggests that it is possible to evaluate the extent to which presidential success – at least in the realm of legislative policy making – is a function of personal characteristics (see Fleisher et al. 2008). Other recent work (Dickinson 2008) seeks to reframe Neustadt's bargaining model for testing with more scientifically oriented methods than Neustadt himself used. If we are trying to understand variations in the effective exercise of presidential authority, Neustadt strongly suggests that we must account for the personal and professional differences between each individual president. At the same time, however, we must be sensitive to potential contextual constraints (and opportunities) that face any president at a particular point in time. Even work focused on the role of president-specific skills in the effective

---

[4] Research on the relationship between the president's professional reputation (another cornerstone of Neustadt's bargaining theory) and presidential policy success is far more limited than research on the relationship between presidential prestige and presidential policy success. Why is this the case? One plausible explanation is the difficulty associated with the adequate measurement of a president's professional reputation. It is not trivially easy to measure public prestige (as we will discuss shortly), but it is far more difficult to develop indicators of professional reputation that are valid and reliable across a set of presidential administrations.

exercise of executive power indicates that presidential policy-making success is contingent on factors beyond the president's control and is wholly unrelated to the president's own individual skills and capabilities (Fleisher et al. 2008).

GOING PUBLIC: A 70S AND 80S STORY

In the mid-1980s, Samuel Kernell wrote a book that would end up refocusing the study of the American presidency and particularly presidential power. Ironically, he began the book by writing that Neustadt was right all along. In the main theory chapter in *Going Public* (1986), Kernell argues that Neustadt's *persuasion* was the lingua franca of the 1950s and early 1960s – exactly the time that Neustadt was writing about. Kernell refers to this as the time of "institutionalized pluralism" (1986). However, according to Kernell, the American political system underwent a transformation beginning in the mid-1960s and culminating in the early 1980s. Kernell refers to this new time period as "individualized pluralism" (1986).

In the era of institutionalized pluralism that Neustadt wrote about so effectively, Kernell argues that a relatively small group of political elite dominated public policy making. Now, by a small group of political elite, neither he nor Neustadt meant a handful of people; think more in terms of several dozen people, maybe a few hundred at the most. These Washington insiders were tied together through a web of trust and reciprocity and an understanding that they were making policy – not necessarily in conflict with the public interest, but certainly without regularized and consistent public input into the details and specifics of the policy-making process. However, these leaders often garnered their position at the bargaining table in the oval office because of their positions as leaders of what Kernell referred to as "protocoalitions" (1986). These protocoalitions were largely inchoate groups of supporters who might be mobilized quickly to support a particular policy initiative espoused by (or sponsored by) their leader.

But times changed, and Kernell argues that the changing times resulted in a changing politics – and a change in the nature of the source of presidential power. The 1960s was a tumultuous time, and the landscape of American society changed dramatically. In a growth trajectory from the beginning of the New Deal, the welfare state experienced particularly strong growth in the aftermath of World War II. This growth led to a concomitant growth and mobilization of significant societal interests well beyond the Washington Beltway. Though interest-group politics were a component of institutionalized pluralism, these new constituencies and interests were far more numerous and far more diverse than those active during the period of institutionalized pluralism. They were also mobilizing at a time in which the political parties – the core of institutionalized pluralism – were fading in power.

This atomization of the national political arena occurred just as modern communication and transportation technology opened up new opportunities for reaching out to the American public. In 1960, we have the first "televised" presidential campaign, and the ability to communicate via television became a particularly important skill for effective presidential candidates to master.[5] Add to the mass political and technological changes, the institutional changes of both the growth in congressional caucuses and the rise of Political Action Committees (PACs), and you have an environment ripe for what Kernell (1986) refers to as "going public." It is a political arena:

> constituted of independent members who have few group or institutional loyalties and who are generally less interested in sacrificing short-run, private career goals for the longer-term benefits of bargaining. Social pluralism and institutional fragmentation guarantee that exchange will remain a ubiquitous activity, but egocentric traders will rarely subscribe to the kinds of commitments and tacit understandings that allow bargains to assume the form of relationships. Instead, these politicians will generally prefer immediate, explicit, and tangible exchanges. (Kernell 1986: 27)

These "immediate, explicit, and tangible exchanges" were the coin of the realm for presidents bent on "going public."

"Going public" is the process of reaching out to the American public to garner support for one's policy position(s) – sufficient support that other public officials will take notice and, due to the pressure of public opinion, support your policies as well. While Kernell focuses on the president's efforts at going public, he also notes that other public leaders – particular prominent members of Congress – may go public as well, often in an effort to counterattack the president. More specifically:

> Going public is a class of activities that presidents engage in as they promote themselves and their policies before the American public .... What these activities have in common is that they are intended principally to place the president and his message before the American

---

[5] Would Calvin Coolidge, Harry Truman, and Dwight Eisenhower have won office during the television era? Maybe, but it is no sure thing.

people in a way that enhances his chances of success in Washington. (Kernell 1986: ix)

While the changed context of national politics, the dramatic growth in the size and variety of the media, and the explosion of interest groups have, according to Kernell, fostered and facilitated presidential efforts to go public, the strategy of going public is not a late-twentieth-century invention. Woodrow Wilson's unsuccessful efforts to build public support for the League of Nations are an early example of going public. However, Kernell argues, the *frequency* with which presidents turn to public appeals is far greater now than it was fifty or a hundred years ago. He writes that, "Forcing compliance from fellow Washingtonians by going over their heads to appeal to their constituents is a tactic not unknown during the first half of the century, but it was seldom attempted" (1986: 2).

Though public prestige is a crucial source of power in Neustadt's bargain theory, there are important differences between using public appeals to outsiders and bargaining with insiders to achieve political goals. Going public is not an exchange-oriented interaction. In fact, going public depends upon a political dynamic that is the inverse of the bargaining dynamic. In a bargaining system, political support (or compliance) generates tangible rewards or benefits. The effectiveness of going public depends not on the distribution of benefits for support but on the imposition of penalties and various forms of punishment (often of an electoral type) for noncompliance. The very nature of the public appeals associated with going public often complicates future bargaining efforts. Staking out very public positions on prominent issues – and forcing one's supporters and opponents to do the same – makes future compromise very difficult for those who must repudiate their former positions. Finally, Kernell argues that going public undermines the inherent legitimacy of those public officials the president means to influence by going public. If the president successfully manipulates the political actions of a legislator through public appeals to the legislator's own constituents, the legitimacy of the legislator's actions is compromised. For a number of important reasons, bargaining and going public are incompatible political strategies.

In the "new" era of individualized pluralism, do presidents still try to bargain to achieve their policy goals? If not, why not? Kernell argues that it is simply too difficult to bargain effectively in the newly atomized, media-dominated political arena. Bargaining with so many independent actors is complicated and costly, and influencing legislators' decision making by reaching beyond them to their constituencies (or threatening to do so) often proves to be a more effective strategy.

What evidence does Kernell present for his contention? Is it similar to the types of evidence Neustadt presents? If not, how is it different? And if it is different, is it more compelling? The empirical case for "going public" is multifaceted. Kernell shows that over the course of the last half of the twentieth century, presidential travel has increased dramatically. Kernell shows that foreign travel has increased eightfold during the last half century.[6] Domestic travel during the same time period increased sixfold.[7] This dramatic increase in presidential travel coincided with a similar increase in public appearances. While Truman averaged fewer than five public appearances during the first three years of his first term, George W. Bush averaged over 140 appearances per year during the first three years of his administration (Kernell 2007). Bush made more than *25 times* the number of public appearances that Truman did (during a similar three-year span). At the very least, the *public* dimension of the presidency became far more prominent over the past half century.

It is somewhat surprising then that the frequency of what Kernell refers to as "major" addresses[8] has not grown at all since the Truman administration. Presidents have tended to make between four and eight major addresses each year, and that range holds true for the entire post–World War II period. Minor addresses have, like travel and public appearances, grown dramatically since the middle of the last century. Harry Truman, who averaged five major addresses a year during the first three years of his first term in office, actually averaged fewer minor addresses. Both Presidents Clinton and Bush, however, gave over 140 minor addresses per year during the first three years of their first terms in office.[9] There was an especially large increase in minor speeches following the Reagan administration – during the early years of which, the average number of minor speeches was 20 or less. Note that this large increase in public activity does not directly demonstrate that Presidents are actually going public with far greater frequency now than they did decades ago. Presidents may make visits or minor speeches for a variety of reasons completely unrelated to a determined effort to win public approval for a controversial policy initiative. However, this data certainly suggests that Presidents go

---

[6] While Eisenhower averaged only four days a year of foreign travel during the first three years of his first term, George W. Bush averaged 32 days a year of foreign travel during the first three years of his first term (Kernell 2007).

[7] Eisenhower averaged 14 days a year while George W. Bush averaged 85 days a year during the first three years of their first term (Kernell 2007).

[8] Major addresses are those in which a president speaks to a national audience on radio and/or television (Kernell 2007).

[9] The presidential address figures are from Kernell (2007).

public far more frequently than they did years ago. At the very least, it appears that presidents are making a more concerted effort to communicate to the public than ever before.

While this quantitative data is different from the types of evidence that Neustadt presents, the three extended case studies from the first term of the Reagan administration are quite similar to the case studies presented by Neustadt. What is interesting is that presidential power (as manifested by the success of attempts to go public) in the Reagan case studies varies greatly from year to year for the same president, a president for whom the term "going public" was invented.

The first Reagan budget is the quintessential case of going public. Reagan comes to office in early 1981 after a sizable victory over then-president Carter in the previous year's general election. Reagan focuses his early energies on – and claims a "mandate" for – the transformation of federal taxing and spending. While proposing dramatic decreases in taxes and domestic spending, Reagan also proposed a dramatic increase in defense spending. The overall shape of the budget implied a significant deficit and a significant increase in the federal debt. Democrats in Congress were none too pleased with Reagan's budget priorities, and they prepared for an extended fight over the budget.

In a series of nationally publicized speeches, Reagan took his case to the American public. Arguing that the decrease in taxes would actually foster greater tax revenue through what were characterized as the dynamics of "supply-side economics," and claiming that the nation's military was insufficient to the task of fighting the ongoing Cold War, Reagan hoped to incite the American public to transfer their attachment to him to his policy objectives. According to Kernell, Reagan's ability to build public support for his budget led to increasing public pressure on the recalcitrant Democrats to pass Reagan's budget. Journalist Steven Roberts summarizes Reagan's public efforts in 1981 as follows:

> Lawmakers believed their constituents supported that [Reagan's] program and they were afraid that Mr. Reagan could galvanize that support through an adroit use of television and punish any dissidents at the polls. (Kernell 2007: 158)

Kernell concludes that

> These [legislators'] fears were not without reason. National polls showed strong support for Reagan as president, for increased defense spending, for elimination of waste, and for lower taxes. Supplementing

these poll data ... were the waves of mail, telegrams, and phone calls that overwhelmed Congress after each presidential address. Reagan's public appeals generated about fifteen million more letters than normally flowed into congressional mailrooms each session. What better testimony to the prowess of the president skilled at going public. (2007: 158–159)

In the end, according to Kernell, Reagan's public efforts in support of his budget – Reagan's efforts to go public – were the deciding factor in his victory in this first budgetary battle.

Reagan's second budget came after a significant deterioration in national economic circumstances. Unemployment during the first quarter of 1982 was higher than at any time since the recession of the mid-1970s. High interest rates posed a significant obstacle to the type of corporate and individual investment that might lead to job growth, and inflation was spiraling out of control. The largest year-on-year percentage increases in the post–World War II consumer price index came during the latter months of 1981 and the first half of 1982. The coincidence of such dire economic circumstances created a "perfect storm" in the American economy, and "[e]ven conservative economists joined in the growing speculation that a full-fledged depression was no longer unthinkable" (Kernell 2007: 160).[10]

The public support Reagan leveraged immediately after his election had evaporated. By early 1982, Reagan's job approval ratings were negative; more people were displeased with Reagan's performance than were pleased with it. The second budget also followed the negative press associated with David Stockman's (then Director of the Office of Management and Budget)[11] criticism of the budget process during Reagan's first year in office in a long interview printed in the *Atlantic Monthly*. Reagan's increasing unpopularity hindered his efforts to maintain the support of rank-in-file Republicans and precluded any efforts to build support among his Democratic opponents. Again, Reagan's budgetary policy objectives conflicted with those of Democrats that controlled the House of Representatives and that posed a significant obstacle (in the minority) in the Senate. Where going public produced a dramatic victory during 1981, Reagan was forced to compromise to a substantially greater degree during 1982. As Kernell

[10] This economic data was gathered from the FRED (Federal Reserve Economic Data) web site of the St. Louis Federal Reserve Bank at http://research.stlouisfed.org/fred2/ (last accessed on December 17, 2009).

[11] The Office of Management and Budget (OMB) is the agency within the Executive Office of the President that is responsible for the development and coordination of the President's budget.

concludes, "President Reagan exerted far less influence over the budget in 1982 – both its substance and politics – than over the one in the previous year" (2007: 166). Even from Kernell's perspective, going public is not an all-powerful weapon in the president's political arsenal.

In the aftermath of significant Republican losses during the 1982 midterm elections, Reagan found himself in an even weaker position than the one in which he struggled during 1982. Though the Republicans retained control of the Senate, they lost more than two dozen seats in the House of Representatives. With the president's public approval at a low point, congressional support for his budgetary initiatives was difficult to obtain even from his own fellow partisans.

Reagan's public efforts in support of his budget were almost wholly ineffective, and he now faced a larger Democratic contingent in both the House and the Senate. In 1983, going public produced little if anything for the president, and the Democrats were able to prevent Reagan from passing "his" budget, for the first time. Significantly, Kernell suggests that during the latter part of 1983, President Reagan focused his public energies on the improvement of his personal popularity (and job approval) than on any particular set of policy initiatives (certainly after the general failure of the 1983 Reagan budget). Reagan found, as did other presidents, that efforts to improve their overall public standing – as opposed to merely building support for particular policy initiatives – are consistently thwarted. On this point, Kernell concludes (at least in the domestic policy arena):

> ... the public president may perform better in the "expenditure," or transference, of popular support than in its resupply. Individualized pluralism helps to explain why he performs well in using his public support, but as a model of Washington politics, it is silent on the subject of what an unpopular president should do to restore the public's confidence. The supply of popular support rests on opinion dynamics over which the president may exercise little direct control. (2007: 175)

Clearly, going public when one is extremely popular is one thing; going public when one is unpopular is something else altogether. But are there certain opportunities that presidents might use to boost their popularity (even if they did not have control over the timing of the opportunity in the first place)? If we look to the context of foreign policy, the answer would appear to be a qualified "yes."

One of the important differences between going public in the domestic policy arena and going public in the foreign policy arena is the potential availability of "rally events" in foreign policy.

International crises tend to result in enhanced popular support for the president, so there is a demonstrable increase in presidential approval (see Kernell 2007). Crises such as the attack on Pearl Harbor, the Bay of Pigs fiasco, the Cuban Missile Crisis, the Gulf War, and the terrorist attack on 9/11 all boosted presidential approval. Note that these crises were not all external threats nor significant policy successes (see the Bay of Pigs fiasco); nevertheless, they all resulted in a boost in presidential support. Though this increase in support was relatively short-lived – rarely longer than 12–18 months – this sort of increase in support can be used to enhance the likelihood that presidential efforts to go public will be successful, especially efforts to go public that are substantively tied to the crises (and thus are inherently foreign policy-oriented).

Kernell argues that Truman was able to trade on his own personal popularity to bring attention to what was perceived as a potential foreign policy crisis with the Soviets on the doorstep of Greece and Turkey. The "Truman Doctrine" speech was widely publicized; Kernell (1976, 2007) cites public evidence that shows a dramatic difference between public concern for foreign policy issues before the speech and after the speech. After the speech, polling data suggest that the public considered foreign policy issues far more significant than they did prior to the speech. Similarly, Truman was most successful in generating support for the Truman Doctrine from voters who already supported the president. Finally, Kernell finds that the most educated segments of the population – and thus, those most likely to be cognizant of the speech, the crisis, and Truman's position on the situation – were most likely to be supportive of the Truman doctrine. All in all, this was a significant case of "going public" in an extreme foreign policy environment.

Though this is only a single case study, it is suggestive of the ability of presidents to mold public opinion during exceptional times to build support for their own policy initiatives. But even in the case of the Truman doctrine, there was no wholesale reevaluation of the president himself nor was there on overall transformation of the broad position of public opinion on the whole range of Truman policy initiatives. Truman's efforts were successful on the specific issue of fighting communism in Europe, particularly in Greece and Turkey. Even in the realm of foreign policy, the ability of presidents to mold public opinion to support the president's policy initiatives is constrained – in some cases, severely.

So what can we say about the significance and general applicability of the "going public" perspective toward presidential power? Before we decide, let's consider the subsequent research on the practice of "going public." The evidence on the general relationship between public support of the president and presidential policy success is mixed. Some analyses suggest the presence of a positive relationship (greater support/more positive public opinion associated with greater policy success); others find no evidence of a relationship. Somewhat surprisingly, what is not at issue is whether or not presidents "go public." Scholars agree that presidents go public, and that they go public far more frequently than they did 50 years ago. Kernell's own observations of this trend are confirmed by other analyses (see Hart 1987; Powell 1999; Ragsdale 1998). As Barrett notes in his recent research on the phenomenon of going public:

> Over the past few decades, going public has become an everyday theory of governing for the president as demonstrated by almost any measure.... modern presidents speak out and participate in public activities at an ever-increasing rate ... presidents go public more than ever. (2004: 339)

But activity is only one aspect of going public; there must also be an appropriate legislative response if presidents are to use going public as a means of exercising power and achieving policy goals. It is the policy impact of the increase in presidential travel, speeches, and public events – that has been so difficult to demonstrate.

At least three plausible explanations for this lack of evidence suggest themselves. First, and most obviously, it may be that going public is not an effective strategy for directly influencing legislative behavior. While it would be odd for presidents to expend so much energy on an activity that is substantively pointless, going public may generate valuable political returns that do not directly and immediately manifest in increased legislative support. For example, Herrnson and Morris (2007) argue that President George W. Bush's campaign visits for House candidates in 2002 (just one aspect of going public) boosted the electoral prospects of those House candidates. In this case, the president is receiving a tangible political benefit, an increased number of fellow partisans in the next Congress, that would not manifest in an immediate change in legislative voting patterns on issues near and dear to the presidents. Here, a certain type of going public helps the president, but in a manner inconsistent with the conventional understanding of the going public dynamic.

Another possible explanation for the dearth of evidence in support of the effectiveness of going public is one or more significant flaws with the analyses of the relationship between going public and subsequent legislative support of the president's policy initiatives. These are just the sort of issues that scientists working in a particular research program are likely to raise. In his recent article entitled, "Gone Public: The Impact of Going public on Presidential Legislative Success," Barrett (2004) makes this argument. He begins by noting that "the study of the effectiveness of going public has been characterized by a lack of strong empirical, quantitative research" (340). He goes on to list the flaws of previous research on going public. They include the following.

1. failure to adequately conceptualize and operationalize just what "constitutes" going public
2. findings based on limited data (either severe temporal limitations, such as a few years from a couple of presidential administrations; limitations on the types of activities that constitute going public, such as focusing solely on nationally televised speeches; or focusing on a very limited number and type of legislative objectives in a severely restricted number of policy areas)
3. failure to adequately test for the presence of a "causal relationship between presidential speeches and presidential legislative success" (340)

In response to these shortcomings, Barrett argues that it is hardly fair to derive a general conclusion about the role of presidential efforts to go public in influencing legislative support for presidential policy objectives. He writes:

> Considering the various weaknesses of the few empirical, quantitative tests of the effectiveness of going public that have been conducted, it is not surprising that these studies have produced conflicting results, with some demonstrating that going public is an effective strategy while others concluding that it is not. (2004: 341)

To effectively address these shortcomings in the scholarly literature (and, more specifically, the research program associated with the theory of going public), Barrett conducts his own analysis. He makes an effort to address each of the shortcomings in the existing literature, and the results of his analysis suggest that "going public is a successful legislative strategy for presidential initiatives and other bills supported by the president" (338). Of course, no analysis is perfect. For example, though Barrett's research covers a relatively long period of time, 1977–1992, and three different presidents (and at least one from each party), there is still the matter of the last 18-plus years. Are these results generalizable to this later time period, the time period that witnessed particularly dramatic growth in various aspects of going public? We must do more research to answer that question.

A final response to the inconclusiveness of the existing research on going public and its impact on legislative support for presidential policy initiatives is to revisit the *contextual* dynamics associated with the likelihood of successful efforts to go public. Maybe presidents do go public and maybe these efforts make a difference on the floor of the House and the Senate. But maybe the likelihood of any particular effort to go public depends upon certain contextual factors that have been overlooked completely or, at the least, received insufficient analytical attention. If that is the case, then it is crucial to identify these contextual factors and account for them in any analysis of going public. On what sort of contextual factors might the effectiveness of going public depend? Extent of the president's popularity? Type of policy? Maybe efforts to go public on defense and security policy issues are more successful than efforts to go public on domestic policy issues? What if the capacity to go public is time-bound? In our media-saturated time, can presidential efforts to direct or mobilize public opinion be successful? And what of tenure in office? Are presidents on their way out able to go public in the same manner as presidents in the earliest days of their administrations?

Until now we have assumed that the causal arrow runs from the president's public appeals to the transformation of public opinion (and the crucial motivation of voters). Presidents go public in order to achieve policy goals. But what if presidents go public for other reasons? What if presidents make public appeals on issues that are *already quite popular* among the citizenry? In this case, the president is following public opinion rather than leading it; if the policy is also inconsistent with the public good, the president is "pandering." Kernell notes that this is a real possibility, and his discussion of pandering suggests that it could be quite prevalent. Some very recent research suggests that it is impossible to distinguish between pandering and going public (Jordan and Primo 2008). In general, it is important to consider the prevalence of pandering because if pandering is misinterpreted as an effective effort to "go public," the researcher overestimates the ability of presidents to use public opinion to achieve their own policy goals and, more generally, the extent of presidential power.

Many recent scientific efforts to examine these issues are based on formal (rational choice) models of presidential politics. Work by Canes-Wrone and her co-authors (Canes-Wrone 2001, 2006; Canes-Wrone and de Marchi 2002; and Canes-Wrone et al. 2001) all attempt to determine the circumstances in which presidents will pander, the circumstances in which presidents will go public, and the contexts in which going public will be successful. There is evidence that these types of theoretical and empirical efforts will be productive, but there is still much we do not know about the nature and usefulness of presidential efforts to use public opinion to achieve policy goals.

PARTIES AND PRESIDENTIAL POWER THROUGH TIME

As we will discuss in the chapter on the president's relationship with Congress, a hot political issue at the end of the twentieth century was legislative gridlock. Conventional wisdom asserts that when different parties control Congress and the White House, policy productivity is limited by *gridlock*: Congressional policy initiatives are thwarted by executive vetoes and presidential policy initiatives fail to win legislative approval. There is considerable disagreement about the actual extent to which this standard story is accurate (a focal point of the chapter on presidential relations with Congress), but there is little question that partisan conflict is a significant component of national politics. For the president, the greater the partisan conflict, the more valuable the support of fellow partisans in Congress.

The most substantial theoretical treatment of the role of partisan dynamics in the determination of presidential power is found in Stephen Skowronek's (1997) book, *The Politics Presidents Make*. In this book, Skowronek argues that presidents govern in *political time* and *secular time*. For Skowronek, a president's power depends upon his position in both of these time frames. Presidents elected during certain eras are in a position to exercise considerably more power and authority than presidents who come to power during other eras. Presidential success (and, implicitly, presidential greatness) is only partly a function of the office holder's individual abilities; presidential success is also a function of the *times* in which a president governs.

The stages of political time follow a predictable cycle. Periods in the cycle include (1) disjunction, (2) reconstruction, and (3) articulation. At times, the cycle is interrupted by what Skowronek refers to as preemption. Any particular president's position in the cycle depends upon the strength and stability of the existing governing regime (*partisan* regime in Skowronek's framework) and the relationship of the president to that governing regime. The politics of *disjunction* manifest when a regime is vulnerable (and in the process of disintegration), and a president allied with the regime struggles to maintain the coalition of political forces that sustains the regime. The politics of *reconstruction* refers to the political dynamics during an era in which a discredited regime is replaced, and a president from the opposing party is elected to build a new regime. Presidents from the dominant regime elected in the wake of reconstruction find themselves in a position to further *articulate* (and advance) the policies of the new regime. Presidents of articulation must elaborate on and fulfill the original mission of the fellow partisan who constructed the current regime. Successive periods of articulation lead, inexorably, to the weakening of the regime and, finally, to the politics of disjunction. At this point, the cycle repeats itself. These distinctive presidential types are illustrated in Table 4-1.

Presidents of reconstruction face dramatic challenges resulting from the failed policies of the previous regime, such as the secession of the Southern states, a deep depression, and interparty conflict so vicious that it led to the passage of the Alien and Sedition Acts. Nevertheless, the presidents of reconstruction are the only presidents in a position to transform the political landscape for the better, and so these presidents are also in a position to build lasting legacies. It is no accident that nearly all presidents ranked in the very top tier were presidents of reconstruction. Jefferson, Lincoln, and Franklin Delano Roosevelt were all presidents of reconstruction.[12]

Reconstructive presidents always owe their electoral victories, at least in part, to the public rejection of the failures of the previous regime. One famous political scientist, V. O. Key (1966) argued that all presidential elections are referenda on the performance of the incumbent (and, by implication, the incumbent's party).[13] While these victories, are not always landslides – FDR's victory was overwhelming; Lincoln won barely 40% of the popular vote – they do provide presidents of reconstruction with the opportunity to transform the political landscape. For Skowronek, to the extent presidents have transformative powers, it is the presidents of reconstruction that wield these powers, and the primary source of these powers is the broad support provided by fellow partisans.

Presidents of articulation find themselves in somewhat less demanding circumstances than presidents of reconstruction. This benefit of articulation is married to an increased constraint on the

---

[12] Washington might be more aptly characterized as a president of "construction" rather than a president of "reconstruction."

[13] This is clearly consistent with our earlier discussion of the relationship between national economic circumstances and presidential election results.

Table 4-1: Skowronek's regime typology

Preexisting Regime Commitments	President's political identity	
	Opposed	Attached
Vulnerable	Politics of reconstruction	Politics of disjunction
Resilient	Politics of preemption	Politics of articulation

exercise of presidential power and authority – particularly the exercise of power and authority to initiate new policies or move off in a different ideological direction. Presidents of articulation are expected to work to fulfill the missions of presidents of reconstruction. Unfortunately, of course, it is theoretically impossible to bring to fruition all of the hopes and dreams of the regime created by one's predecessor. Inevitably, politics is a frustrating endeavor, and regardless of the political genius of the president of reconstruction, the president of articulation will come face to face the practical exigencies of politics. And over time, more and more supporters of the regime will become frustrated, disenchanted, and disillusioned. The erosion of support may take many years, but it starts early, and as Skowronek argues, the seeds of the regime's disintegration are sown during the process of reconstruction. They grow, however, during the process of articulation. They mature during the process of disjunction.

Presidents of articulation find themselves in a political context in which they are expected to fulfill the promise of the administration of reconstruction with which they are aligned by party and in time. Every president of reconstruction (with the exception of Abraham Lincoln) has been immediately followed by at least one president of articulation: James Madison and James Monroe followed Thomas Jefferson; James Polk followed Andrew Jackson; and Franklin Roosevelt was followed by Harry Truman. Let us consider several examples of articulation in more detail.

James K. Polk was not only a supporter of Andrew Jackson, he was also a personal friend. Polk had a significant political career prior to his campaign for the presidency, having served several terms in Congress (including several years as Speaker of the House) and a term as governor of Jackson's home state of Tennessee. Jackson's own personal support for Polk's candidacy – especially Polk's expansionist intentions with regard to Oregon and Texas – was instrumental in Polk's efforts to win the Democratic Party's nomination for the presidency.

More than any other Democrat between Jackson and the Civil War, Polk worked to realize "manifest destiny" – the dramatic geographic expansion of the United States. In particular, the annexation of Texas was a prominent plank in the Polk platform. As Skowronek writes, "Andrew Jackson had been as passionate about the annexation of Texas as Jefferson had been about the acquisition of Florida. Indeed, Jackson was one of those who believed that in settling the Florida question and negotiating the Transcontinental Treaty in 1819, John Quincy Adams had sold out the nation's clear title to Texas" (1997: 158–159). Polk followed Jackson's lead here, and less than two years into his administration, Polk was able to deliver Texas (as the spoils of a war with Mexico), Oregon, and a variety of domestic policy objectives dear to the heart of his fellow Democratic partisans.

Unfortunately for Polk, and Skowronek argues that this is an inherent difficulty in even the most successful presidencies of articulation, the full promise of the Jackson program (or regime) could not be satisfied. Eventually, and inexorably, various constituencies within the Democratic Party became disenchanted and disillusioned because of slights (whether real or perceived) to their own particular interests. In fact, Polk's own successes – especially the effective annexation of Texas – brought new issues for which the Jackson "orthodoxy" (see Skowronek) was fully unprepared. The latent rift within the Democratic Party between North and South was activated by the introduction of the Wilmot Proviso in the House in August of 1846. The Proviso, an amendment to an appropriation bill, precluded the extension of slavery into any of the new lands received from Mexico. Had it passed (which it did in the House but not in the Senate), this amendment would have ensured that Texas would enter the Union as a free state. Though Polk did not support the Proviso, southern Democrats became increasingly disenchanted with the Polk administration. For other reasons, western Democrats also found considerable fault with the Polk administration and its policies. The irony, of course, is that on any reasonable scale, the first 18 months of the Polk administration had been a dramatic success – if not the near-complete fulfillment of the most significant goals of the Jacksonian Democratic Party. But as Polk was to discover, the promises made by presidents of reconstruction are always too grand to be fully realized by the subsequent administrations of presidents of articulation. As Skowronek writes of Polk:

> A master manipulator of the abstract scheme, he again found himself at a loss when confronted with the real political consequences of his own actions. ... What he failed to perceive, or at least could not

acknowledge, was how thoroughly his own schemes had transformed the political calculations of others. (1997: 174–175)

Theodore Roosevelt also found himself in the position of articulating (and finally realizing) the goals and promise of a president of reconstruction. In this case, the president of reconstruction was Abraham Lincoln (rather than Andrew Jackson), and in this case it is the articulation of Republican Party goals and objectives rather than the articulation of the goals and objectives of the Democratic Party. Roosevelt's articulation of a previous reconstruction is also different from Polk's because of the long time span between the Lincoln reconstruction and the articulation of the Lincoln reconstruction by T.R.[14]

T.R. became president following the assassination of William McKinley, the third president to be assassinated in less than 40 years. As the youngest person to rise to the office of the president, T.R. was not only a product of the Lincoln reconstruction, he was also a product of William McKinley's articulation of the Lincoln reconstruction. T.R. was instrumental in the development not only of the institutional power and prerogative of the executive branch but also of the power and prerogative of the national government more generally. Though a president of articulation within the Skowronek framework, T.R.'s vision of presidential authority was singular – he was the embodiment of the "stewardship" orientation toward the extent and exercise of presidential power.[15]

T.R. brought to the White House an understanding of presidential authority – and a sense of the active exercise of that authority and power – which exceeded that of any of his predecessors.[16] T.R. brought this expansive understanding of presidential authority to the office at what might be considered the peak of Republican power. According to Skowronek:

> [Roosevelt] appreciated that the Republican party had never stood on more solid ground than it did at the moment of McKinley's assassination. It had attained a lock on national power unseen since the days of the Jeffersonians. (1997: 235)

But T.R.'s realization of the Republican party's position of power did not preclude his frustration with his assessment of the political

---

[14] Note that presidents of reconstruction may be followed by presidents of articulation for decades.

[15] See our previous discussion of T.R.'s *stewardship* interpretation of presidential power in Chapter 3.

[16] Lincoln is the one potential exception.

direction of the Republican Party. T.R. took seriously the articulation of the quite radical message of Lincoln's reconstruction: the expansion of the power of the president and the federal government to meet the growing demands of the transforming American economy and polity. T.R. was the first *progressive* president; unfortunately for him, his progressivism was quite controversial within his Republican Party. His own final efforts to regain the presidency came on the platform of a personal party – the Bull Moose Party – and resulted in the victory of Democrat Woodrow Wilson, a president of preemption.

After a period of articulation – articulation that increasingly frustrates ever larger portions of the original regime constituency, because it is simply impossible to live up to the promise of the dream of the original reconstruction – the reconstructive foundation crumbles, and the regime is at risk. At this point, the politics of disjunction overwhelm presidential policy making. Presidents during periods of disjunction find the regime coalitions that supported the policy initiatives of their fellow partisans have disintegrated, and in response, presidents of disjunction tend to turn to institutional prerogatives and administrative procedures to achieve what they can. Whatever transformative energy remained during articulation is fully dissipated during disjunction. And the end result of disjunction is always the repudiation of the ruling regime; often disjunction also manifests in a national calamity of some sort (such as secession and civil war or a depression). Every president of reconstruction is eventually followed by a president of disjunction: John Quincy Adams followed Thomas Jefferson; Franklin Pierce followed Andrew Jackson; Abraham Lincoln was followed by Herbert Hoover; and Franklin Roosevelt was followed by Jimmy Carter. Let's consider several of these examples of disjunction in more detail.

The first presidency of disjunction following Jefferson's creation of a national political party in 1800 was the presidency of John Quincy Adams. The regional schism within the party that Jefferson had created was so serious that in the election of 1824, the only candidates who ran were all Democratic–Republicans, and not a single one received a majority of the electors in the Electoral College. The political infighting intensified when the election devolved to the House of Representatives. Though four Democratic–Republicans had run in the national election (Andrew Jackson, John Quincy Adams, William Crawford, and Henry Clay), the Constitution limited the contestants for election by the House to the top three vote-getters, and thus Clay was unable to continue his campaign. However, Clay was at that time the Speaker of the House, and his personal and political predilections (politically he was closest to Adams, and he had a great personal dislike for Jackson) led him to support Adams in the House election. Clay's support was instrumental in Adams election on the first House ballot. When Clay became Adams' Secretary of State shortly thereafter, the appearance (at least) of a questionable political deal made the reconciliation of the increasingly disparate regional wings of the Democratic–Republican party all but unthinkable.[17]

Ironically, Adams' foreign and domestic policy initiatives called for a significant increase in the size and scope of the national government. In this respect, his policy orientation as president was a repudiation of the Jeffersonian ideal of limited government. But his own attachment to the ideals (largely aristocratic) of a dying regime (and political party) prevented any serious effort to provide the necessary *political* foundation for the new regime that he had at least partially conceived. Skowronek's concise characterization of the Adams' problem – and the more general difficulty which hounds all presidents of disjunction – is as follows:

> … Adams had himself assembled so many of the ingredients of a great political reconstruction…. What he did not bring was a consistent and compelling political rationale for reconstructing the polity. Instead of each aspect of his leadership project reinforcing the message of the others and galvanizing the legitimacy of political action, they operated at cross purposes to leave him impotent and instill in his opponent the reconstructive authority he lacked. (1997: 126)

Herbert Hoover also stepped into a difficult situation as president from a party with a long history of electoral success but with a considerable number of new political obstacles to its continuation. Though the Republican regime had survived the Wilson interregnum (and T.R.'s Bull Moose Party), it struggled through Harding's scandal-ridden presidency without ever fully recovering its earlier strength. Hoover was – like John Quincy Adams – an odd mixture of new energy and new policy initiatives and a strong attachment to the existing partisan regime. While Hoover was a progressive and a strong believer in the power of administration (at the national level) to solve serious public problems, he was also a strong supporter of market economics and "voluntarism and local autonomy" (Skowronek 1997: 267). As Skowronek describes this apparent inconsistency, "Hoover went to the people

---

[17] Howe (2007) provides an insightful description of this electoral episode *What Hath God Wrought: The Transformation of America, 1815–1848.*

affirming both the creative potential of the national government *and* the "genius of modern business" (1997: 270, emphasis in original).

His responses to the Great Depression that began during his first term in office ran the gamut from solidifying and extending the power of the federal government (sometimes in a progressive manner, sometimes not) and a reemphasis of the foundational importance of free markets. Unfortunately for Hoover, this "middle way" was deeply unsatisfying to large segments of his party. As is conventional in presidencies of disjunction, the promises and commitments of the past to the various constituencies of the regime come due, and there are never sufficient resources to pay them. Though a tariff supporter, Hoover sought a new tariff that would be less onerous to certain particular constituencies, particularly agricultural interests. Once the Hoover tariff reached Congress, however, the components designed to provide relief for agricultural interests were eviscerated, and the result was one of the most protectionist tariffs in American history, the Smoot-Hawley Tariff of 1930.

Skowronek argues that even in those cases in which Hoover's policy initiatives were significant and progressive departures from the status quo of the Republican regime, Hoover was never committed to communicating and emphasizing this break with the past. Whether on issues related to labor (such as the Wagner Act for which he received no credit) or his various efforts to rebuild the financial sector in the U.S. (his negotiation, with private bankers, for the creation of the National Credit Corporation or the creation of the Reconstruction Finance Corporation), his efforts were always interpreted by his opponents in both parties as insufficient efforts tied inextricably to the limitations of the old regime. Hoover, for his part, was unwilling to make a consistent effort to fight these characterizations of his efforts. For Skowronek:

> Hoover's inability to take the final step in innovation and repudiate the system he was transforming served his critics well.... Hoover would later lament the people's failure to appreciate the significance of his policies, and yet he was the first to deny it. (1997: 284)

Hoover found himself in the difficult situation shared by all presidents serving at a time of national economic crisis; barring a successful escape well in advance of the next election, the administration is doomed.[18] Since Hoover was unwilling to repudiate the Republican

---

[18] It is important to note that the same cannot necessarily be said for foreign policy crises, though voters do tend to expect to see progress in wars begun during the

regime with which he was related – his only chance at reelection given the continuation of the Depression – he was not in a position to win in 1932. His electoral weakness in 1932 made it much easier for fellow partisans (especially those in Congress) to distance themselves from him and his policies in an effort to protect their own electoral fortunes. Again, Hoover found himself fighting a devastating economic crisis with a party organization that was rife with existing conflict. This is the standard script for disjunction (and the end of the dominant regime), and that is just what happened.

Occasionally, a president not attached to a stable regime will find his way to the White House. Skowronek refers to these as presidents of preemption. Examples include Andrew Johnson, Grover Cleveland, Woodrow Wilson, and Dwight Eisenhower. Andrew Johnson was a unique vice president. For the first and only time since the ratification of the Twelfth Amendment (which required separate ballots for president and vice president), the president and the vice president were, at least by background, from distinct parties. Choosing Johnson in an effort to extend the political base of the Republican party, Lincoln chose the only senator from a southern state (Tennessee) who did not leave his seat at the start of the Civil War. Johnson's appeal to other Democrats who supported the war, while important, did not endear him to the Radical Republicans who intended to press for every advantage in any postwar negotiations with the former members of the Confederacy. How Lincoln would have handled Reconstruction is still an open question, but with his assassination just days after Lee's surrender at Appomattox, it became a moot point.

Johnson's management of the early reconstruction efforts were very unpopular with the Radical Republicans, and when they increased their advantage in the House and the Senate in 1866, Johnson's efforts at conciliation with the former Confederate states were actively opposed by Congress. The conflict between Johnson and the Republican Congress became so serious that Johnson was eventually impeached. While he survived the threat of removal, he did so by only a single vote. His influence over subsequent Reconstruction policies was quite limited, and his more general policy-making influence was, at best, negligible. He was an unsuccessful candidate for the Democratic Party nomination in 1868, and he was replaced by Ulysses S. Grant – a Republican – in 1869. Unlike most presidents of preemption, Johnson did not win

administration prior to the next election. This is why Lincoln's reelection was open to question before the Union victories during the spring and summer of 1864, and why Johnson could not reasonably expect to win reelection in 1968 given the situation in Viet Nam.

an election because of a schism in the dominant party regime. The absence of this ideological fissure made his job – as a president of preemption – just that much more difficult.

Republican Dwight Eisenhower did not owe his rise to the presidency in 1952 to a schism in the Democratic Party. Adlai Stevenson, the Democratic candidate, actually received nearly all of his electoral votes from states of the former confederacy. However, an unpopular war, years of Democratic control of the White House, and suggestions of corruption in the Truman administration resulted in a landslide victory for Eisenhower. As is common with presidents of preemption, none are content to follow a traditional party line in their policy initiatives. Since these presidents serve at a time when the dominant party regime is neither weak nor struggling, they realize that their election is not a result of a sweeping repudiation of their opponents' policy objectives nor an overwhelming acceptance of their own party's policy objectives. According to Skowronek, the presidents of preemption:

> … were opposition leaders in the sense that they rode into power with parties opposed to a previously dominant regime. But each was careful to assert his independence from the alternative thought to be harbored by that opposition party and to project some new accommodation with received priorities. (1997: 450)

For Eisenhower, the most dramatic departure from the Republican orthodoxy was in foreign affairs. While the Republican party of the 1940s and early 1950s had a strong isolationist bent, Eisenhower was an internationalist. He rejected the "Fortress America" perspective and actively engaged the international community. He ended the war in Korea and made a number of diplomatic advances to the Soviet Union. On domestic policy, his objectives were somewhat more conventional, even from a partisan standpoint. While he was a supporter of a balanced budget, he made no attempt to roll back the programmatic innovations of the New Deal. He was arguably the most politically successful preemption president – Skowronek concludes that "Dwight Eisenhower, the first Republican to come to power after the New Deal reconstruction, remains the most successful of our preemptive leaders to date" (1997: 45). But his own personal political success was insufficient to wrest the power from the dominant Democratic regime, nor was it even enough for his vice president Richard Nixon to win the presidential election in 1960.[19]

---

[19] It was, admittedly, a very close election.

Historically, presidents of preemption were rare,[20] but Skowronek argues that they may have become increasingly common. To understand the significance of the new prevalence of the presidents of preemption, we must first understand and discuss Skowronek's second temporal dimension: *secular* time. While political time cycles through the series of disjunction, reconstruction, and articulation, secular time moves apace in linear fashion; there is no cycle. According to Skowronek, presidents find themselves in both political time and secular time. In political time, their power and authority is a function of the stability of the dominant regime and their relationship to the regime (a member of the regime or a member of the opposition). In secular time, presidents' power and authority is a function of the development of the institution, so while Jefferson, Lincoln, and FDR were all presidents during periods of reconstruction, the powers and authorities available to them were vastly different because of the sequence of their presidencies in secular time.

The same can be said for presidents in each of the other categories as well. Presidents of articulation have, over time, come to enjoy the increasing capabilities of the office of the president. Enhanced authority and expanded power have not, however, come without a cost. The crux of the problem of articulation is that it is ultimately impossible; presidents of articulation cannot fully honor the commitments and promise of the original reconstruction because the varying interpretations of the reconstruction *within* the dominant regime ignored the unavoidable tradeoffs that would have to be made to realize *any* practical conceptualization of the original reconstruction. Tradeoffs only become obvious (and necessary) as dreams meet the everyday realities of politics. And presidents of articulation must fulfill the promise of the original reconstruction – however defined or conceptualized – in a new and different political world. These efforts to realize the old dream in the practical political realm of a new world result, unavoidably for Skowronek, in political actions and policy initiatives that both support *and* undermine the old regime. This conflict between old and new is most dramatic in the presidencies of articulation furthest along in secular time. As Skowronek writes in the particular case of Lyndon Johnson:

> ... the two most resolute commitments of Johnson's presidency – the one to Vietnam, the other to civil rights – held in their balance the order-affirming and order-shattering elements of presidential action.... With

---

[20] Woodrow Wilson was another example.

his resolute defense of the cornerstone of the old order and his equally resolute pursuit of the cornerstone of a new one, Johnson led himself into a time warp where he became vulnerable to charges of betrayal on all sides. (1997: 346)

The enhancements in institutional power and authority that presidents increasingly enjoy over the course of secular time offer no protection from the conflicts and inconsistencies inherent in the partisan dynamics of presidencies of articulation.

The political dynamics of the presidencies of disjunction are also influenced by the passage of Skowronek's secular time. Presidents presiding over the final disintegration of the partisan regime to which they are attached will tend to latch onto what Skowronek refers to as "the machinery of government" (1997: 393). In the absence of sufficient political power to achieve their policy goals and objectives, they turn to administration and management – venues in which their authority and control does not depend upon the strength and stability of their partisan regime – to affect policy. Obviously, as secular time runs its course, the administrative and managerial outlets available to the president increase dramatically. So it is no wonder that the managerial and administrative options available to Hoover and Carter far exceeded those available to John Quincy Adams and Franklin Pierce.

Somewhat ironically, Skowronek wonders about the possibility that political time is actually fading away and that all presidents will soon be sufficiently empowered by the institutional developments through secular time that all will serve during periods of preemption. Rather than sustained partisan regimes that survive a set of presidencies, the new personalistic "regimes" will last no longer than an administration. The presumptive ending of political time almost certainly underestimates the power and significance of partisan attachments here in the entryway to the twenty-first century, but there is little question that the institution of the presidency has undergone a radical transformation in *secular* time.

Of the theories of presidential power that we have discussed so far – Neustadt's bargaining theory, Kernell's conceptualization of "going public," and Skowronek's partisan theory – Skowronek's is the most difficult to translate into the terms of scientific analysis. Part of the difficulty with Skowronek's theory is its implicitly historical focus. The attention to historical detail and nuance provides a very rich characterization of a particular time and place (or a particular president or presidency); it does not, however, lend itself to straightforward inference. The second difficulty with Skowronek's perspective is the nature of the change (transformation) of its foundational theoretical concepts over the course of time.

Political time is a cycle between stages (disjunction, reconstruction, articulation, and occasionally, preemption) with specific political characteristics. These political characteristics are largely determined by the status of party relations and the power and stability of the existing partisan regime. These partisan political characteristics determine (to a large extent) the *opportunities* for the exercise of presidential power and authority that will exist for any particular president. According to the logic of political time, presidents attached to the dominant regime are in their weakest position during periods of disjunction. The greatest opportunities for the exercise of power come during periods of reconstruction. Though Skowronek suggests that presidents have some limited control over which stage of the process will characterize their presidency, he provides no examples of situations in which presidents clearly and successfully chose a political path inconsistent with their position in political time. So, while Skowronek argues that Hoover might have become a president of reconstruction (even though he was technically a member of the dominant Republican regime), he did not escape the politics of disjunction that he appeared destined to play out.

Even if we assume that presidents are not in a position to choose (or influence) their position in political time, we still have the difficulty of the interaction between political time and secular time. Why is this a difficulty? Because we must understand the relationship between political time and secular time to generate any hypotheses for new data. If we could focus solely on political time (or secular time, for that matter), then it would be far easier to predict the power relations of future presidents. These power relations would depend inherently on the stability and strength of the partisan coalition to which they are attached. The most expansive authority would be available to presidents in a position to respond to the disintegration of an opponents' partisan regime with a reconstruction of their own partisan regime. Presidents of articulation would be somewhat more limited in the exercise of their own power and authority – partly due to the limitations of the commitments of the reconstruction to which they are tied and partly due to the unavoidable fraying of the fabric of the regime that begins during reconstruction – but they would still be better off than presidents of disjunction. The power expectations of presidents of preemption are most difficult to assess because they are outside (or exceptions to) the cycle of political time. That Skowronek spends far less time dealing with presidents of preemption is also a difficulty.

While there are full-chapter descriptions of multiple presidents of reconstruction, articulation, and disjunction, there isn't a single full-chapter description of a president of preemption.

It is the theoretical integration of political and secular time that makes it so difficult to identify the presidential power implications of Skowronek's theory for the future. Fitting the joint trajectories of the cycle of political time and the trend of secular time to historical data is one thing; discerning the future pattern of these joint trajectories is quite another. It would be sufficiently difficult if Skowronek were clear about the integrated trajectory of political and secular time, but he is not. He suggests that the trajectory of secular time might eventually *end* political time, but he is unwilling to commit to this position, and he is unclear about what this might mean for future presidential power relations. His recent characterization of George W. Bush's administration is instructive. In *Presidential Leadership in Political Time: Reprise and Reappraisal*, Skowronek (2008) reflects on the cycle of political time and its potential relevance for our understanding of future presidencies and the nature of presidential power in the twenty-first century. Ironically, his primary criticism of his original argument (made in *The Politics the Presidents Make*) is not that the conceptualization of political time was flawed; his primary contention is that the effects of secular time were overemphasized. Rather than waning to the point of dissolution, the dynamics of the cycle of political time are as patently manifest as ever. Accordingly, he writes:

> I wrote of the "waning of political time," .... [but] these presidencies seem to have exaggerated their most bizarre and worrisome elements.... initiatives that stand out in contemporary America as weird political distractions and intolerable political blunders – initiatives like Clinton's impeachment and Bush's war in Iraq – are, in political time, all too true to form. (2008: xii)

Skowronek attributes this "mistaken" overemphasis on secular time to a surprising rebirth of the American party system. Though he does not make this connection in either the original book or the reappraisal, it is clear that an important component of secular time during the twentieth century was the gradual ebbing of cohesive, distinct political parties. As the power of parties waned, so too (apparently) did the relevance of the cycle of political time to the scope of presidential power and authority. Now that parties have undergone a renaissance, the wheel of political time turns again – and it turns on parties and the strength and stability of partisan regimes.

Now it is possible that the twenty-first century will see a new form of presidential politics inconsistent with the character of Skowronek's political time. Historically, partisan regimes are long-standing. Jackson's regime lasted over 30 years, and Lincoln's reconstruction did not fully disintegrate until FDR's election in 1932, more than 70 years after Lincoln's election. Even the partisan regime created by FDR lasted nearly a half-century. Reagan's partisan regime will be the shortest since that of Thomas Jefferson.[21] If the logic of political time still plays a role in presidential politics, it is highly unlikely – especially given the strength of party organizations today – that it is the same cyclical dynamic that ran through the substance of the nineteenth- and twentieth-century presidential politics.

Even if we are unsatisfied with Skowronek's conceptualization of the role of party organizations and party regimes in the determination of presidential power and authority, his work provides a useful starting point for understanding the role of parties in presidential politics. It is a particularly useful starting point if we are willing to focus on the implications of political time rather than secular time. Given Skowronek's recent conclusions about his own previous work – and his reconsideration of the relative significance of political time and secular time given the Clinton and George W. Bush presidencies, the focus on political time is more than justified, as is his focus on the role of partisan regimes and inter- and intraparty relations on the effective exercise of presidential power. While Skowronek's theory is not the only partisan theory of presidential power, it effectively highlights the significance of partisan relations in the exercise of presidential power.

OLD STYLE PRESIDENTIAL POLITICS?: THE IMPERIAL PRESIDENCY

One of the clear implications of the theories of the sources of presidential power previously discussed is the inherent contingency of power and control. Neustadt's theory of presidential persuasion and effective bargaining is explicitly oriented toward the explanation of the special (and rather unusual) circumstances that tend to produce an active

---

[21] Significantly, it will have been of exactly the same length. Jefferson was elected in 1800, and his partisan regime ended with Jackson's election in 1828. One important difference between the Jefferson and Reagan regimes is the fact that the Jefferson regime was uninterrupted while the Reagan regime was interrupted by Clinton's two-term administration. Whether Obama is a president of reconstruction or a president of preemption remains to be seen.

and effective presidency. In response to the question of whether the president is a clerk or king, Neustadt clearly comes down on the side of the clerk. Efforts to move beyond "clerkhood" take unusual skill and capability – and some degree of good fortune. And these efforts, in the end, are extraordinarily difficult to maintain.

If possible, Kernell offers an even more pessimistic perspective toward the likelihood that the president will be able to exercise broad powers and garner effective control. For Kernell (1986), the insular world of "beltway politics" – what he refers to as "institutionalized pluralism" – has given way to "individualized pluralism" – an atomistic, complicated politics composed of a myriad of interest groups all focused on individual objectives. The disintegration of institutionalized pluralism sounded the death knell for policy making through bargaining and the subsequent persuasion of Washington insiders. For presidents, there were simply too many interest-group mouths to feed to expect to buy off supporters for any extended period of effective policy making. So presidents turned to the general public and began frequent efforts to leverage their own (the president's) personal popularity – "go public" – to build support for their own (the president's) policy initiatives so that members of Congress (in particular) would support these same presidential initiatives to avoid the electoral repercussions of open conflict with a popular president during the next election cycle. But presidents are not always popular (as Ronald Reagan would learn shortly after his first year in office), and "going public" is difficult (and often costly) even for popular presidents. Efforts to mold (or activate) public opinion in the absence of considerable popularity are often disastrous.[22] Again, power and control that may be gained under the best of circumstances may dissipate just as easily when time marches on and things change. For Neustadt and Kernell, the important matters that might change were arguably different, but that the conditions for the effective exercise of significant power and control were ephemeral was plainly shared between them.

Ironically, though Skowronek's conceptualization of the nature of presidential power and authority is explicitly temporal, his characterization of the ebb and flow of power is somewhat more ambiguous than that of Neustadt or Kernell. This is manifest in his discussion of the concomitant "times": political time and secular time. Political time is cyclical. The stages of political time – reconstruction, articulation,

---

[22] Woodrow Wilson's efforts on behalf of U.S. entry into the League of Nations is just a prominent early example of this fact.

and disjunction – follow each other in a cycle, and though there are the occasional interruptions – the politics of preemption – these inter-regna are rarely long and never permanent. Drawing conclusions only on the basis of political time, it is clear that presidential power and control is episodic, it ebbs and flows, though with some admit-ted inconsistency. But political time is not the only temporal course charted by Skowronek; there is also secular time. Secular time does not have an obvious cycle; in fact, there is an inexorability about it that is difficult to interpret.

Skowronek argues that secular time is eroding the distinctive-ness of the stages of political time. At one point, he suggests that we are now likely to have a series of presidents of preemption (regard-less of party or united/divided government). But this is merely a sug-gestion, and so the implications of the erosion of the distinctiveness of the stages of political time for our understanding of presidential power are unclear. Are presidents now in a position to exert consistent and extensive control, or is the era of the expansive interpretation of executive authority of the reconstructive president is now behind us? The issue remains unsettled even in his recent discussion of presiden-tial power (Skowronek 2008). He does, however, raise the "specter" of the *imperial presidency* – an interpretation of executive authority based primarily on institutional prerogatives (particularly war pow-ers) that suggests we are in the latter stages of the full development of the "command and control" potential of the executive office. For the institutionally oriented proponents of the *imperial presidency* perspective, the ebb and flow of power common to other theoretical characterizations of presidential power is greatly constrained, if not completely eliminated. It is to this understanding of executive author-ity and power that we now turn.

Defining and Describing the "Imperial Presidency"

Arthur Schlesinger described the imperial presidency as.

> ... a conception of presidential power so spacious and peremptory as to imply a radical transformation of the traditional polity. In the last years presidential primacy, so indispensable to the political order, has turned into presidential supremacy. The *constitutional* Presidency – as events so apparently disparate as the Indochina War and Watergate affair showed – has become the imperial presidency and threatens to become the revolutionary presidency. (1973: viii, emphasis added)

For Schlesinger, the imperial presidency resulted from "the shift in the *constitutional* [emphasis in original] balance ... the appropriation by the Presidency, and particularly by the contemporary Presidency, of powers reserved by the Constitution *and long historical practice* [emphasis added] to Congress" (1973: viii).

The defining characteristics of the imperial presidency include the following:

1. Presidents take sole responsibility for policy-making powers that are traditionally shared by the Congress and the President.
2. Presidents implement policies through the agencies and bureaucracies of the Executive branch and the Executive Office of the President that exceed the constitutional boundaries of the limits of federal government action (beyond even congressional authority).
3. Presidents make a concerted effort to hide – usually under the pretense of executive privilege or the needs of national security – the most egregious instances of the exercise of extralegal authority.

Schlesinger even allows for the possibility of a presidency so domineering that it exceeds the bounds of even the imperial presidency. This extraordinary – and plainly illegal – usurpation of power is referred to as the "revolutionary presidency." The distinctive characteristics of the revolutionary presidency are as follows:

1. Complete concentration of significant executive branch decision making in the EOP (Executive Office of the President) in general and the White House staff more specifically. In particular, the shift toward decision making and presidential advising by an extraordinarily small number of subordinates, which is a component of the imperial presidency, reaches its zenith in the revolutionary presidency.
2. The broad extension of presidential authority into policy prerogatives plainly associated with and historically exercised by Congress or the Court.
3. Use of executive privilege and claims of national security to control information relevant to domestic policy making.
4. The use of federal agencies – particularly investigative agencies – to combat domestic political opponents without regard for widely accepted legal conventions.

The revolutionary presidency is the imperial presidency taken to its logical conclusion. Schlesinger describes the archetypical revolutionary president, Nixon, in these terms:

He was not a man given to political philosophizing. But he was heading toward a new balance of constitutional powers, an audacious and imaginative reconstruction of the American Constitution. He did indeed contemplate, as he said in his 1971 State of the Union message, a New American Revolution. But the essence of this revolution was not, as he said at the time, power to the people. The essence was power to the Presidency. (1973: 252)

Institutional Prerogatives, War Powers, and Domestic Policy Control

The expansive powers of the imperial presidency are based on the formal construction of the executive branch in the Constitution and the latitude for interpretation provided by the ambiguous semantics of important aspects of the first two articles of the Constitution. The Constitutional clauses most relevant to the development of the imperial presidency deal with the war powers of the president (and Congress). Schlesinger is very clear about the foundation of the powers of the imperial presidency. The source of the imperial president's exceptional authority is the explicit war powers provided by the Constitution. He writes:

> ... historians and political scientists, this writer among them, contributed to the rise of the presidential mystique. But the imperial Presidency received its decisive impetus, I believe, from foreign policy; above all, from the capture by the Presidency of the most vital of national decisions, the decision to go to war. (1973: ix)

He goes on to argue that:

> The assertions of sweeping and unilateral presidential authority remained official doctrine in foreign affairs. And, if the President were conceded these life-and-death decisions abroad, how could he be restrained from gathering unto himself the less fateful powers of the national polity. (1973: ix)

The primary issue for proponents of the imperial presidency theory is the explanation of the ebb and flow of presidential power – and even the theory's most ardent supporters would agree that presidential power and authority has not been constant nor has its realization been an uninterrupted increase – during a period of formal constitutional stasis. Technically, the Constitution has not remained unchanged from the ratification to the present day; after all, there are 27 amendments. However, none of the amendments includes a new and explicit grant of presidential authority. So, at least from a *formal* standpoint, the powers of the president remain unaltered.[23]

Presidential power and authority have waxed and waned over the more than two centuries since Washington's inauguration. Historically, there is no constancy in presidential authority. So how could formal institutions and formal powers provide any leverage in our efforts to understand the waxing and waning of presidential power? Isn't it more likely that presidential power varies because of personal capabilities, or public popularity, or partisan strength? Possibly, but one could also argue that none of those other variables (and related theories) captures the nub of the problem directly addressed by the imperial presidency.

The literature on presidential power tends to focus on the means (bargaining and persuasion, the support of public opinion, partisan support in Congress) by which presidents build coalitions to achieve their policy goals. While the coalition may include a wide range of political actors both inside and outside government, the main coalition of concern is nearly always a legislative coalition. Much of the literature on presidential power revolves around the cultivation and development of the means necessary to build majority (and in some cases, super majority) coalitions in Congress.[24] In these standard cases it is the president who faces the costs and difficulties of building a coalition.

---

[23] The power and authority of the national government have been enhanced through the amendment process – the Sixteenth Amendment, the income tax amendment – is just one example. However, the grant of authority to the national government was not a direct grant of additional authority to the president. In most cases, if a grant of authority is made, it is most directly affecting the power and authority of the legislative branch, which is certainly the case with the 16th Amendment. That presidential authority might have been enhanced indirectly – through, for example, the increase in the size of the executive branch enabled by the levy of an income tax – is certainly possible. Still, there is no direct grant of authority to the executive branch.

[24] Why would a president ever need a super majority in Congress? Assuming away the veto – why would the president oppose his own legislation – under what circumstances would the president need more than a simple majority in either house of Congress? The President will need a super majority in situations in which it is necessary to invoke cloture – and thus end a filibuster (a standard delay tactic designed to kill legislation) – in the Senate. Cloture requires a three-fifth's majority; and in cases where a filibuster is threatened or implemented, a simple majority is insufficient to head it off or stop it. Absent the votes necessary to invoke cloture, a determined filibuster can kill the targeted piece of legislation. For issues with a significant budgetary component, the reconciliation process provides an alternative for majorities which are not filibuster proof. Use of reconciliation procedures are, however, controversial.

But what if the Constitution (or, more accurately, the widely accepted interpretation of the Constitution) provided the authority for the President to act unilaterally? If the President is in a position to affect policy change unilaterally, then the costs and difficulties of coalition building fall onto his opponents. In this case, the relative power and authority of the President is far more substantial than in the (more standard) case in which the President must build the coalition to affect policy change. Students of the presidency have begun to take these possibilities far more seriously in the post–9/11 world, and an increasing volume of rigorous, scientifically oriented work suggests that institutional prerogatives – apart from bargaining skill, public opinion, and even partisan support – provide the president with an increasingly wide range of opportunities to wield authoritative power.

Recent work on the reinvigoration of the imperial presidency focuses on the use of varied means of the unilateral exercise of executive authority (see Rudalevige 2005). Presidents enjoy a variety of institutional prerogatives that they may implement unilaterally. These include the veto, executive agreements, executive orders, and signing statements that we discussed in Chapter 3.

Before we move on, it is important to distinguish between two closely related concepts – the *imperial presidency* and the theory of the *unitary executive*. The term "imperial presidency" was intended as, and is generally taken to be, pejorative. Schlesinger's imperial president was an executive wielding exceptional power well beyond the bounds of the Constitution. His research on the imperial presidency describes how this situation occurs, why it is a serious threat to popular government, and how it might be averted in the future. The theory of the unitary executive, on the other hand, explicitly attributes all executive authority to the president, and proponents of this theory (at least the strong version of this theory) tend to favor this extensive grant of power to the president.[25] Supporters of the unitary executive perspective cite two clauses in Article II of the Constitution as *prima facie* evidence that the Founders placed the entire executive authority in the hands of the president: the vesting clause and the

---

[25] According to Lessig and Sunstein (1994), there is little question that the Founders created some form of a unitary executive. The question is the extent to which the exercise of the executive powers may be (should be) effectively constrained by the legislative branch through its law-making powers. Supporters of the "strong" version of this theory presume a dramatically circumscribed legislative authority; weaker versions of the theory imagine a more dynamic and powerful legislative authority capable of checking the executive authority.

"take care" clause. The vesting clause, at the very beginning of section 1, reads "The executive Power shall be vested in a President of the United States of America" (U.S. Constitution). The "take care" clause, in section 3, reads that "he shall take Care that the Laws be faithfully executed" (U.S. Constitution). Though these passages imply that the executive power resides solely in the president, other aspects of the constitution – including the advice and consent requirements for presidential appointments and treaties – suggest the sharing of executive power. Recently, at least since the Reagan presidency, the presidential assertion of authority consistent with a unitary executive has become more common (Kelley 2006). Significantly, a growing body of work also warns of the reemergence of the imperial presidency (see, in particular, Rudalevige 2005).

An important additional distinction between the imperial presidency and unitary executive perspectives is the relative significance of the roles of Congress and the Supreme Court in restraining the abuses of presidential power. Research on the imperial presidency – both the work by Schlesinger and the more recent work – identifies Congress as the primary bulwark against the exercise of excessive power by the president. For these scholars, Congress must rise to the challenge and exercise its full constitutional authority (particularly in the area of oversight and budgeting) to maintain the balance of powers between the branches of government.

Proponents of the unitary executive perspective, on the other hand, do not recognize Congress as having any executive powers or responsibilities, so it is particularly difficult for Congress to restrain the executive in those policy arenas in which oversight is most difficult and in which the threat of the budgetary axe is a relatively inefficient means of control. New programs and new policy initiatives can be very expensive. Even if presidents control the executive branch, new funding always requires legislative action. Signing statements (which we learned about earlier in the "nuts and bolts" chapter) cannot add funds to the bottom line appropriations for a federal program, but they can indicate in detail the ways in which the president will (and will not) interpret the authorizing the legislation for the funded program. It is no surprise then, that research on the unitary executive focuses on those policy areas most difficult to control via budgetary politics – foreign policy (particularly during a time of war), domestic security (during a war on terrorism), regulatory policy, and civil rights and civil liberties.

Within the context of the theory of the unitary executive, the responsibility for restraining the president falls primary to the Supreme

Court. If the president wields the full executive authority of the federal government, then only the Court may constrain him, and this constraint comes through the interpretation of the constitutional boundaries of the executive authority. In short, the president may reach for as much power as the Court will allow. The people are also responsible for restraining a power-hungry president, but there opportunities to do so only come once every four years. And in the most extreme cases, Congress may censure, impeach, and remove a president, but in more than two centuries, a president has never been removed from office. For all practical purposes, as the proponents of the theory of the imperial presidency depend on Congress to maintain an effective balance of power, so the supporters of the unitary executive theory view the Court as the only rightful arbiter of the extent of presidential power.

It is worth noting, and it is no accident, that the fullest manifestation of both the imperial presidency and the unitary executive comes in the arena of foreign policy and national security. Schlesinger clearly describes the role of Vietnam-era foreign policy dynamics in the development of the imperial presidency under Johnson and Nixon. More recently, Rudalevige (2005, 2009) argues that the imperial presidency reemerged during the George W. Bush administration in the aftermath of the terrorist attacks of 9/11. Historically, the imperial presidency depended, to a significant extent, on the acceptance of a semipermanent state of emergency (or at least a heightened security threat), so the imperial presidency theory implies that the power of the modern president waxes and wanes with (1) the personal ambition of the president and (2) the perceived level of national security. Both extreme presidential ambition and a significant perceived threat are necessary for the manifestation of imperial presidential authority and the absence of significant congressional restraint. Whether or not dire economic circumstances will also enable the growth of imperial presidential authority remains to be seen, but the Obama administration may well test this possibility.[26] Though the tenets of the imperial presidency do not lend themselves to rigorous empirical testing, partly because of the relatively small number of presidencies for which the preconditions for an imperial presidency are met, we should expect to see a direct relationship between the perception of a significant security threat (and possibly the realization of an economic threat) and the aggrandizement of presidential power.

---

[26] Though FDR faced more severe economic circumstances, his administration began before the full realization of the administrative state. As Schlesinger notes, the imperial presidency depends upon a substantial, mature bureaucracy.

Though related to the imperial presidency perspective, the theory of the unitary executive is not an empirical theory. The unitary executive perspective is a normative theory focused on the proper locus of executive power. There is no way to prove (or disprove) the Founders' intentions (with regard to presidential authority) or to prove (or disprove) the proper interpretation of the constitutional delineation of executive authority. But it is possible to evaluate the role of the Court in limiting presidential authority, and rigorous empirical analysis of the practical political implications of Court rulings for the exercise of presidential authority have the potential to make an important contribution to our understanding of presidential power.

PRESIDENTIAL POWER: PERSUASION, GOING PUBLIC, PARTISANSHIP, AND IMPERIAL POWER IN THE TWENTY-FIRST CENTURY

As social scientists, how do we deal with the diversity of perspectives toward presidential power? How do we evaluate the empirical content of distinct theories that were, in most cases, not designed with a scientific perspective in mind? We start with the following:

1. *Focus on the primary independent variables in each theory.* Neustadt focuses on persuasion and bargaining; his theory tells us to look for the exercise of presidential power in deals cut with insiders and trades made with other policymakers. He also reminds us that personal skills matter a great deal, that all presidents do not share these in the same order, and so *who* the president is, the specific man or woman, also matters a lot. Kernell finds the source of presidential power in public opinion, in popular support for a president's own policy initiatives – a popular support curried by the president himself. Skowronek reminds us that presidents live in a partisan world, and presidential power may ebb and flow with party fortunes. Finally, Schlesinger reminds us that institutions should not be ignored. Under certain (dire) circumstances, these institutions may provide for the dramatic expansion of presidential power.

2. *Derive testable hypotheses from the various theories that focus on the effects of the primary independent variables. Realize that additional theory development may depend upon the judicious integration of these basic theories (i.e., a theory that examines the integrated effects of partisan dynamics and bargaining/persuasion).*

Regardless of the aspect of the presidency on which you concentrate, avoid idiosyncratic explanations. Attempt to understand what you see by constructing potential explanations from the building blocks of one (or two) of these theories. Then extend these explanations to new data through the development of more general hypotheses.

3. *Test these hypotheses in a variety of temporal and institutional contexts. Realize that you may not always be able to distinguish between the effects of different independent variables.* If you were initially interested in understanding the role of the president in recent health-care policy making, consider extending your scope of analysis to additional time periods or to other policy domains. Be sure to consider alternative explanations and remember that your ability to distinguish between alternative explanations may depend upon the size of your sample – in this case, the extent of the time period you are analyzing. For example, at the beginning of the Obama administration, one could argue that each theory discussed above predicted the opportunity for the expansive use of presidential power. President Obama was quite popular. He enjoyed majorities in both houses of Congress, just as one would expect of a president of reconstruction. The institutional architecture upon which the imperial presidency depends is in place, and the country faces not only a terrorist threat but also grave economic circumstances. And President Obama would appear to have just the skills that Neustadt touted in *Presidential Power*. He may lack the experience, but time will provide that. How then do you distinguish between the distinct effects of each variable? You look to the past and keep up with the future as it unfolds. The conditions will not always be so conducive to the exercise of extensive presidential power.

4. *Finally, evaluate the results in the light of Lakatos' distinction between **productive research programmes** and **degenerating research programmes**. Powerful theories (and useful theories) apply in an increasingly wide array of contexts.* As your work progresses, you will gain insight about the *general* applicability of one or more of these theories (or, possibly, one of your own). This insight will be very useful. It is the knowledge that provides the foundation for an understanding of the fundamental nature of presidential power and the knowledge that can productively inform our choice of presidents, expectations of sitting presidents, and reforms of the office and the executive branch. It is knowledge – scientific knowledge – that can be put to use.

IMPORTANT TERMS

going public
imperial presidency
individualized pluralism
institutionalized pluralism
Marbury v. Madison
political time
- reconstruction
- articulation
- preemption
- disjunction

power to persuade
presidency-centered
president-centered
professional reputation
protocoalitions
public prestige
rally event
revolutionary presidency
secular time
self-executing order
signing statements
unitary executive
war powers

5

Electing a President

The October 2008 edition of the journal *PS: Political Science and Politics* included a symposium entitled "Forecasting the 2008 National Elections." This symposium included a set of articles in which more than a dozen political scientists predicted the outcome of the presidential election (who would win and by what percentage of the popular vote).[1] Though the articles were published in October, because of the time necessary to review and edit the manuscripts and prepare them for publication, they were all completed by the middle of the summer. In fact, all of the data on which the predictions were based was available prior to Labor Day, the traditional beginning of the general election campaigns. This is important because it indicates that all of the predictions in each of the articles *preceded* the beginning of the general election, so neither the general election campaign of then-Senator Obama nor Senator McCain influenced the results or predictions in any way.

As each article included its own particular model for predicting the partisan distribution of the popular vote, it should come as no surprise that there was some variation in the predictions. While some symposium participants thought the election would result in a relatively easy victory for Obama (see Abramowitz 2008, Holbrook 2008), others thought Obama would win in a nailbiter (see Cuzan and Bundrick 2008; Norpoth 2008). The editor of the symposium, James Campbell, actually predicted a very close McCain victory. What is most interesting about the symposium results – which, while somewhat varied, were surprisingly consistent for a set of precampaign election predictions – is the average prediction: an Obama victory

---

[1] Several scholars also made predictions about the partisan distribution of seats in the House and Senate following the 2008 election, but those are not our focus at this time.

with 53.7% of the two-party popular vote, the exact outcome to the tenth of a percentage point. This is a strikingly accurate prediction if it were made any time before election day; that this average "prediction" is based on data and analyses that preceded the entire general election campaign is especially surprising.

And this was not a run-of-the-mill presidential election. To say that the campaigns leading up to Election Day 2008 were unique is all but an understatement. Consider the following unconventional aspects of just some of the candidates for the presidency and the vice presidency during the 2008 primary and general election campaigns:

1. The first major party African American presidential candidate (and, eventually, president).
2. The first significant female candidate for a major party nomination (who happened, also, to be the wife of a former president).
3. A major party candidate who would have become the oldest person ever to become president (and the first president to be born outside the 50 states).
4. Only the second major party female vice presidential candidate in American history (and the first major party candidate for president or vice president from Alaska).
5. Finally, this was by far the most expensive presidential campaign in American history.[2] Presidential candidates spent more than $1.3 billion during the 2008 election, a dramatic increase on the previous high of $718 million in 2005.[3]

This is far from an exhaustive list of the unusual or uncharacteristic aspects of the 2008 electoral season, but it clearly suggests that this presidential campaign was like none other. And yet, there were those predictions, and they were so accurate. How is it possible to make such good predictions about such an unusual race?

The fact that experts can predict the outcome of presidential elections in advance of the start of the campaign strongly suggests that campaigns have little or no effect on the final outcome (and maybe even the final margin). Yet the vastness of the resources expended during presidential campaigns would seem to suggest that someone thinks the campaigns matter. Millions of dollars spent by both Senator McCain and then-Senator Obama in the last few days of the campaign also suggest not only that campaigns matter but that the last few campaign

[2] This campaign was also the most expensive election in American history.
[3] See other historical data on the Center for Responsive Politics web site at http://www.opensecrets.org/pres08/totals.php?cycle=2008 (last accessed on December 17, 2009).

activities matter – even in an election that would be decided by over 190 electoral votes and nearly 10 million popular votes.

Now, no one is suggesting that campaigns are irrelevant in the very closest presidential elections. Given the final margin of victory in the presidential election of 2000 – a five-vote margin in the Electoral College that was dependent upon a popular vote margin of 537 votes in Florida – it is impossible to completely discount campaign effects.[4] But the 2000 election was arguably the closest in American history. It was certainly the closest, in terms of electoral votes, since the presidential election of 1876. More generally, the outcomes of very close elections are almost certainly subject to some sort of campaign effects. Most presidential elections, however, are not particularly close. Most presidential elections are decided by a million or more popular votes and dozens of votes in the Electoral College. During the post–World War II era, the average margin of victory has been 248 electoral votes and 8.5% of the popular vote. Not close; not close at all.

Given the rarity of close, competitive presidential elections, the apparent inconsistency of the juxtaposition of intense and expensive campaigning in the face of strikingly predictable outcomes leads us to several research questions:

1. How predictable are presidential elections? Are presidential elections as predictable as we think?
2. What evidence suggests that campaigns matter?
3. Are predictable elections and intense, meaningful campaigns mutually exclusive?

The significance of American presidential elections has led to substantial scholarly interest in research questions such as those above. So what does the research on presidential elections suggest? Are they predictable? Quite predictable? And do campaigns matter? And if so, how? And finally, is it possible to have meaningful and outcome-relevant campaigns in the context of predictable elections?

In the next section, we take a look at what political scientists have to say about the predictability (or unpredictability) of presidential elections and the role that campaigns appear to have on the outcomes of presidential elections. Throughout the discussion, we will make an effort to identify those positions and perspectives that are most controversial (giving equal time, ideally to the various alternatives) and

---

[4] For information on the 2000-vote totals for each of the presidential candidates, see the web site of the National Archives at http://www.archives.gov/federal-register/electoral-college/2000/popular_vote.html (last viewed on December 17, 2009).

those perspectives for which there is a consensus. As you go through this literature review, think about the following questions:

1. Which perspectives do I find most compelling?
2. What data might I use to test the hypotheses associated with one or more of these perspectives?
3. What tests or analyses might provide for a more complete assessment of the hypotheses associated with one or more of these perspectives?
4. What results would convince me to change my own position on the issues of election predictability and campaign significance?

REVIEWING THE LITERATURE(S)

Predicting general election outcomes

Predicting presidential elections is something of a political junkie pastime. For example, during 2008, the *Washington Post* sponsored a "Pick Your President Contest" in which entrants submitted their estimates of the distribution of Electoral College votes between presidential candidates Obama and McCain. Though the development of the Internet has certainly facilitated the availability of various types of data and information that might be used to predict the outcome of national elections, the practice of handicapping the "horse race" of the presidential campaign is a tried and true aspect of American political history.

Historically speaking, it appears to be the predictions that are most erroneous that are remembered longest. Most famous was the *Literary Digest*'s prediction that Alf Landon (Republican senator for Kansas) would defeat incumbent Franklin Delano Roosevelt in a landslide in 1936. Roosevelt would end up winning the election with more than 60% of the popular vote, and he won the Electoral College ballot 523–8. Of the 48 states, Landon would carry only two (Maine and Vermont).[5] From the standpoint of both the popular vote and the Electoral College tally, the presidential election in 1936 was one of the most one-sided in American history.

Why were the results of the *Literary Digest* poll so far wrong? Certainly, the *Literary Digest* pollsters cannot be faulted for too small a sample. A large national sample today would be no more than 2,500–3,000 respondents. The *Digest* sample was composed of over 2 *million*

---

[5] Landon failed to capture his home state of Kansas.

respondents. However, the sample was not random; it suffered from significant class and partisan bias and response bias. The survey was distributed only to readers of the *Digest*, a magazine with a far wealthier and far more Republican readership than the general population. So the *Digest* began by greatly oversampling individuals who were most likely to support the Republican Landon. Second, among the readership, participation was a result of self-selection; to participate in the survey, you had to fill out the survey card and mail it to the *Digest*. This self-selection mechanism tends to bias the sample toward the most ideological and partisan subjects in the sample because it is the most ideological and partisan individuals who are most likely to participate in these sorts of political activities. The *Digest* started with a sample of individuals predisposed (because of class and partisan leanings) to support Landon and then increased the bias in the sample by using a self-selection participation procedure that was most likely to draw the most conservative and most Republican voters into the sample. These severe sample biases cannot be overcome by even the very largest of sample sizes.[6]

Equally famous, though not as dramatically errant, was the faulty, but widespread, expectation that Thomas Dewey (Republican governor of New York) would defeat incumbent Harry S. Truman in 1948. This is the background result for the famous picture of a smiling Truman disembarking from Air Force 1 holding aloft a copy of the *Chicago Daily Tribune* with the headline – in bold – "DEWEY DEFEATS TRUMAN." In the end, the election was not especially close. Truman won by over 2 million votes, and he won over 60% of the votes in the Electoral College. Unlike the *Literary Digest* prediction in 1936, the expectation of a Dewey victory was widespread, and Truman was *generally* given little chance to win reelection.

The midterm election in 1946 had resulted in a significant increase in the number of Republicans in both the House (55 more Republican representatives) and the Senate (13 more Republican senators). The Republicans took control of both the House and the Senate for the first time since Roosevelt's election in 1932. Truman' unpopularity was considered an important factor in the especially poor showing of congressional Democrats in 1946, and Truman's continued unpopularity

---

[6] Though based on a far smaller sample, a 1936 survey by George Gallup correctly predicted a Roosevelt victory. Gallup's work and the responses to the polling errors of the *Digest* survey in 1936 are viewed as the beginning of a scientific orientation to opinion sampling. Ironically, the *Digest* had correctly predicted the previous five elections. Squire (1988) provides a detailed analysis of the *Digest's* 1936 sample and survey and the various reasons for its flawed prediction.

lead to an intense competition for the Republican presidential nomination (for so many hoped to take advantage of Truman's weakness) and surprisingly strong competition for his own party's nomination. An additional problem for Truman was Strom Thurmond's Dixiecrat candidacy, an overt effort to draw southern Democrats away from Truman. In the end, Thurmond carried only four states, and the support for Dewey (the Republican candidate) was not as strong as expected, so Truman's victory, at least in hindsight, was relatively comfortable.

In 1936, the *Literary Digest* poll garnered a considerable amount of attention, both for the size of its sample and for the dramatic inaccuracy of its distinctive prediction. In 1948, pollsters *generally* expected Dewey to defeat Truman, and they based these expectations on a number of conventionally sized polls. Why did polling miss the Truman victory in 1948? There are several potential explanations. First, polling practices over a decade following the *Literary Digest* debacle tended to oversample voters who were more likely to support Republicans – voters with telephones, for example. Today, cell phones are ubiquitous; in 1948, many working class and middle class homes – homes that, at least from a class standpoint, would be more likely to vote Democrat – were without telephones. Also, several weeks before the 1948 election, Dewey's lead was generally viewed as insurmountable. Given the size of the lead and the clear expectation of a Dewey victory, relatively few polls were fielded during the final weeks of the election. During these final days, however, there was a significant shift of support to Truman. Since so few polls were fielded during this time period, this shift in support went unnoticed.

Both of these errant predictions were based on what was assumed to be the best polling technology of the day. At the very least, both predictions were based on polling data. Today, our polling technology and methods for assessing public opinion are far more sophisticated than they were in either 1936 or 1948. Still, polling data – even that collected on the very eve of an election – is a surprisingly imperfect tool for predicting presidential elections. Even in recent years and even for polls taken very, very close to Election Day (certainly no more than a day or two before), there has been considerable variation in the predictions of the popular vote and a considerable amount of error.

At first glance, this is somewhat surprising. On closer inspection, explanations for this sort of variation in estimates – and the level of error in a large proportion of predictions based on polls – are not difficult to find. First, every poll has some explicit margin of error. For conventionally sized samples (between 1,000 and 2,000 respondents), the margin of error is around 3–3.5 percentage points. This means that two identical polls fielded at exactly the same time to two different (but identically sized) samples might yield vote percentage predictions that are half a dozen points apart – say, one poll predicts Candidate A will receive 47% of the vote and the other predicts Candidate A will receive 53% of the vote. Thus, given a 3.5 percentage point margin of error, the results from the first poll imply that the actual vote percentage (the percentage predicted for the population of voters, not just this sample) is somewhere between 43.5% and 50.5%. For the second sample, that range would be from 49.5% to 56.5%. Because these *confidence intervals* overlap, we cannot distinguish, at least in a meaningful way, between the estimates of the two polls. They are not, statistically speaking, distinct. So, in any polling environment, sampling error (due to the variations in the samples) will produce variation in the polling results and thus the predictions based upon the polls. This is unavoidable. Unfortunately, in close elections (or even relatively close elections), the break-even point will often be within the confidence interval, and in these cases we cannot confidently predict which candidate will win.

These statistical issues do not touch on two other issues that complicate the use of polls to predict election outcomes. First, as is obvious from most poll reports, there are often a significant percentage of undecided voters. Again, in close elections, the winner is often determined by (1) whether or not these "undecideds" vote and (2) which candidate wins the larger portion of the undecided voters. Rarely do voters who are undecided shortly before the election split evenly between the two major party candidates. We will discuss this in more detail below. Second, vote choice polls are only useful if they are sampling individuals who will end up voting. While it is impossible to perfectly predict who will vote (and who will not), pollsters make an effort to sample "likely voters." This is an important strategy because a large portion of the voting-age population does not vote (no less than 30–35% in most presidential elections), and traditionally, there are some important demographic differences between voters and nonvoters. Voters tend to be more highly educated, wealthier, and older than nonvoters. These differences – differences that tend to have important political implications – require that pollsters make an effort to focus on that group of potential voters who are likely to go to the polls. To accurately predict population outcomes, it is crucial that samples are as representative as possible. Unfortunately, small errors in the "likely voter" predictions (or models on which the predictions are based) may generate sizable errors in the predictions based on the poll results from the flawed sample. Underestimating (or overestimating) the turnout of a particularly partisan voting bloc – such as African Americans – may lead to a set of errant state-level predictions, and thus the expected Electoral College result might be off by dozens of electoral votes.

Political scientists do have alternative strategies for predicting presidential election results. Predictions based on polling data are generated from *individual-level* data – a collection of distinct data from a set of individual respondents. Since the object of the prediction is the outcome of a simple aggregation[7] of millions of individual votes, this would seem to be a reasonable strategy. But as we discussed above, it does have certain important flaws. An alternative strategy, one that does not attempt to predict the vote choices of more than 100 million Americans from a sample of less than 2,500 potential voters, focuses on aggregate-level data to predict presidential election outcomes. These aggregate models of presidential election outcomes tend to focus on economic circumstances and their historical impact on the distribution of votes between the candidate from the incumbent party (whether or not the candidate is actually the incumbent president) and the candidate from the challenging party. The expectation is that voters will punish incumbents (and incumbent parties) for bad economic circumstances. So high inflation and low income growth (or no income growth, as in a recession or depression) tend to lead voters to support the challenging party (and its candidate) rather than the incumbent.

Historically, there is a strong relationship between economic circumstances during an administration, particularly in the last few quarters prior to the election, and the level of support the party of the administration receives on Election Day. Probably the most famous economic model of presidential election returns is the Fair model developed by Princeton economist Ray Fair.[8] His statistical model (technically, a regression model) estimates the relationship between various economic variables (recent inflation, recent income growth, and the number of quarters of good income growth over the president's term of office) and the percentage of the vote received by the incumbent party (whether or not the incumbent party's candidate is actually

---

[7] At this point, let us ignore the complications and complexity of the Electoral College. Nearly all election-oriented predictive analysis focuses on the distribution of popular votes between the two major party candidates. This is true for poll-based individual-level data/models and economy-based aggregate-level data/models.

[8] The original model was published in Fair (1978). More recent versions of this model can be found in Fair (2002) and online at http://fairmodel.econ.yale.edu/vote2008/computev.htm (last viewed on December 17, 2009).

the incumbent president) over time.[9] The strong evidence of a relationship between aggregate economic indicators and the distribution of the vote between the two major parties has not resulted in a consensus on the particular economic variables to include in the analysis (and thus form the basis of the electoral prediction), nor is there a consensus on the specific operationalization of the variables chosen for the analysis (and the predictive model). Some scholars include measures of unemployment or other indicators of inflation or income growth. But these subtle differences in modeling strategy do not obscure the strength of the general relationship between these economic factors and the presidential vote.

Aggregate-level models of the presidential vote are not limited to economic variables. Some aggregate models include a measure of the public support for the current incumbent, normally measured during the summer of the election year (Cuzan and Bundrick 2008; Lewis-Beck and Tien 2008). The greater the public support for the incumbent president, often operationalized as the percentage of Americans who give the president good marks on a job approval survey, the higher the voter support for the incumbent's party during the fall election. It is also fairly common for aggregate models not limited to economic variables to include a measure for tenure in office. A tenure-in-office variable normally takes the form of a counter for the number of years that a party has been in power or an indicator of whether or not a party is currently seeking a third or higher term. Generally, the longer a particular party has been in office, the less support that party will receive in a presidential election.

One of the most interesting aspects of the aggregate-level model is that even when it incorporates some type of polling data (in the form of job approval ratings for the incumbent presidency, for example), nearly all of the data on which the aggregate model predictions are based are from the time period prior to the traditional beginning of the general election campaign (Labor Day of the election year). If one can accurately predict the winner of the general election and the margin of victory with information that is completely unaffected by any general election campaign – in fact, technically precedes the general

---

[9] Fair operationalizes inflation as the annualized growth in the gross domestic product (GDP) deflator over the first three quarters of the election year. Income growth is operationalized as the annualized growth in GDP over the first three quarters of the election year, and what Fair refers to as the "good news" variable – an indicator of the frequency of a relatively high level of income growth – is operationalized as the number of quarters, out of the first 15 of the current president's term – in which annualized growth was at or above 3%.

election campaign – then how important is the role of the campaign in determining the outcome of the presidential election? More specifically, what, if any, are the primary campaign effects for presidential elections? We turn to this question in the next section.

Do campaigns matter?

Scholars who study American political behavior have developed at least three prominent explanations for vote choice; these explanations are based primarily on economic, sociological, and psychological factors. Proponents of an economic model of voting behavior focus their research on the relationship between individual-level economic circumstances and vote choice or aggregate economic circumstances and vote choice. Somewhat surprisingly, individual-level economic factors such as short-term changes in wealth or income, employment status, and subjective evaluations of individual economic circumstances have relatively little impact on vote choices. On the other hand, individuals' evaluations of aggregate economic circumstances – their perceptions of the quality of the national economy, for example – are strongly tied to vote choice. Scholars call this sociotropic voting, and its prevalence is one of the reasons for the predictability of presidential elections. If economic factors dominate individual-level vote choice, campaign effects are likely to be relatively limited. Some very recent research suggests that candidates may occasionally be in a position to influence the relative significance of the economy in some voters' minds (see Vavreck 2009), but generally, if the economic voting model is accurate, campaign effects are likely to be quite limited.

Sociological models of voting focus on the relationship between individuals' vote choices and their demographic characteristics. Going back to at least the 1940s and 1950s, books like *The People's Choice* (Lazarsfeld et al. 1944) and *Voting* (Berelson et al. 1954) demonstrated the ways in which social characteristics such as class, race, and union membership influenced vote patterns. Even today, there are strong correlations between certain demographic factors and partisan vote choice. African Americans and Jews, for example, are overwhelmingly Democratic and supportive of Democratic candidates, particularly in presidential elections. To the extent that vote choice is primarily a function of sociological or demographic characteristics, campaigns are unlikely to alter vote choices. The stability of vote choice does not preclude the possibility that campaigns might have turnout effects – one campaign may be relatively more effective at generating supporter turnout than another campaign – but given the variety of factors that determine individual-level turnout that are unrelated to campaign dynamics, these differential turnout effects are likely to be limited.

Finally, we come to the psychological model of vote choice epitomized by the research of Campbell et al. (1960) in *The American Voter*. The psychological model focuses on the significance of partisanship in the determination of vote choice – Democrats will vote for Democratic candidates and Republicans will vote for Republican candidates. From the standpoint of campaign effects, it is important to note that partisanship is a particularly stable personal characteristic. While there are demographic shifts in partisanship that occur over decades (what is often referred to as a *partisan realignment*) – the shift of white southern Democrats to the Republican party over the course of the last half of the twentieth century is one example of this phenomenon – these shifts are relatively rare and often depend upon replacement rather than transition. In the southern example just referenced, replacement would occur when a relatively old Democrat leaves the voting population only to be replaced by a young Republican. Individual-level partisanship is quite stable. Strong Democrats rarely become strong Republicans.

Proponents of the psychological perspective note that even though voters are partisan, they are not particularly ideological – that is, their understanding of policy issues is relatively limited and any new political information they might receive is incorporated inefficiently, if at all (Converse 1964). The most informed and sophisticated voters are also the most partisan, and these strong partisans are likely to filter the information they do receive through their own partisan lens (Zaller 1992). The least partisan voters are the least likely to process new political information (Zaller 1992). So the voters who are most likely to perceive and process campaign messages are least likely to change their minds, and voters who are most likely to change their minds in response to campaign messages are least likely to perceive and process these messages (Zaller 1992). These dynamics do not preclude the possibility of significant campaign effects – there are certainly voters in the "middle level" who may hear campaign messages and who are not so partisan as to ignore them outright (see Shaw 2006; Zaller 1992) – but this is a small portion of the voting population, and as political partisans become increasingly polarized, it is an ever-shrinking portion of the population. Still, the psychological model of voting does allow for the possibility of significant campaign effects.

What types of campaign activities might produce these campaign effects? The literature on campaign effects focuses on a variety of campaign activities. These include: (1) conventions, (2) debates, (3) campaign advertising, (4) candidate events, (5) media effects, and (6) mobilization efforts.

During each presidential election year, both major parties stage elaborate party conventions during which thousands of party leaders from all across the United States gather to hear speeches, adopt a platform, and finalize the nomination of their candidates for the presidency and the vice presidency. Before the development of the modern primary/caucus system for allocating delegates to presidential candidates, nominees were actually chosen at party conventions. Today, the likelihood that none of the potential nominees would have a majority of the committed delegates prior to the beginning of the convention is quite small,[10] so the delegate vote in most modern conventions is merely the final ratification of a decision made weeks (if not months) in advance. What conventions lack in true political drama they make up for with the spectacle of speeches and speakers including the keynote address (often given by a prime candidate-to-be or former party great)[11] and the acceptance speeches of the vice presidential and presidential nominees.

Conventional wisdom suggests that presidential candidates receive what is referred to as a convention "bump" in public support immediately following their party's convention. Academic research on the convention bump indicates that candidates do receive a boost in popular support following their own party conventions (see Campbell et al. 1992). However, these bumps are of relatively limited size (rarely more than 5–7%) (Campbell et al. 1992). The bumps are subject to being offset by a comparably sized bump received by the opposing party following their own convention, and the bumps are quite temporary, rarely lasting more than two weeks (Campbell et al. 1992). If the impact of convention bumps – bumps that occur at the very beginning of the general election campaign – is inherently limited in the manners indicated above, the overall significance of the campaign effects produced by conventions is, likewise, quite minimal.

Presidential candidates have participated in debates in every election year since 1956,[12] and particularly in more recent years, with the

---

[10] Even in the exceedingly close and contentious contest between Barack Obama and Hillary Clinton in 2008, Obama had commitments from a majority of all delegates in advance of the convention.

[11] An example of the candidate-to-be keynote speaker was Barack Obama in 2004. A former party great keynote speaker was Bill Clinton in 2008.

[12] The first presidential debates were held in 1948. There were no debates during the presidential election of 1952. For more information on presidential debates, see the web site of the Commission on Presidential Debates at http://www.debates.org/ (last viewed on December 17, 2009).

full-blown development of effective overnight polling, efforts to estimate the effects of debate performances on electoral prospects have
dramatically increased. The vast scholarly literature on presidential
debates ranges from analyses of particular debates – the Kennedy-
Nixon debate is a particularly popular topic (see Druckman 2003;
Kraus 1996; Windt 1994) – to research on rhetorical style and dynamics (Dailey et al. 2007; Friedenberg 1997) to the effect of debate content
and performance on public policy attitudes (Holbrook 1999), candidate evaluations (Geer 1988), and election outcomes (Holbrook 1996).[13]
Individual debates do have limited short-term effects on candidate
support for certain voters, but the overall impact of candidates' performances in presidential debates on the final vote is quite limited (see,
in particular, Holbrook 1996). The limited size of this effect would
not preclude the possibility that an election might turn on a debate or
set of debates – especially in extraordinarily close elections – but the
likelihood of this type of significant effect is small.

If the net effects (final effects on aggregate vote choice) of conventions and debates are limited, the most recent research suggests that
the effects of smaller, individual campaign events (such as candidate
speeches) are even more limited. At most, the effect of campaign events
besides conventions and debates is much more sensitive to the political context in which they occur, the particular character of the event
(public gaffe or dramatic scandal), and their proximity to Election Day
(see Shaw 1999, 2006). Recent research does suggest that campaigns
implement advertising and candidate scheduling strategies that are
sensitive to state-specific support levels (and Electoral College dynamics), and there is some limited evidence that these strategies influence
state-level outcomes on election day (see Shaw 2006).

Even if we were to accept the power of economic models of the
aggregate vote, there may be room for the type of campaign effects
that have received the most recent scholarly attention. If campaigns
focus on a relatively small number of battleground states, then we do
not expect to see campaign effects in the other states. Also, unless one
campaign is strategically and organizationally dominant, we would
not expect to see their efforts win the day in each of the contested
states. However, if more effective campaigning produced a set of subtle
advantages in a majority of the contested states, a close election might
well be decided by the work of a superior campaigning effort. This
conclusion is consistent with an increasing body of recent research

---

[13] Note that these references are only a small sample of the large literature on presidential debates.

(see, among others, Hillygus and Jackman 2003; Hillygus and Shields 2008; Holbrook 1996; Wlezien and Erikson 2001).

These campaign effects tend to be produced by three types of campaign activities: (1) participation in campaign events such as conventions and debates, (2) subnational media campaigns, and (3) candidate or "surrogate" visits and local mobilization efforts. Significantly, research in this vein tends to focus on immediate or short-term effects rather than long-term effects. Note that these campaign efforts are not all designed to produce the same effect. While some campaign events and campaign advertising are designed to draw voters away from one party and to the other, other events and advertising are designed to mobilize supporters, drawing partisan supporters from the ranks of the uninvolved to the polling booth. Partisanship is widely viewed as one of the most enduring political attachments (far more stable than ideological orientation), and as voters have become increasingly partisan – and parties have become increasingly polarized – campaigns have become increasingly interested in investing in a variety of mobilization efforts to bring their partisans to the polls. Election outcomes sometimes ride on the success of these efforts.[14]

Overall, the evidence suggests that the boundaries for campaign effects are from 1 to 4% points (Shaw 2006). Obviously, in very close presidential elections, these effects could determine the outcome. However, unless we are willing to assume that all of the possible effects flow in the direction of a single candidate, the likely *net* effects in the overwhelming majority of presidential elections is well smaller than 4%. If we assume an average net effect of 2% – and we assume that net effect goes to the winner (not necessarily the case) – then we might say that campaign effects have significantly influenced the outcome of five elections since the turn of the twentieth century: 1916, 1960, 1976, 2000, and 2004. Not a trivial number, but far from a majority of presidential elections.

A middle ground: significant campaigns and (generally) predictable elections

Finally, there are some scholars who admit that campaign effects play a role in determining the outcome of presidential elections, but that

[14] The standard treatment of the significance of partisanship in American politics is the *American Voter* (Campbell et al. 1960). Though this important work is not without its critics, the conceptual and practical prominence of partisanship is still reflected in prominent recent work on issue voting (Zaller 1992) and partisanship (Green et al. 2002). Research on campaigns and their mobilization effects is

the effects occur at the margins and that they are, at least in large part, predictable. Consistent with the research on the economic dynamics of aggregate vote models, Campbell (2003) argues that the broad parameters of a presidential election are determined by three primary structural factors months in advance of Election Day: (1) the state of the national economy, (2) public approval of the sitting president, and (3) the length of time the party of the current administration has held the White House.

These economic and political "fundamentals" largely determine whether or not an election will be competitive and, if it is not competitive, who will win. The latter scenarios include situations where a popular incumbent president enjoying a strong economy is running for only his party's second consecutive term in office[15] in a row. Recent examples of this type of scenario included Reagan in 1984 and Clinton in 1996. Alternatively, an unpopular president facing a weak economy and attempting to win a third (or higher) term for his party is often at a severe electoral disadvantage. Hoover in 1932 is only the most obvious example.

But these fundamentals – measured months before the election – may not provide sufficiently detailed information to determine the outcome of a race we expect to be very close. These races are determined by what Campbell refers to as "predictable" effects and "unpredictable" effects. Campbell argues that the predictable campaign effects provide consistent pressure over the course of the final two months of the campaign for a closing of the gap between the frontrunner and her opponent. Some of the predictable effects that tend to narrow the margin between the candidates are as follows:

1. Trailing candidates catch up because they are able to recover from split conventions.
2. Leading candidates fall back because they receive an inordinate amount of media criticism.
3. Undecided voters tend to split relatively evenly in the later portion of the campaign.
4. If they vote, partisans tend to return to the fold.
5. The majority of partisans make up their minds before the general election campaign begins.

also growing (see Gerber and Green 2000, 2001; Green and Gerber 2005; Krasno and Green 2008; Middleton and Green 2008; Panagopolous and Green 2008).

[15] Campbell (2003) has argued that political parties face a third-term penalty when competing for a third (or more) straight term in office. The presumption is that, *ceteris paribus*, voters prefer a change in partisan control rather than an extended period of one-party dominance, and there is some evidence confirming this position (see Campbell 2003).

Not all elections manifest each of these effects, but each tends to occur relatively frequently. Up until the Obama campaign's decision to reject federal funding for the general election campaign, we could also assume that neither presidential candidate would have a significant fundraising advantage during the general election, another reason we would not expect an ever-widening margin over the course of the last two months of the campaign.

However, even with these predictable effects, there is still room for unpredictable effects – those unknown (or at least unexpected) factors that produce a final outcome that deviates from the expected outcome (based on economic and political fundamentals) and predictable campaign effects. The average percentage of the vote that Campbell attributes to these unpredictable effects is approximately 2–3%. Notice that this percentage is more than enough to change the outcome in several recent presidential elections. It is also comparable to Shaw's (2006) claims about the average size of campaign effects. So we might need to ask ourselves the extent to which these "unpredictable" effects really are unpredictable.

CONCLUSION

We began this chapter with the mention, and subsequent discussion, of a puzzle. Put simply, the puzzle is "Why was the outcome of the 2008 presidential election, though distinctive (unique) in so many ways, so predictable?" How you respond to this puzzle depends upon your position on the significance of presidential campaigns. You may consider economic and political fundamentals so important to presidential election outcomes that even distinctive (or especially unusual) campaigns only serve to reinforce an underlying strategic advantage (as a result of the fundamentals) that determines the outcome of the race itself. As a scientist, further investigation of this conjecture would require more consistently precise predictions, and it would also include a more effective distinction between those precampaign economic and political variables that actually influence electoral outcomes (in the aggregate) and those which do not.

If you find the research on significant campaign effects more compelling, then you would want to be able to show that campaign effects are less ephemeral than we now believe. The ephemeral effects of a convention bounce or a strong performance during a debate happen long before Election Day. To make a case for their role in electoral outcomes, the connection between the response to the event and the final vote would need to be analyzed in more detail. Also, the electoral effects of campaign strategies designed to win particular battleground states in the fight for 270 votes in the Electoral College should be evident in elections that go back well before those of the twenty-first century. Extending the sample of elections studied back into the 1980s and earlier – and evaluating the strategic dynamics of future elections as they occur – would provide additional opportunities to bolster the support for this perspective and more fully demonstrate that it is a productive research program.

Finally, if you are most convinced by the theory of "predictable" elections, you must be prepared to respond to the subsequent research of the proponents of the alternate perspectives. As the predictions of the economic models become more precise (if they do) and the research on campaign effects demonstrates the increasingly important role of campaign events and campaign strategies in determining electoral outcomes, the size and significance of the "unpredictable" effects may well wither away. To the extent this happens, we may someday find that the answer to our earlier puzzle is that (1) the distinctive aspects of the campaign had no effect on the underlying economic fundamentals, or (2) the distinctive aspects of the election did not alter the campaign in such a way as to produce an unpredictable outcome. If the first is true, presidential elections are quite predictable. If the second is true, the predictability of a unique campaign tells us little about the predictability of more conventional campaigns. Only time (and analysis) will tell.

GUIDED RESEARCH EXERCISES

Guided research exercises for this chapter focus on the evaluation of the relationship between economic conditions and the presidential vote. You have learned about the relationship between these variables during your reading, and this is your chance to examine this relationship on your own.

Data sources

For these exercises, you will need data on a variety of macroeconomic variables and data on presidential election returns from at least 1948 (the first postwar election, a common starting point for analyses of this type) to 2008. You may also be interested in extending the timeframe of your analysis, and in that case you will need the same data for earlier years as well.

Official election results may be obtained from the Office of the Federal Register at the National Archives (see http://www.archives.

gov/).[16] There are also a variety of other sources for this information, but authoritative sources are preferred. Data on inflation and income growth are available from the FRED (Federal Reserve Economic Data) web site at the St. Louis Federal Reserve Bank (http://research.stlouis-fed.org/fred2/).[17] Unemployment data is available from the Bureau of Labor Statistics' *Current Population Survey* web site (http://www.bls.gov/cps/).[18] The variables you will need for each set of exercises are listed below.

EXERCISES

A. Bivariate Exercises

1. Descriptive Exercises

a. Hypotheses

(1) The percentage of the two-party presidential vote received by the candidate of the incumbent party is *inversely* related to the percentage change in the consumer price index (inflation rate) during the 1948–2008 time period.

(2) The percentage of the two-party presidential vote received by the candidate of the incumbent party is *inversely* related to the unemployment rate during the 1948–2008 time period.

(3) The percentage of the two-party presidential vote received by the candidate of the incumbent party is *directly* related to growth in disposable personal income during the 1948–2008 time period.

b. Analysis

(1) Collect and organize the variables listed above from the indicated web sites.

(2) Create the following separate scatter plots. Note that in each case, the percentage of the two-party presidential vote received by the candidate from the incumbent party is the x-axis variable whereas the relevant economic variable is placed along the y-axis.

---

[16] For most data available online, I have provided a base web site only. Variable-specific web sites are much more likely to change than base web sites, and so only the base web sites are provided in an effort to limit incorrect (outdated) information. Once you get to the base web site, you are expected to locate the particular variables of interest on your own.

[17] Last accessed on December 17, 2009.

[18] Last accessed on December 17, 2009.

        (a) inflation x incumbent party vote percentage

        (b) unemployment x incumbent party vote percentage

        (c) disposable personal income growth x incumbent party vote percentage

    (3) Draw (estimate) a regression line for each scatter plot.

  c. Response to results

    (1) Describe the slope of the line in each graph. Is the line flat or steep? Does it slope down or slope up?

    (2) Determine whether your results are consistent or inconsistent with each of your hypotheses.

    (3) Explain your conclusions.

  2. Inferential Exercises

    a. Hypotheses[19]

      (1) The percentage of the two-party presidential vote received by the candidate of the incumbent party is *inversely* related to the percentage change in the consumer price index (inflation rate).

      (2) The percentage of the two-party presidential vote received by the candidate of the incumbent party is *inversely* related to the unemployment rate.

      (3) The percentage of the two-party presidential vote received by the candidate of the incumbent party is *directly* related to growth in disposable personal income.

    b. Analysis

      (1) Complete the descriptive exercises above.

      (2) Compute the standard error for the slope coefficient of each regression line calculated above and report the p-value for each coefficient.

    c. Response to results

      (1) Determine whether your results are consistent or inconsistent with each of your hypotheses.

      (2) Explain your conclusions.

B. Multivariate Exercises

What if the relationship between economic circumstances and the presidential vote varies across elections that involve an incumbent and those that do not? In this set of exercises you will investigate this possibility.

---

[19] Note that these hypotheses are more general than the hypotheses listed in the descriptive exercises section. These hypotheses are not limited to a particular time period.

1. Descriptive Exercise

    a. Hypothesis – The relationship between the two-party percentage of the presidential vote and growth in disposable personal income during the 1948–2008 time period is stronger for elections that include an incumbent president.[20]

    b. Analysis

        (1) Divide the elections in your sample between those that include an incumbent and those that do not.

        (2) Create the following scatter plot – disposable personal income growth by the incumbent party vote percentage – for each sample.

        (3) Draw (estimate) a regression line for each scatter plot.

    c. Response to results

        (1) Compare the slopes of the two regression lines. Do both slope in the same direction? Is one steeper than the other?

        (2) Determine whether your results are consistent or inconsistent with each of your hypotheses.

        (3) Explain your conclusions.

2. Inferential Exercise

    a. Hypothesis – The relationship between the two-party percentage of the presidential vote and growth in disposable personal income is stronger for elections that include an incumbent president.

    b. Analysis

        (1) Complete the descriptive exercises above.

        (2) Compute the standard error for the slope coefficient of each regression line calculated above and report the p-value for each coefficient.

    c. Response to results

        (1) Determine whether your results are consistent or inconsistent with each of your hypotheses.

        (2) Explain your conclusions.

IMPORTANT TERMS

aggregate data
campaign advertising

---

[20] The same multivariate analysis could be conducted with either of the other economic variables from the bivariate analysis.

campaign effects
confidence interval
convention bump
debates
economic model of voting
Electoral College
individual-level data
media effects
mobilization effects
partisan realignment
pollsters
population
predictable effects
psychological model of voting
response bias
sample
sociological model of voting
unpredictable effects

6

Congress and the President

Research on the historic relationship between Congress and the president is often dominated by a focus on interparty conflict, and this conflict has become more prevalent in recent years because of the increasing frequency of divided government. One of the presumptive effects of interparty conflict during periods of divided government is "gridlock" – a significant obstruction to the development and passage of significant legislation of any type (see Gilmour 1995).

Recently, however, the divided government explanation for gridlock has come under significantly more analytical scrutiny, and the most recent and thorough research on the causes of gridlock have produced a puzzling result: the absence of a relationship between partisan control of the legislative and executive branches and legislative productivity. In short, prominent recent research (Mayhew 1991) suggests that the rate of development and passage of significant/major legislation is the same during periods of divided government as it is during periods of united government. For those who take partisan conflict seriously, this is a *puzzling* result. Likewise, if partisan relationships are the foundation of presidential power (as Skowronek suggests), these results are a puzzle that must be solved.

With this puzzle in mind, let us take a closer look at the recent research on interparty conflict and relations between Congress and the president. After we review this literature, we will return to this puzzle and identify several relevant research questions and some hypothetical answers to those research questions. Then we will move on to our own analysis and efforts to answer one or more of these research questions and test our hypotheses. But first, let's take a closer look at the research on which this *puzzle* is based.

GRIDLOCK, UNINTENDED CONSEQUENCES, AND
UNEXPECTED RESULTS

Regardless of our preference for unified or divided government, since the late-1960s we have had far more divided government (in one form or another) than we have had unified government. From 1969 through 2008, there were a dozen years of united government – four during the Carter administration, the first two years of the Clinton administration, and the first six years of the second Bush administration – and 28 years of divided government.

Divided government has taken a variety of forms; as Mayhew (1991) notes in *Divided We Govern*,[1] we have actually had every single type of divided government since 1980.[2] For much of the post–FDR era of the modern presidency, federal government has been a divided government. It is important to note that this is a relatively rare state of affairs throughout American history. Prior to 1969, unified government was far more common than divided government.

According to Mayhew, the standard story of the role of partisanship and partisan conflict in the relationship between Congress and the president is that divided government tends to (1) inhibit legislative productivity and (2) constrain the exercise of executive authority. Legislative productivity is limited because parties have distinct policy objectives, and the separation of powers and system of checks and balances installed by the Constitution make it very difficult for a single branch to dominate policy making.[3] Presidential proposals that are legislatively unpopular – due to the distinct policy objectives of

---

[1] It is worth noting that this book received the 1992 Richard E. Neustadt Award given by the Presidency Studies Section of the American Political Science Association for the best book on the American presidency.

[2] The two forms of divided government that are least evident (or least common) are DRD (Democratic president and House and Republican Senate) and DDR (Democratic president and Senate and Republican House). As Mayhew (2005) notes, DRD occurred briefly immediately prior to George W. Bush's inauguration, and DDR occurred briefly immediately prior to the inauguration of Ronald Reagan.

[3] Michael Munger and I argue that true congressional dominance is theoretically possible (Morris and Munger 1998), but the practical situations in which it is likely to occur – in which a cohesive party holds an overwhelming majority of seats in the House and the Senate, certainly more than enough to override a presidential veto in both chambers or invoke cloture in the Senate – are rare. The latter part of Andrew Johnson's administration might be one example, though an odd one as Johnson was the vice president of a president from the dominant party. Recent efforts to develop a working theory of a "unitary executive" must also provide a theoretical rationale for the dominance of a single branch, in this case the presidency, in a separation of powers/checks and balances system.

the different parties controlling the White House and the chambers of Congress – tend to wither and die in Congress, either in committee or on the floor.[4] Legislation unpopular with the president risks a presidential veto, and partisan majorities that are large enough to override a presidential veto (two-thirds of both chambers) are historically rare. So there is a relatively straightforward logic to the conventional association of divided government with gridlock.

This logic is also consistent with Skowronek's conceptualization of partisan regimes and their impact on presidential power. Strong, stable regimes will tend to produce united government. That has been true for every major party regime, from the Jeffersonian regime to the Roosevelt regime, until the most recent regime, the Reagan regime. Divided government during the earlier regimes could easily be viewed as a sign of weakness and instability on the part of the dominant regime. The same is true for more recent times. So, for example, divided government preceded the presidencies of preemption of Eisenhower and Clinton, and Obama's victory in 2008 signals a second preemption, if not the end, of the Reagan regime. In the context of political time, to the extent that legislative productivity might be viewed as a rough indicator of presidential power, divided government should inhibit legislative productivity as united government fosters legislative productivity.[5]

Much of the existing literature suggests that executive power is constrained because of the increase in legislative oversight during

---

[4] In *Strategic Disagreement: Stalemate in American Politics*, John Gilmour (1995) argues that even in situations in which some reasonable negotiation might result in lawmaking beneficial to both parties, there are still significant incentives to avoid compromise.

[5] Reasonable arguments may be made on both sides of the issue of whether or not legislative productivity is an indicator of presidential power. As presidents have other means of achieving certain types of policy goals – through administrative action, for example – a president might be said to exercise power and authority even in the absence of a record of significant legislative accomplishment. This position is largely consistent with the institutionalist understanding of presidential power reflected in both the imperial presidency literature and the unitary executive literature. However, there is a traditional link between legislative productivity (or at least some measure of legislative *accomplishment*) associated with presidential power (at least in the domestic realm). If we associate presidential power with the broad authority of reconstructive presidencies, then *all* manifest nontrivial legislative productivity (even in war time). That many of these legislative accomplishments were *congressional* initiatives (rather than presidential initiatives), particularly during the nineteenth century, is true. But powerful presidents in the twentieth century – reconstructionist or not – have tended to produce a considerable amount of significant legislation (consider, for example, the records of both Roosevelt's and the early Johnson administration).

periods of divided government. Somewhat ironically, the period of the 1950s and early 1960s –a time period of relatively weak parties – was an era largely dominated by "partisan" theorists. In 1950, the APSA Committee on Parties concluded:

> Historical and other factors have caused the American two-party system to operate as two loose associations of state and local organizations, with very little national machinery and very little national cohesion. As a result, either major party, when in power, is ill-equipped to organize its members in the legislative and executive branches into a government held together and guided by the party program. Party responsibility at the polls thus tends to vanish. This is a very serious matter, for it affects the very heartbeat of American democracy. It also poses grave problems of domestic and foreign policy in an era when it is no longer safe for the nation to deal piecemeal with issues that can be disposed of only on the basis of coherent programs. (1950: v)

For the party-oriented theorists of the time, the absence of cohesive, distinct, well-organized parties implied that Americans were left without a true choice in national politics. For these scholars, it was as if the public's options were limited to Alice's Tweedledum and Tweedledee. Without distinctive choices, it was not possible for the public to move their elected officials in a new direction or, at the extreme, to motivate their public officials at all. Absent a serious alternative, the idea of "responsible" parties (or responsible public officials) was specious.

Ironically, as the political parties began to present increasingly distinct options to the American public, divided government became increasingly common. In the 48 years between the election of Warren G. Harding and Richard Nixon, there are only eight years of divided government.[6] In the four decades since Nixon's election, government was divided more than half of the time.[7] In fact, during the entire span of the Reagan and George H. W. Bush administrations, no party ever controlled both chambers of Congress and the White House; this 12-year interregnum for united government was (and is) a record.[8]

---

[6] A government is "divided" when at least one chamber of Congress is controlled by a party other than the one controlling the White House.

[7] Twenty-two years of divided government even if we ignore the portions of the 107th Congress during which government was divided because of the short overlap of the presidential term and the congressional term (approximately two and a half weeks in January during which outgoing vice president Al Gore was the deciding vote due to the 50–50 partisan split of the seats) and Senator Jim Jeffords (VT) decision to switch from Republican to Independent caucusing with the Democrats.

[8] Mayhew highlights this point in the preface to the second edition of *Divided We Govern* (2005).

Clearly divided government has been far more prevalent during the time of increasingly powerful parties than it was during the time of relatively weak parties.[9]

Recently, this standard characterization of the effect of divided government on legislative productivity has come under attack. In 1991, David Mayhew published *Divided We Govern: Party Control, Lawmaking, and Investigations, 1946–1990*, a thorough examination of the hypothesis that Congress produces more significant legislation during periods of unified government than during periods of divided government. A corollary of this hypothesis is that congressional investigations of the president and members of the executive branch tend to be more common during periods of divided government than they are during periods of united government. Surprisingly, Mayhew finds no evidence for either contention. Specifically, he writes:

> ... the main argument in the following pages will be that unified as opposed to divided control has not made an important difference in recent times in the incidence of two particular kinds of [legislative] activity. These are, first, high-publicity investigations in which congressional committees expose alleged misbehavior in the executive branch.... And second, the enactment of a standard kind of important legislation: From the Taft-Hartley Act ... [to the] $490 billion deficit-reduction package of 1990, important laws have materialized at a rate largely unrelated to conditions of party control. (2005: 4)

In a 2005 updating of his early 1990s analysis, Mayhew finds largely the same relationship between divided government and legislative productivity, though he also finds – and for the first time – a strong relationship between divided/unified government and legislative investigations. During the most recent time period, the legislative productivity of Congress is unrelated to whether or not the legislative and executive branches are held by the same party. On the other hand, legislative investigations are far more common during periods of divided government than during periods of united government.

These results – particularly those from the earlier time period (1946–1990) – have generated a considerable degree of interest and reanalysis. However, to understand the responses to Mayhew's work, we must first understand the nature of his argument and the character of his evidence. As a scientist, if you wished to study the relationship between divided/unified government and legislative productivity,

---

[9] As Mayhew notes, "Until the 2002 midterm, I was encountering undergraduates and even young graduate students who seemed to view unified party control as a rare event on the order of the eclipse of the moon" (2005: x).

how would you do it? First, you would need some sort of theory to help you understand what sort of relationship is likely to exist between legislative productivity and divided government (and why). As we know from our previous discussions of presidential power, partisan dynamics are commonly used to understand variations in presidential power (recall Skowronek's theory of political time). If partisanship is related to presidential power, then this suggests that presidents will realize the most success with their legislative agendas during those periods in which their party also controls the House and the Senate. On the other hand, when the president must deal with a House and a Senate dominated by the opposing party, we would expect the president to be far less successful in passing his legislative agenda. From a partisan perspective, united government breeds legislative success (and legislative productivity) and divided government restricts legislative success. So, we have a hypothesis: legislative productivity will be greater during periods of united government than during periods of divided government.

Next, we need to operationalize our key concepts: divided government and legislative productivity. To see how we might choose to do this, let's consider the operationalizations Mayhew used for these theoretical concepts. First, consider divided government. The answer here would appear to be straightforward. The operational distinction between divided and unified government is apparently simple; the president's party either controls both chambers of Congress (united government) or it doesn't (divided government). However, that operationalization lumps different types of divided government together (president's party controls the House but not the Senate, president's party controls the Senate but not the House, president's party controls neither the Senate nor the House). Does that make sense? Is that what Mayhew did?

Theoretically, if we take a presidential perspective, there is a reasonable justification for lumping together the various types of divided government. If we assume that it is the president's agenda that Congress debates, amends, and then accepts or rejects, and that fellow partisans are more supportive of each other's policy goals than opposing partisans, then unified government will provide opportunities for significant legislative policy making unavailable (or rarely available) during periods of divided government. Unified government would not guarantee significant policy productivity, even fellow partisans often disagree, sometimes significantly, but it would tend to be more conducive to important policy making than divided government. Party theorist V. O. Key put it succinctly with "Common partisan control of executive and legislature does not assure energetic government, but division of party control precludes it" (as quoted in Mayhew 2005: 2).

The reason that divided party control is such a serious obstacle to significant legislative policy making is the ability of either the executive or either chamber of Congress to block the policy initiatives of the others. The blocking power does not depend upon the acquiescence or support of the branch (or chamber, in the case of the House or Senate). Given the independent ability to block legislation, any deviation from unified government is likely to be significant. If, for example, a presidential policy initiative is opposed by a sufficient number of representatives, the Senate's level of support for that initiative is practically and politically irrelevant. Adding Senate opposition does not magnify the legislation's defeat. A loss is a loss, and what is key is that the opposition of a single chamber (or the president if it is a congressional policy initiative) is sufficient for defeat. Given that dynamic, it would seem that most important distinction is between unified government and the various types of divided government.

Empirically, there are some difficulties associated with a full separation of the various types of divided government, especially if we must also concern ourselves with the question of whether or not the party of the president (Democrat or Republican) has an impact on legislative productivity. Though every distinct type of unified or divided government has occurred during the time period of Mayhew's analysis, some of the types of divided government have been very short-lived.[10] Thus, because of the limited number of observations of several of the party control patterns, there is insufficient empirical leverage to effectively distinguish between the independent effects of each of the various patterns of divided government on legislative productivity.

"Legislative productivity" (or even "lawmaking") is a more nebulous term than divided government. How should we go about operationalizing this term? How did Mayhew operationalize this term? Let's start by considering our options. What do we mean by "legislative productivity" or "lawmaking"? Well, we almost certainly mean the passage of new laws. One way to operationalize legislative productivity is to count the number of new laws produced each year (or, more appropriately given our context, each Congress). This would also be easy to

---

[10] As Mayhew notes, a Democratic president–Republican House–Democratic Senate existed for less than a month in early January 2001 (after the beginning of the 107th Congress but prior to the inauguration of George W. Bush), and the Democratic president–Democratic House–Republican Senate also existed for less than a month in January 1981 for similar reasons (2005: x). This was the only time either of these party control patterns existed during the 1946–2002 time period.

do because the information needed to count the number of new laws passed by each Congress is readily available. The Library of Congress publishes the *Congressional Record*, a "record" of the proceedings of the House and the Senate (including a list of votes on legislation), and this resource could by searched (by Congress) for a list of new legislation passed.[11] But would we really want to count all new laws? Should we have some sort of rule for determining the difference between significant legislation and other types of lawmaking? For Mayhew, the distinction is crucial; in fact, he argues that his "study requires, *above all*, some plausible ways of identifying important investigations and laws" (2005: 6, emphasis added). He also notes that the great bulk of previous research on lawmaking fails to account for what he considers the crucial distinction between significant and insignificant legislation. He writes, "for all of the work done on legislative behavior, laws and investigations are seldom tackled in a way that is reasonably systematic yet tries to sort out the significant from the trivial" (2005: 6).

Mayhew realizes that the critical response to his argument (and the results upon which it is based) will depend on the acceptance of the way he defines and operationalizes the primary variables of interest: divided government and legislative productivity. While his handling of divided government is more or less standard, his treatment of legislative productivity is not, as is made clear by his own critique of previous research. To the extent that his understanding and measurement of legislative productivity departs from the standards and practices of previous research, he must make a concerted attempt to justify his choices and their variance from those on which the existing literature is based. He does that in an extensive discussion in Chapter 3. His creative operationalization of "significant legislation" is novel, theoretically justifiable, and empirically useful, so as a good example of an important part of the scientific process, it's worth discussing in some detail.

To distinguish between significant and insignificant legislation, Mayhew uses two methods for the legislation from the 1946–1990 time period – what he refers to as "Sweep One" and "Sweep Two" (2005: Chapter 3). Sweep One bases the determination of significance

---

[11] A number of years of the *Congressional Record* can be searched online at the web site hosted by the Library of Congress at http://thomas.loc.gov/home/r110query. html. A complete list of the current laws – regardless of the year (or Congress) during which they were passed can be found in the U.S. Code (online at http://uscode. house.gov/about/info.shtml, a web site hosted by the Office of Law Revision Counsel, an agency of the House of Representatives). Both web sites were last accessed on December 17, 2009.

on contemporaneous evaluations of the importance of the legislation; in essence, did expert observers, at the time of passage, consider the legislation significant? So Mayhew argues, "The best source of such judgments is the journalist's annual end-of-session wrap-up story, ordinarily written as a Congress is adjourning" (2005: 37). The experts on whose observations Mayhew depends are the journalists for the *New York Times* and the *Washington Post*, who filed the year-end (or congress-end) reports published by their respective papers. Mayhew adds that these journalistic sources were "supplemented where possible by books or articles that discuss the overall legislative records of particular Congresses and, in doing so, pick up or embody judgments that observers or participants expressed during those congresses about the importance of enactments" (2005: 39).

"Sweep Two" is based on subsequent evaluations of the historical significance of the legislation produced during different congresses. Rather than focusing on the analysts' immediate evaluations of the significance of legislation, the second sweep focuses on the evaluation of legislative significance with the benefit of historical hindsight. More specifically, "By drawing on long-term perspectives of policy specialists about what enactments have counted most in their areas, it [the second sweep] adds a dimension of expertise" (2005: 44). Though there are distinctions between the two lists of legislation (or "sweeps"), there is considerable overlap; in fact, the total number of laws generated from Sweep Two is (203) is within 4% of the total number of laws generated from Sweep One (211) (Mayhew 2005: 50).

After operationalizing his two key analytical variables, what sort of analysis does Mayhew execute to test his hypothesis? Though the analysis is extensive, it is also surprisingly straightforward. Mayhew provides an extensive amount of tabular data that clearly suggest the absence of a significant difference between legislative productivity during divided government and unified government. After a table listing all of the legislation identified by Sweep One and Sweep Two, by president, Mayhew includes tables illustrating the differences between divided government and unified government legislative productivity while accounting for other potential explanatory variables. So, in one table Mayhew limits the legislation considered to social programs and new regulatory programs (including the creation of new regulatory agencies). The idea here is that maybe for certain types of policies – for example. the Great Society programs of the Johnson administration – there is an important difference between divided and unified government. The table, however, shows that there is little difference. There are considerable differences by president – the majority of new programs and agencies were created during the Johnson and Nixon administration – but the distinction between divided and unified government provides no additional explanatory leverage. Mayhew also shows that significant legislation is more frequently passed during the first two years of an administration than the last two years, but there is still no divided/unified distinction. Mayhew also presents evidence that suggests that important legislation tends to pass by overwhelming majorities; if this is the case, the president's need for partisan control of the House and the Senate may be less significant than previously realized. Finally, Mayhew estimates a multivariate model and the results from this model provide no support for the presence of a relationship between divided/unified government and legislative productivity.

Mayhew's quantitative data is accompanied by a considerable amount of historical analysis, and Mayhew makes a concerted attempt to evaluate alternative hypotheses for the variation in legislative productivity over time. In fact, his efforts to assess alternative hypotheses include two full chapters, one entitled "Explaining the Patterns, I" and one entitled "Explaining the Patterns, II" (2005).[12] Among the potential explanations that Mayhew considers besides divided/unified government are:

1. *Electoral incentives.* Mayhew's most famous work, *Congress: The Electoral Connection* (1974) was a groundbreaking work that demonstrated how one could explain the structure and behavior of Congress (as a whole) from one straightforward assumption – that members of Congress are "single-minded seekers for reelection" (Mayhew 1974). In *Divided we Govern*, Mayhew argues that the types of activities in which electorally oriented members of Congress participate tend to lead to consistent policy productivity. Members of Congress will always need to provide specific benefits to their districts, and so this type of policy making will likely occur under both divided and unified government. Likewise, there will always be some small number of legislators who are preparing to run for the presidency. These members of Congress (senators, usually) must demonstrate that they can produce results; and in legislative terms, "results" equal policy. Presidential aspirations are not limited to either party, nor are they limited to periods of divided or unified government. This is again a dynamic that should produce policy consistency. Finally, if credit claiming is a core activity of members of Congress seeking reelection (Mayhew 1974), then

---

[12] The second edition of *Divided We Govern* (2005) includes, as the first seven chapters and appendices A, B, and D, the full text of the first edition (1991).

there may be occasions in which a certain type of divided government (one party controls the House, the other party controls the Senate) results in the passage of more important legislation than the typical divided government/unified government distinction would suggest. In these particular cases, both parties might reasonably be able to claim credit for legislation. When both parties can claim credit, the impetus to produce legislation increases, and it increases at a time of divided government.

2. *Presidential* and *congressional leadership*. Some presidents (and possibly some prominent legislators) may simply be more successful leaders than other presidents (or other legislators). Although these differences in "leadership" might be explained by bargaining or public opinion theories of presidential power, Mayhew references neither Neustadt (at least in this context) nor Kernell. These differences in leadership may produce what Mayhew refers to as *"alternative variation"* (2005: 176, emphasis in the original). This alternative variation might cloud or obscure the potentially significant effects of divided government. So, for example, if divided government *and* presidential leadership have an effect on legislative productivity, it is possible that one effect might hide the effect of the other. To avoid this inferential problem, it is important to consider the effects of both variables simultaneously.

3. *The presence of "broad majorities."* If legislators have a preference for large majorities (majorities of both parties) when enacting laws, the subtle shifts in party power – the subtle shifts that would often determine whether or not the government is united – would likely have little impact on policy making. The preference for broad majorities will tend to mitigate whatever differences do exist between legislative productivity during divided government and united government. Why would lawmakers prefer broad majorities? Mayhew suggests two reasons: (1) an orientation toward problem solving and (2) the inherent difficulty of passing legislation even during periods of unified government. If lawmakers have a collective sense of a pressing issue that requires a response, partisan differences may not be a significant obstacle to meaningful legislation. Likewise, if the nature of the legislative process is such that relatively large majorities are consistently required for the passage of significant legislation, the simple unification of government (often with slim majorities in both chambers) will be insufficient to produce a dramatic increase in the volume of legislation.

4. *External events*. Certain external events, such as the assassinations of President Kennedy or Dr. Martin Luther King, Jr., might have

prompted the passage of relevant significant legislation. But Mayhew argues that it is difficult to see how external events would produce greater legislative consistency across time (and thus dampen the potential effects of partisan divisions) or generate a significant amount of alternative variation in legislative productivity across time (and thus obscure the possible legislative effects of partisan divisions). What is most likely is that a limited set of idiosyncratic (or random) effects on legislative productivity result from external events. These sorts of infrequent random effects should not, then, obscure the effects of partisan divisions (if they actually exist).

5. *Issue cleavages.* In some cases, prominent issues may induce intraparty divisions. On this type of issue, there are proponents of both sides of the debate in both parties. Civil rights during much of the latter part of the twentieth century was this type of issue (with Southern Democrats tending to be far more conservative than Northern Democrats), and Mayhew argues that foreign policy (particularly security and defense policy) was this type of issue during the same time period. Beyond the Cold War consensus (large majorities of both parties favored the containment of communism), both parties included *internationalists* (supporters of international engagement) and *isolationists* (opponents of international engagement). Issue cleavages, to the extent they are present, tend to mitigate the influence of divided/unified government on legislative productivity.

6. *Public mood.* It is possible that strong, ideologically oriented *waves* of interest in and attention to certain public policy issues or problems periodically sweep over the American people, producing potentially dramatic shifts in *public mood*. These sweeping changes cross party lines; they also provide a source for alternative variation and an alternative to the divided government/unified government explanation for the variance in legislative productivity. These public moods are difficult to describe and measure,[13] and they may be produced by a variety of different forces – Mayhew's own list includes "leadership, war, a cyclical impulse, and changes in economic conditions" (2005: 170) – so it is difficult to estimate their impact on policy making. Nevertheless, they provide another possible source of alternative variation in policy productivity.[14]

---

[13] Mayhew laments that "A 'mood' seems to be one of those phenomena that drive political scientists to despair by being at once important and elusive" (2005: 160).

[14] The most important analysis of public moods can be found in Stimson (2004) and Carmines and Stimson (1989).

Mayhew finds some evidence that presidential leadership and congressional leadership influence legislative productivity, but he also admits to the difficulty in adequately and rigorously measuring leadership, or what he refers to as "levels of agenda, will, or skill" (2005: 114). He also argues that even if variation in leadership does influence legislative productivity, there is little reason to expect that leadership would vary with unified/divided government. Similarly, the presence of broad majorities occurs during both divided and unified government. Even if congressional behavior suggests a preference for large or "broad" majorities, they provide no counterexplanation for why Mayhew fails to find a divided/unified government effect. The same is largely true for the effects of external events and crosscutting issue cleavages – what limited influence they have on legislative productivity is insufficient to account for the absence of a divided/unified government effect. Only public mood has a clear and demonstrable effect on legislative productivity, but even when accounting for the effect of public mood, there is no evidence that legislative productivity is higher during periods of united government than during periods of divided government (at least for the 1946–1990 time period).

What about the more modern era, the 1991–2002 time period? Again, Mayhew provides a complete list of all significant legislation by president. In this case, because the time period is so recent, it is not possible to conduct a historically oriented "Sweep Two," so the list depends only upon a Sweep One analysis comparable to that conducted for the 1946–1990 time period. Though the quantitative analysis is somewhat more limited – only a couple of tables not related to joint resolutions on foreign policy or legislative investigations – the general conclusion is the same; there is still little difference between legislative productivity during times of divided government and legislative productivity during times of united government. As Mayhew writes, "For 1991–2002, the overall verdict on differences between conditions of party control seems to be: no on legislative volume, somewhat on legislative content ..." (2005: 226).[15]

Mayhew's work in *Divided We Govern* clearly has a scientific orientation. He directly tests a prominent hypothesis based on a partisan theory of presidential–legislative relations and federal policy

---

[15] Significantly, Mayhew notes that there were considerable differences between divided and unified government during the later time period (1991–2002) in interbranch conflict (greater conflict between the president and Congress during divided government) and congressional investigations (significantly more frequent during divided government than during united government). These are two important differences between the 1946–1990 time period and the 1991–2002 time period.

making: Does divided government produce gridlock? Mayhew's data suggests that there is no relationship between the presence of divided government and the manifestation of gridlock. He finds no evidence that divided government inhibits legislative productivity (at least as long as we focus on "significant" legislation). Does Mayhew offer an alternative perspective? In a way, yes. Each of the alternative explanations listed previously provides the basis for an alternative explanation, an explanation for why there is *no* relationship between divided/unified government and legislative productivity. Note that these are theoretical rationales for the absence of an actual relationship between divided/unified government and legislative productivity. As with any analysis, there are limits to Mayhew's empirical evidence; the actual relationship between divided/unified government and legislative productivity may be stronger than these results suggest. Why? For one or more of the following reasons:

1. *The operationalization of "legislative productivity" is flawed or incomplete.*[16] The overall volume of legislation is, at best, only one aspect of legislative productivity. Another potential component of legislative productivity is the extent to which a legislative agenda is successfully translated into law. A raw count of the number of pieces of significant legislation would not effectively capture the proportion of the agenda made into law. A more accurate indicator of this conceptualization of (or aspect of) legislative productivity would be a percentage measure – the proportion of agenda items made into law. The number of significant pieces of legislation and the percentage of agenda items passed into law may be highly correlated, but there is no guarantee of this relationship, nor is a high correlation the same as a perfect correlation.

2. *The result is sensitive to time period.* It is possible that Mayhew's original result is not robust across time. Even his updated analysis (Mayhew 2005) suggests the significance of divided government varies across time. While the absence of a relationship between divided government and legislative productivity remains even when adding additional years at the end of the twentieth century and the very beginning of the twenty-first century (1991–2002), there is evidence of a new relationship between divided government and congressional investigations during this time period. If the relationship between divided government and congressional investigations may change over time, might we find the same type of variation in

---

[16] Research by Edwards and Barrett (2000) and Edwards et al. (1997) makes this argument.

the relationship between divided government and legislative productivity if we extend the time frame even further? There is ample evidence that the political parties have become more polarized and more cohesive since the latter part of the twentieth century. We do not know if Mayhew's result holds for the most recent years of highly polarized parties.

3. *The analysis is flawed.* Mayhew's original (and updated) analysis may not fully account for alternative explanations of legislative productivity. For example, suppose the true explanation for the variation in legislative productivity (Mayhew's conceptualization of legislative productivity) is the ideological divergence between the chambers of congress and the intrachamber ideological dispersion of the members rather than the nominal partisan control of the White House and Congress. According to this perspective, legislative productivity is hindered by significant ideological differences between chambers and within chambers. This possibility has played an important role in recent research on this topic (see Binder 1999, 2003, and 2008; Chiou and Rothenberg 2008a and 2008b) This is an option that is not effectively accounted for in Mayhew's analysis (1991 or 2005). Failing to account for the effect of this possibility may lead us to underestimate the real effect of divided government. It is possible that both the ideological model and the divided government model explain some significant portion of the variation in legislative productivity. However, empirical models that do not include both potential effects are *underspecified,* and if an empirical model is underspecified, we can have no confidence in the results generated for the variables actually included in the model.

As scientists, how might we respond to Mayhew's conclusion and to the potential flaws in Mayhew's argument listed above? How might we respond to the *puzzle* of the insignificance of divided government in an era of increasing partisanship? We might do the following:

1. Conduct a more complete examination of the relationship between various conceptualizations of *legislative productivity.* We would need to evaluate the extent to which the competing measures of legislative productivity are related (or not). Then if the measures are not related, we would need to understand why (possibly the result of significant variation in the size of the president's legislative agenda). And then we would want to be able to determine whether or not the reasons for the differences in indicators of legislative productivity have a partisan foundation. If partisan dynamics can explain why there is variation in different indicators of legislative productivity,

then it may be possible to reconcile Mayhew's results with the growth in partisan polarization over the past three decades.

2. The appropriate empirical response to the question of the robustness of the Mayhew results across time is an extension of the analysis to a larger sample (longer time period). If Mayhew's theoretical perspective is the foundation for a productive research program, then the same result (or absence of a result) should be manifest in more recent data.

3. The appropriate analytical response to an underspecified model is a reanalysis of the data with a properly specified model.

Practically speaking, implementation of analytical responses 1 and 3 from the last list require a significant amount of specialized theoretical and methodological expertise. However, we can conduct several straightforward tests for Mayhew's thesis on new data, and the following guided research exercises focus on these tests.

GUIDED RESEARCH EXERCISES

The guided research exercises for this chapter focus on the evaluation of the relationship between divided government and legislative productivity. You have learned about the relationship between these variables while reading this chapter, and this is your chance to examine this relationship on your own.

Data sources

For the exercise in this chapter, you will need data on legislative productivity for the time period from 1946–2008. This data may be obtained directly from Mayhew's web site at http://pantheon.yale. edu/~dmayhew/data3.html.[17] You will also need data on divided government for this time period. This information may be gathered from a variety of sources, but easily accessible, authoritative sources include:

1. The Clerk of the House of Representatives web site at http://clerk. house.gov/art_history/house_history/partyDiv.html.[18] This site provides the partisan breakdown for the House from the first Congress to the present day.

---

[17] Last accessed on December 17, 2009.
[18] Last accessed on December 17, 2009.

2. The U.S. Senate web site at http://www.senate.gov/pagelayout/history/one_item_and_teasers/partydiv.htm.[19] This site provides the partisan breakdown for the Senate from the first Congress to the present day.

3. The White House web site at http://www.whitehouse.gov/about/presidents/.[20] This site provides a list of all U.S. presidents with information about the time periods of their administrations.

EXERCISES

A. Bivariate Exercises

1. Descriptive Exercises

a. Hypotheses

(1) Legislative productivity is greater during periods of united government than during periods of divided government for the 1946–2008 time period.

(2) Legislative productivity is greater during periods of united government than during periods of divided government for the 1981–2008 time period (a time period of significant growth in partisan polarization).

b. Analysis

(1) Collect and organize the variables listed above from the indicated web sites.

(2) Create the following separate bar graphs.

(a) Legislative productivity by divided government for 1946–2008 time period.

(b) Legislative productivity by divided government for 1981–2008 time period.

c. Response to results

(1) Describe the graphic results for the 1946–2008 time period.

(2) Describe the graphic results for the 1981–2008 time period.

(3) Determine whether your results are consistent or inconsistent with each of your hypotheses.

(4) Explain your conclusions.

2. Inferential Exercises

a. Hypothesis[21]

---

[19] Last accessed on December 17, 2009.
[20] Last accessed on December 17, 2009.
[21] Note that this hypothesis is more general than the hypotheses listed in the descriptive exercises section. This hypothesis is not limited to a particular time period.

        (1) Legislative productivity is greater during periods of united government than during periods of divided government.

    b. Analysis

        (1) Complete the descriptive exercises above.

        (2) Compute the difference of means test statistic for both analyses.

    c. Response to results

        (1) Determine whether your results are consistent or inconsistent with each of your hypotheses.

        (2) Explain your conclusions.

B. Multivariate Exercises

What if the relationship between legislative productivity and divided government varies by the partisanship of the president (i.e., Democratic presidents are significantly more/less successful at achieving their legislative goals than their Republican counterparts)? You will examine this possibility in the following exercises.

1. Descriptive Exercise

    a. Hypothesis – The difference between the legislative productivity of Republican presidents during periods of united government and periods of divided government is greater than the difference for Democratic presidents for the 1946–2008 time period.

    b. Analysis – Create the same bar graph as in 2a earlier but separate the results for Democratic and Republican presidents. Note that this will result in four separate bars in the graph.

    c. Response to results – Compare the difference between the Republican bars and the Democratic bars. Which difference is larger? Is this difference consistent with the hypothesized relationship? Explain your conclusion.

2. Inferential Exercise

    a. Hypothesis – The difference between the legislative productivity of Republican presidents during periods of united government and periods of divided government is greater than the difference for Democratic presidents.

    b. Analysis

        (1) Complete the descriptive/graphical exercises above.

        (2) Compute the difference of means test for the party-specific differences in legislative productivity across divided/unified government.

    c. Response to results

        (1) Determine whether your results are consistent or inconsistent with each of your hypotheses.

        (2) Explain your conclusions.

IMPORTANT TERMS

alternative variation
credit claiming
divided government
gridlock
internationalists
isolationists
legislative productivity
public mood
"significant legislation"
Sweep One/Sweep Two

7

☆ ☆ ☆

The Supreme Court and the President

During the second term, particularly the latter part of the second term, of George W. Bush's administration, the content of the Bush "legacy" frequently arose as a topic of conversation among political pundits and as the focus for op-ed pieces in major national newspapers. Political scientists and legal scholars were also interested in the potential role of the second Bush administration in charting the future ideological course of the Supreme Court. Initial returns suggest that there is a wide perception that George W. Bush's influence on the Court will be felt for quite some time. According to David Yalof, a prominent student of the relationship between the presidency and the judiciary:

> As George W. Bush approaches the final year of his presidency, pundits are considering what legacy the 43rd president will leave to the nation.... one area where scholars are in a better position right now to assess the Bush legacy is his impact on the federal judiciary and, indirectly, on the state of constitutional law. Stated simply, George W. Bush may have done more to transform the constitutional landscape in a conservative direction than any president in the past century, including Ronald Reagan and Richard Nixon. (2007)

This characterization of Bush's legacy is not unique to Yalof; it is an increasingly common contention among scholars and journalists from both the right and the left. Maggie Barron argues that Bush's final State of the Union address:

> ... was about legacy-building. But the President spent only a moment of his hour-long speech on a subject that could be his most enduring legacy of all, one that will have an impact long after troops are out of Iraq and the housing market has recovered – the makeup of the judicial branch. (2008)

When presidents speak of their judicial legacy, they are rarely, if ever, referring to the sway of the quality of their own legal arguments (or even those of their subordinates, such as the Solicitor General). Presidents (and presidential scholars) measure judicial legacies in terms of appointments to the Supreme Court. The puzzling aspect of the early assessments of the significance of George W. Bush's judicial legacy is that is based on so few appointees. George W. Bush successfully appointed two justices: John Roberts, currently the Chief Justice, and Samuel Alito, currently an Associate Justice. Historically, the first 42 presidents (counting Grover Cleveland twice) have appointed 108 justices, which works out to just over 2.5 justices per president. This figure suggests that Bush did not nominate an unusually large number of justices; in fact, his number of nominations is below average. If we also consider the fact that a justice is appointed once every two years (approximately), and we remember that Bush served two full terms, it is clear that Bush had few opportunities, in terms of open seats on the Court, to alter the ideological landscape of the Court's decision-making process. Why is this apparently minimal slate of appointments considered such an important aspect of the George W. Bush legacy? More generally, is the president often in a position to control (or significantly influence) the decision making of the federal judiciary – particularly the Supreme Court?

If control over Supreme Court decision making is a manifestation of presidential power, what perspective toward presidential power might be the most useful for explaining the variation in this type of control? Assuming for the moment that the key to this presidential influence is the appointment power, what perspective toward presidential politics would be most useful in helping us understand the dynamics of "appointment politics"? Recent research on the appointment power (and appointment politics) will help us begin to answer these questions.

The literature on the Supreme Court appointment power is vast and, for political science, relatively old. It goes back at least to David Danelski's *A Supreme Court Justice is Appointed* (1964) in the early sixties. However, the scientifically oriented work on the politics of judicial appointments is far newer, only going back to the 1980s. From the standpoint of presidential power, the focus of much of the more recent research on Court appointments has been institutional. This is not a foregone conclusion. It is relatively easy to outline pathways of presidential influence on the Court – through the use of the appointment power – that are based on each of the other sources of presidential power: partisanship (and large numbers of fellow partisans in the Senate), public opinion, and bargaining ability.

The president might attempt to "pack the Court" with his own fellow partisans and, if the Senate is amenable, the president might be successful. After packing the Court in this manner, we might expect the Court to provide the president with very favorable rulings on a consistent basis. But until relatively recently, American political parties have been neither especially cohesive (i.e., partisans all have very similar policy preferences) nor distinctive (i.e., the parties offer substantially different policy platforms). So the appointment of fellow partisans in an era of weak parties would not necessarily result in increased support for the president's position on cases before the Court. In the famous example of Eisenhower's appointment of Earl Warren, the relatively conservative Republican president appointed a Republican governor of California to the Court (as Chief Justice). But shortly after his confirmation, Warren led the Court through one of its most liberal eras.[1] So appointing fellow partisans does not always go as expected. There is some recent evidence that suggests that the straying of presidential appointments is more common than generally thought (Segal et al. 2000).

Presidents might also expect that their own high job approval would translate into support for the president's position in cases on which the Court makes a ruling. Research on the relationship between Court rulings and public opinion more generally (i.e., polling data on the policy preferences of the public rather than polling data on the public's support for the president) is extensive. The evidence on the direct relationship between public opinion and Court rulings is mixed, but the most recent evidence tends to suggest a positive relationship – as the public tends toward the liberal or conservative end of the ideological spectrum, the Court tends to follow.[2] What has received relatively little attention is the relationship between public support for the president and the consistency of Court rulings and presidential policy objectives.[3] This is certainly an interesting topic for future research,

---

[1] Eisenhower's own self-criticism for the appointment of Warren is legendary.

[2] See McGuire and Stimson (2004) for a useful description of the literature on this question and some interesting recent results.

[3] There is significant research on the relationship between presidential approval and Court treatment of cases relating to the exercise of presidential authority. For example, Yates' *Popular Justice: Presidential Prestige and Executive Success at the Supreme Court* is an important work on the relationship between presidential approval and Supreme Court rulings on cases relating directly to the extent of presidential powers. However, there is very little comparable research on the more general relationship between presidential approval and the extent to which Court rulings are consistent with broader presidential policy objectives.

but absent the analysis, we can draw no conclusions about possible relationships between the variables.

Likewise, even if we are unwilling to accept the possibility of direct bargaining with sitting justices for favorable rulings, there is no reason to ignore the possibility that presidents lobby senators for support of the president's most favored judicial nominees. There is some descriptive historical work that suggests these types of negotiations occur, but there is no general analysis of their frequency or political significance.

The primary focus of much of the recent research on the relationship between the president and the Court has focused on the appointment process. In this explicitly institutional context, the focus has been on the relationship between the ideological orientations of the nominating president, the Senate, the Court, and potential nominees. It is a gross simplification to suggest that the ideological orientations of the justices determine their decision-making patterns. Certainly, a variety of factors – many of them case-specific – enter into justices' decision making. One theory of judicial decision making, often referred to as the legal or case-specific perspective, focuses on the role of case characteristics and the details of the existing law to explain judicial decisions. Another theory of judicial decision making focuses on the role of contextual effects – such as political contexts – on judicial decision making. These efforts would obviously be more straightforward (and more compelling) in those contexts in which a Court decision was overwhelming (ideally, unanimous). If the facts of the case are the primary determinants of judicial decisions, how do we explain split decisions, especially the tight 5–4 majorities?[4] For both the case-specific and contextual perspectives, explaining the variation in justices' opinions on the same case at the same time is not easy. Case-specific information is not irrelevant – at the most basic level, how could it be? – and there is some evidence that political contexts, especially state-level political contexts, play an important role in judicial decision making in tribunals below the Supreme Court.[5] But our focus is on the Court (and the president), and the most prominent models for explaining the voting patterns of Supreme Court justices are the ideological or attitudinal model and the strategic model.

---

[4] Though not especially common, even close votes may mask differences of opinion that are only fully evident after inspecting a set of distinct concurrences and dissents.

[5] For very useful descriptions of the case-specific and contextual perspectives (and efforts to integrate these orientations with the attitudinal model), see Brace and Hall (1993, 1997).

The attitudinal model of judicial decision making posits that all justices have distinct and discernable ideological orientations, meaning that some justices are conservative, some are moderate, and some are liberal. Proponents of the attitudinal model then go on to posit that these ideological orientations influence the voting patterns of the justices on cases heard by the Court. These ideological orientations should be discernable in advance of the justice's confirmation to the Court, so journalists and scholars examining the professional record of nominees should be able to identify which will tend to have liberal voting patterns on the Court, which will be more conservative, and which will have moderate voting records. Ideological consistency is a crucial component of the attitudinal model. If individual justices' voting patterns range across the ideological spectrum from year to year, then their political orientations or attitudes cannot be the determining factor in their voting calculus. This does not preclude occasional deviations from an established voting pattern – or votes taken on cases that do not easily fit into ideological categories – but consistent and pervasive ideological behavior is the cornerstone of the attitudinal model.

The strategic model of judicial decision making also presumes that justices have stable ideological orientations (Epstein and Knight 1998).[6] In the attitudinal voting model, justices' votes are assumed to reflect their underlying ideology in a straightforward manner: Liberal justices cast liberal votes; conservative justices cast conservative votes. In the strategic model, justices' votes are not necessarily an obvious reflection of their underlying ideological orientations. While justices are goal-oriented and are attempting to achieve the particular policy goals associated with their own ideological or policy orientations, they are also making collective decisions with eight other justices, and these decisions (and the opinions explaining them) will be used by other political actors in their own efforts to achieve their own policy goals. The strategic model highlights the possibility that a justice may have an incentive to cast a vote that is strategic (rather than a sincere reflection of her own policy orientation) to achieve a subsequent policy goal. So, a judge might cast a vote for *certiorari* or a preliminary vote in deliberation that is significantly more conservative (or significantly more liberal) than their underlying ideology in an effort to strategically advance her own favored final outcome. The attitudinal model posits the consistent and sincere reflection of a justice's ideology in each decision-making setting; the strategic model

---

[6] Or, if not technically ideological orientations, then stable policy preferences.

posits that a justice will cast whatever vote is necessary – regardless of the ideological cast – to achieve the final result that is most consistent with her preferences. In many cases, the voting predictions for the attitudinal model and strategic model will be the same, but in some cases, the predictions will vary. Significantly, a justices' ideology plays an important role in both models.

Some recent research has also focused on the role of the ideology of the retiring justice (relative to the ideology of the Court as a whole) in at least partially determining the extent to which the successful nominee will reflect the president's ideological orientation. These institutionally oriented analyses tend to be (increasingly) based on spatial models of the appointment process. These spatial models are an example of a formal model based on game theory.

What is a spatial model of the appointment process? Let me describe it. Suppose we draw a straight line and say that the line represents a single ideological dimension ranging from most liberal on the left end of the line to most conservative on the right end of the line. The center of the line will represent a moderate position. Then let us assume that each significant political "player" in the appointment "game" (the president, senators, current Supreme Court justices, and potential presidential nominees) has an ideological orientation that is consistent with (and can be accurately characterized by) a single position on the line. If that is the case, then every actor can be placed at some point on the line (which, for us, represents ideology).

Let us also assume that when a choice must be made between two positions on the line (say, positions that represent the ideological orientations of two potential Supreme Court nominees, for example), then players always choose the position on the line (or the nominee) that is closest to their own position (or in game theory terminology, "ideal point"). Also, from previous research on the character of games of this type,[7] the winning position in a vote between two options (two potential nominees or a nominee and the sitting justice about to retire) is the one that captures the *median* voter.[8] It is the choice of the median voter, the senator at the center of the ideological distribution of senators, who casts the deciding vote between (1) confirmation of a new

---

[7] Technically, games in a single dimension in which all actors have "single-peaked" preferences. For a general discussion of games of this type – and game theory more generally – see McCarty and Meirowitz (2007), Morrow (1994), and Osborne (2004).

[8] For more information on the *median voter theorem*, see Downs (1957), Enelow and Hinich (1984, 1990), and Hinich and Munger (1997).

←-------J1---J2------J3----------J4----SM-----J5-----J6----J7----P---------J8-----------J9-----→

Figure 7-1: Supreme Court Appointment Scenario 1.

justice or (2) rejection of the appointee (in favor of the continued tenure of the sitting justice planning to retire).

Finally, we will assume that both the president and all of the senators care only about the ideological tenor of the overall Court and
thus the ideological content of the rulings they hand down. The ideological orientation of the appointee only matters to the extent that it
alters the ideological disposition of the decision-making member of
the Court. Who is the decision-making member? It is the tie-breaker,
the median voter among the nine justices. In fact, in some research
on the appointment power and Supreme Court decision making, the
game on which theoretical predictions are based is referred to as the
"move-the-median game" (Krehbiel 2007).[9]

The stages (or "moves") in our game are as follows:

1. A prospective opening on the Court becomes available when a sitting justice announces her or his intended retirement. The justice
   agrees to remain on the Court until a replacement is confirmed.
2. The president nominates a replacement.
3. The Senate confirms or rejects the nominee. If the nominee is confirmed, the retiring justice is replaced. If the nominee is rejected,
   the retiring justice remains on the Court, and the nomination process begins again.

Consider the distribution of preferences depicted in Figure 7-1.

J1-J9 are the ideal points of nine hypothetical Supreme Court justices. The most liberal justice, J1, is furthest to the left, while the most
conservative justice, J9, is furthest to the right. SM is the ideal point for
the median senator (assuming the vice president is counted as a voting
senator for tie-breaking purposes), and P is the ideal point of the president. In the current configuration, J5 is the median justice. Assuming,
as we do above, that Court decisions reflect the ideological orientation
of the median justice, the president's ability to influence the ideological cant of future Court decisions depends upon her ability to shift the
Court median. The Court median may shift for one of two reasons: (1)
the median justice retires and is replaced by someone with a more
liberal (conservative) orientation, or (2) another member of the Court

---

[9] Rohde and Shepsle (2007) present a similar but somewhat more complicated game
that includes multiple cloture voters (the 60th senators – one from the right and
one from the left). Moraski and Shipan's (1999) model is also similar.

←-------J1 ---J2------J3 ---------J4 -----------J5-----J6-SM-J7----P---------J8-----------J9-----→

Figure 7-2: Supreme Court Appointment Scenario 2.

retires, and that justice is replaced by a member with a sufficiently different ideological orientation that a different justice becomes the new median voter. Ideologically speaking, whether the new median justice is a new appointee or a sitting member of the Court does not matter. What matters, from a policy-making standpoint (and thus, for the president), is the ideological position of the new median justice.

Whether or not a president will be able to shift the median justice depends upon the position of the president and the median senator, as well as the ideological distribution of the sitting justices. This last detail is of particular importance. Consider the scenario above. If J5 plans to retire, how much ideological movement will the president be able to generate with a new appointee? The answer is "none." As long as the median senator and the president are on opposite sides of the median justice, neither will agree to a replacement for the retiring justice that shifts the balance of the Court, the median justice, away from the status quo. The president has no incentive to nominate a justice to the left of J5 because that would shift the median away from the president's ideal point, and the president is better off if J5 remains on the Court.[10] If the president nominates a justice with a more conservative orientation (i.e., farther to the right) than J5, then the median voter in the Senate will not support the nominee, and the nomination will fail, because the median senator prefers the median at J5 to any position further to the right (away from the median senator's ideal point). As long as the ideal point of the median justice is bounded by the ideal points of the median senator and the president (and the retiring senator remains on the Court until her replacement is confirmed), this theory suggests that the president can do nothing to change the policy-making orientation of the Court.

However, if the median senator's position shifts toward the president, as it might if the president's party were to win a number of Senate seats in a successful election, then the retirement of the same justice might well provide the president with the opportunity to significantly influence the ideological tenor of the Court's rulings. See the scenario depicted in Figure 7-2.

The only difference between the preference distribution in Figures 7-1 and 7-2 is the location of the median senator. SM has moved

---

[10] Remember that we are assuming, for the sake of simplicity, that a retiring member will remain on the Court until her replacement is confirmed.

←-------J1---J2---J3—J4—J5------------------------SM—J6-P---J7----J8-----------J9-----→

Figure 7-3: Supreme Court Appointment Scenario 3.

well to the right of her original position, and this movement dramatically alters the strategic opportunities available to the president. The president may now nominate a jurist that shares the president's ideal point, and the Senate will confirm this appointee because the median senator prefers the new Court median (J6) to the old Court median (J5). In this case, the president is able to influence the ideological disposition of the Court with only a single successful nomination, but you should note that the Court's shift in orientation does not result in a Court median consistent with the president's own ideal point. It is possible for a president to move the Court median to her own ideal point, but the circumstances that would allow for that type of shift are quite restrictive. In this case, for example, the president's preference would have to be very near the Court median to begin with – specifically between J4 and J6 – for the president to be able to successfully nominate a new justice that would result in the Court median matching the president's ideal point.

There are two other types of appointment/confirmation scenarios of particular interest. In one, we have the same distribution of preferences as depicted in Figure 7-2, but this time, the retiring justice comes from the set J6–J9. In this case, even though both the president and the median senator would prefer a more conservative Court than the one in which J5 is the median voter, since the retirements come on the conservative side of the spectrum, replacements will not alter the location of the median voter. In the second, imagine a scenario like the one pictured in Figure 7-3.

Assuming that J5 is (again) the retiring justice, a single vacancy will be filled with a successful nominee whose ideological position would be no less conservative than J6.[11] In this case, the replacement for a single retirement dramatically alters the ideological orientation of the Court. It is the absence of moderates – the empty middle space – that allows for the magnitude of this change. Note also that this dramatic shift does not depend upon the retirement of J5; the retirement of any justice from the J1–J5 set would have produced the same result.

---

[11] To see this, consider the choice the median senator has between J5 and J6; clearly, she prefers J6. The president also clearly prefers the position of J6 to any position to the left of J6. As the president has no incentive to nominate someone to the left of J6, and the Senate will confirm a nominee at J6 (because of the preferences of the median senator), then the president may nominate someone at least as conservative as J6.

←-----TM---WBR-----------------JPS -----HB----------MS-BW-LP -PS-----WBU-----WR-RR --→

Figure 7-4: O'Connor Appointment Scenario 1.

Here we see a case where a single appointment might reasonably be said to produce a substantial (and potentially lasting) impact on the Court. The president making this appointment might well see it as an important part of her *legacy*.

Let's consider a real-world example. In 1981, Reagan made good on his campaign promise to appoint the first woman to the Supreme Court when he selected Sandra Day O'Connor to replace the retiring Potter Stewart. O'Connor was a popular choice – second in her class (to then-sitting justice William Rehnquist) at Stanford's law school – and she was confirmed by a vote of 99–0. Early in his presidency and supported by a Republican Senate, Reagan might have been expected to choose a conservative ideologue as his first Supreme Court appointee, but he actually chose a relative moderate. Why? Our simple spatial model provides a clue.

Using ideal point estimates for President Reagan, the median Senator in 1981, and the justices in 1981, we can see the strategic context which Reagan faced.[12] Figure 7-4 is a depiction of the ideal points of all of the relevant actors prior to the resignation of Potter Stewart in 1981. See Figure 7-4.[13] In this scenario, three justices have ideal points that are extraordinarily close together – White, Powell, and Stewart. So, while the technical median justice is White, what you see is a set of centrist justices that are very similar. Note that Reagan's ideal point is slightly farther to the right (more conservative) than that of the most conservative justice (Rehnquist).

When Stewart retires – and only eight justices remain – the median shifts to the space between Blackmun and White. Splitting the difference, the estimated median is now to the left of the ideal point of the median Senator. Given the location of Reagan's ideal point, the model suggests that the next appointee will be to the *right* of the eight-justice median. Theoretically, we should expect the new appointee to have an ideal point that is indistinguishable from that of the median Senator, but because White's ideal point is nearly indistinguishable from the

---

[12] The ideal point estimates are taken from Michael Bailey's data. See the guided research exercises at the end of this chapter for more information on this data.

[13] The key to the abbreviations is as follows: TM=Thurgood Marshall, WBR=William Brennan, JPS=John Paul Stevens, HB=Harry Blackmun, MS=Median Senator, BW=Byron White, LP=Lewis Powell, PS=Potter Stewart, WBU=Warren Burger, WR=William Rehnquist, and RR=Ronald Reagan.

←-----TM---WBR----------------JPS-----HB----------MS-BW-LP--SDO----WBU-----WR-RR--→

Figure 7-5: O'Connor Appointment Scenario 2.

ideal point of the median Senator, Reagan has somewhat more latitude to appoint a conservative. See Figure 7-5.[14]

While slightly more conservative than Stewart, O'Connor takes exactly his ordinal position in the decision-making space. Why does the Senate allow the appointment of a slightly more conservative candidate than they would ideally prefer? Because the appointment and confirmation of O'Connor shifts the Court median back to its previous point, a point preferred by the median Senator to the median in the eight-justice Court. Why doesn't Reagan push his advantage and select a conservative ideologue? Because there is little to be gained (at least in the short term) – White would still become the median voter – and much to be lost if a bitter Senate fight developed. This is just a single case, but it does nicely illustrate the real-world strategic dynamics captured by this simple spatial model.

More generally, the implications of this simple model suggest the following about the ability of the president to influence or manipulate the Court solely through the use of the appointment power:

1. The ideological orientation of the person(s) leaving the bench (relative to that of those remaining) is at least as important as the ideology of the new appointee/justice. If a very liberal president is simply replacing a very liberal justice, that alone does nothing to shift the overall balance of opinion on the Court. The same is true if a very conservative president is simply replacing a very conservative justice. When presidents replace justices who are moderates (relative to the other members of the Court), the change in the ideological balance of the Court may be dramatic. This is particularly true when the president is appointing the replacement of the median voter on the Court, especially if none of the remaining justices are ideologically similar to the departing justice.

2. A president on one end of the ideological spectrum (either very liberal or very conservative) – even when facing a Senate that shares her ideological orientation – may find herself in a situation in which an appointment *cannot* result in a significant shift in Court ideology. If a very liberal (conservative) president is replacing a very liberal (conservative) justice, the new appointee – even if very liberal (conservative) – will not alter the ideological balance of the Court.

---

[14] SDO represents the ideal point of Sandra Day O'Connor.

3. Those situations in which a president is most likely to be able to shift the ideological position of the Court – when a moderate or a justice with an opposing ideological orientation retires – are the circumstances in which an ideologically opposed Senate proves to be the most significant obstacle to change.

While this is an interesting theory, it is just a theory. What sort of empirical tests have been conducted on the hypotheses derived from this theory? Because the implications of the theory are sensitive to the specific ideological dispositions of not only the president, the senators, and the nominee, but also of all of the justices on the Court, including the retiring member, empirical testing is neither easy nor straightforward. There is some evidence that the Court appointment process is broadly consistent with the dynamics outlined in the spatial theory above. Empirical research on the Court appointment process consistently demonstrates that presidents tend to nominate justices with ideological orientations consistent with their own. Senators are also sensitive to the ideological orientation of justices, favoring those whose perspectives are similar, and senators apparently pay attention to qualifications and expertise as well. Nominees facing ethics probes or those with low American Bar Association (ABA) qualification scores tend to face greater scrutiny (and a significantly more difficult nomination process) than their more highly qualified (and less ethically questionable) colleagues.[15]

These empirical results, while generally consistent with the implications of the spatial model presented above, are also consistent with much simpler models, models which do not account for the positioning of the retiring justice or the specific relative position of the median senator, the president, the retiring justice, and the nominee. For the spatial model to demonstrate its theoretical and empirical usefulness, we must be able to evaluate the distinctive implications of the model. Some anecdotal evidence suggests that models of this type do capture an important aspect of the political dynamics of the Court appointment process (see Moraski and Shipan 1999).

Though limited, recent quantitative analyses also provide support for the "move the median" model presented earlier (Krehbiel 2007). As noted above, the most straightforward tests of the implications of the model would require valid and reliable measures of the ideological ideal points of the sitting members of the Court (including the retiree),

---

[15] See Epstein and Segal (2005) for an overview and description of this evidence. Other important references include Segal et al. (1989, 1992) and Moraski and Shipan (1999).

the members of the Senate (including the median Senator), and the president in the same policy space. It is not easy to order the justices in the same space, but scholars have developed several methods for estimating the ideal points of the members of the Court. One method is based on a content analysis of newspaper articles and editorials about each justice prior to their confirmation to the Court (Segal and Cover 1989). By counting the relative frequency of the mention of ideological terms such as "liberal" or "conservative" in the description of each justice's political orientation, researchers can gauge the relative liberalism/conservatism of each justice.[16] Overall, this institutionally oriented perspective toward the politics of appointments suggests that there are significant constraints on the effective use of the appointment power to influence or manipulate the ideological orientation of the Supreme Court, especially in the short term. This is not to suggest that the cumulative effect of a set of ideologically extreme justices will not alter the overall ideological disposition of the Court (and the character of the Court's rulings). As Krehbiel notes, "The overwhelming consensus of observers of the Supreme Court is that appointments have important consequences for public policy, at least *in the aggregate* and over the *long term*" (2007: 238, emphasis added). But John Maynard Keynes' observation about the long run – "in the long run, we are all dead" is relevant for presidents – in the long run, they are no longer in office. If the effects of appointments are only fully realized in the long run, then a president's legacy may have a significantly greater impact on Court rulings than the limited effects during a president's administration might suggest.

So how does this model allow us to address the puzzle presented at the beginning of this chapter? It helps us understand that a president's ability to influence the Court is not solely a function of the number of justices she is able to appoint. It is not enough to know who is joining the Court; one must also know who is leaving. And even if a liberal (conservative) president is in a position to replace a staunch ideological opponent with a fellow ideologue, the president must have a Senate (or median senator) disposed to allow the replacement. And the political dispositions of the other justices must be such that this new appointment is able to "move the median" on the Court. It is not at all difficult to imagine a scenario in which a president makes multiple successful appointments to the Court and the

---

[16] A list of the ideological scores for past and current justices based on this method can be found at www.sunysb.edu/polsci/jsegal/qualtable.pdf (last accessed on December 17, 2009).

Court median does not move at all. Numbers alone are not enough. More generally, "the average appointment opportunity is likely *not* to be of great consequence for immediate policy outcomes" (Krehbiel 2007: 238).

Occasionally, however, presidents find themselves in a situation where a single well-considered appointment (or two) might make a dramatic difference in the current and future ideological character of Court opinions. This model helps us understand why George W. Bush might well have been in one of those situations during his presidency. First, Bush was able to appoint a Chief Justice, an opportunity few presidents receive. Chief justices have an influence over Court proceedings and decisions that exceeds that of any of the associate justices, and so the opportunity to appoint a Chief Justice during a time when your party controls the Senate is a significant advantage from the standpoint of a judicial legacy.[17] Second, Bush was able to replace one of the moderates on the Court, Justice Sandra Day O'Connor – and often the hypothetical median voter on 5–4 decisions – with a significantly more conservative justice, Samuel Alito. One of the reasons Bush was able to replace a moderate with a staunch conservative was the fact that his party controlled the Senate at the time of the Alito confirmation hearings. So the appointment of Alito to replace O'Connor certainly provided Bush with the opportunity to put his stamp on the Court for some years to come. So if the model presented above captures the important political dynamics of the Supreme Court appointment process, then it is possible to see how Bush's two appointments could be perceived as having such an impact on the Court that it would make sense to speak of the Bush "legacy."

Significant though it is, we are only talking about two appointments, and while the model helps us make sense of these two appointments, these two cases hardly pose a sufficient test for the broader generalizability of the implications of the model. In the guided research exercises that follow, you will have an opportunity to test the model using real-world data on the ideological dispositions of other justices (and nominees whose confirmations were not so successful). See how often the model's predictions accord with the actual data and then draw some conclusions about whether or not this model might form the foundation for a progressive research program.

---

[17] Of course, no appointment strategy is perfect. Remember Eisenhower's appointment of Chief Justice Earl Warren.

GUIDED RESEARCH EXERCISES

Data sources

The guided research exercises for this chapter involve the use of estimate of the ideological "ideal points" of the president, senators, Supreme Court justices, and Supreme Court appointees who were not confirmed. To use the "move the median" model above to precisely specify the likely ideological orientation of a new appointee, one must have ideal point estimates for the president, each senator (so it will be possible to determine the median senator), and each sitting justice (so that it will be possible to determine the actual Court median and the potential shift in the Court median with a particular retirement). Fortunately, the technology for estimating ideal points across institutions (presidency, Senate, Court) has developed to the point that we have estimates for each of the necessary players for the last half of the twentieth century. These ideal point scores are available from the web site of Michael A. Bailey, professor of government at Georgetown University.[18] Unfortunately, this data does not include ideal points for unsuccessful nominees. For the exercises dealing with failed appointments, you will need ideal point data for these nominees. Ideal point data for all Supreme Court justices and failed nominees for the latter half of the twentieth century can be obtained at the web site of Jeffrey Segal, a professor of political science at SUNY–Stony Brook.[19]

You will also need to know the nomination and confirmation dates for each justice, the name of the justice who the new justice replaced, and the names of the other members of the Court at the time of appointment and confirmation. That information can be gathered from the Supreme Court web site.[20]

EXERCISES

1. Consider the following hypothetical scenario. Assume that the positions and specific ideal points for the sitting justices, median senator, and president are as depicted in Figure 7-6.

---

[18] The data are available at http://www9.georgetown.edu/faculty/baileyma/Data.htm (last viewed on December 17, 2009). For a detailed description of the procedure used by Bailey to generate these ideal points, see Michael Bailey (2007).

[19] The data are available at http://www.sunysb.edu/polsci/jsegal/qualtable.pdf (last viewed on December 17, 2009).

[20] The specific site is http://www.supremecourtus.gov/about/members.pdf (last viewed on December 17, 2009). This site also provides the name of the nominating president.

←-------J1---J2---J3—J4—J5------------------------SM—J6-P---J7----J8-----------J9-----→

Figure 7-6: Supreme Court Appointment Scenario 4.

Further assume that the specific ideal point for the sitting justices, median senator, and president are as follows:

J1 = .1
J2 = .15
J3 = .2
J4 = .25
J5 = .3
J6 = .58
J7 = .65
J8 = .75
J9 = .9
SM = .55
P = .60

Given this scenario, what would be the predicted ideal point for a successful appointee if J3 retired? As the Court median is J5 and the median senator and the president both prefer J6 to J5, the model suggests the new appointee will have an ideal point of no less than .58. Note that in some cases, the model will predict a specific ideal point and in other cases it will suggest a range. In the case of a range, choose the ideal point in the range closest to that of the appointing president.

Now choose any six justices appointed between 1951 and 2002. Using the Bailey data, calculate an estimated ideal point for each of these justices based on the Court to which they were being appointed, the ideal point of the president and the median senator, and the ideological disposition of the justice who each was replacing. Using the example above as a guide, estimate an ideal point for each of the justices you chose and compare the actual ideal point with the predicted ideal point. Plot the predicted ideal points against the actual ideal points? Is there a direct relationship? Is the slope close to 1? Does it come closer to one if you add additional observations? What does this comparison of the model predictions with the actual data tell you about the usefulness of the model?

2. Estimate the predicted ideal point for each of the *failed* nominees over the last 50 years. To do this, use the data from the Segal web site (so that a comparison with the empirical ideal point for the failed nominee will be possible). Since comparable ideal points are not available for median senators and presidents when using the

Segal data, use .7 for Democrats (senators and presidents) and .3 for Republicans (senators and presidents). Graph the predicted ideal point against the actual ideal point as in the exercise above. Is there a relationship between the predicted and actual ideal points for *failed* nominees? Should we expect to see a relationship? Why or why not? What do these results imply about the usefulness of this model for understanding the dynamics of failed (as well as successful) Supreme Court nominations?

IMPORTANT TERMS

Associate Justice
attitudinal model
certiorari
Chief Justice
Confirmation
ideal point
median voter
nomination
"pack the Court"
strategic model
Supreme Court

8

The President and the Executive Branch

The rise of a professionalized bureaucracy and the concomitant growth of the American administrative state are arguably the most significant institutional developments at the national level since the Civil War. This is not to say that the legislative branch and the judicial branch have not evolved over the course of nearly 150 years, but the term "evolution" simply does not do justice to the dramatic transformation of the executive branch over this time period. The broad outlines of this transformation – in magnitude and content – are described in the section on the executive branch in Chapter 3.

In this chapter, we focus specifically on the president's relationship with the agencies and bureaucracies in the executive branch and the scholarship that examines this relationship. A quick review of this scholarship provides us, immediately, with an interesting and important *puzzle* relating to the ability of the president to effectively manage the executive branch. Simply put, there is a puzzling lack of consistency in scholarly accounts of the president's relationship with the executive bureaucracy. Some scholars focus on the president's domineering control over the bureaucracy. Other research suggests that the executive branch is structurally uncontrollable. An additional strain of research focuses on the legislative control of federal agencies. We will examine these inconsistencies and consider possible explanations for them. Then you will have an opportunity to examine one particular manifestation of the president's relationship with the executive branch – the president's influence over the policy-making activities of the Federal Open Market Committee (FOMC), an important policy-making committee within the Federal Reserve System.[1]

---

[1] We will discuss the Federal Reserve System (and the FOMC) in greater detail in Chapter 10.

THEORIES OF BUREAUCRATIC POLICY MAKING

Max Weber provides the foundational conceptualization for the modern bureaucracy. From Weber's perspective, *bureaucracy* was the organizational structure resulting from the rationalization of governance and governmental functions over time. The distinctive characteristics of Weber's bureaucracy include.

1. a chain of command that clearly delineates the formal relationship between subordinates and superiors
2. standard operating procedures that guide the work activities of the bureaucrats and the bureaucracy
3. extensive recordkeeping
4. position-specific skills and training
5. clear specification of job responsibilities and requirements
6. hiring and professional advancement determined by skills and professional performance (as opposed to personal characteristics or political relationships)[2]

What you should notice about these characteristics of bureaucracy is that they are *not* consistent with the structure and organization of the executive branch during the era of the spoils system. The focus on job-specific training and expertise and the practice of hiring and promotion based on professional skills and performance are patently inconsistent with a system of political patronage based on personal political support. On the other hand, Weber's characterization of bureaucracy is clearly consistent with the civil service system established in the latter half of the nineteenth century.

In addition to his delineation and examination of the fundamental characteristics of bureaucracy, Weber also analyzed the difficulties associated with the political control of bureaucracies. For Weber, authority and power relations are based on one of three sources: tradition, charisma, and law or reason (see Weber 1978). Traditional rule corresponds to the divine right of kings and familial monarchies. Charismatic rule corresponds to the temporary rule of leaders with particularly intense personal followings, and legal rule is based on a system of laws, constitutions, and administrative bodies and procedures. Weber argued that over time, the increasing complexity of the modern world and the inherent instability of charismatic regimes would lead to the displacement of traditional and charismatic regimes

---

[2] See Weber's *Economy and Society* (1978) for a detailed and comprehensive statement of his perspective on bureaucracies and the bureaucratization of society.

with legal regimes, and maturation of legal regimes would result in increasing rationalization (Weber 1978). For Weber, this rationalization and bureaucratization was not costless. He was greatly concerned with the potential for a dramatic increase in the authority of (unelected) bureaucrats at the expense of properly elected public officials. Note that this aggrandizement of bureaucratic authority is not, necessarily, the result of explicit bureaucratic efforts to usurp political power. The growth of bureaucratic authority is simply a result of the needs of effective governance of an increasingly complex modern society. As complexity grows, the expertise necessary to govern grows. As the gap between the expertise of bureaucrats and elected officials grows – as it must in a political system with a properly functioning bureaucracy – politicians find it ever more difficult to control the bureaucrats. At the extreme, Weber argues, it is the bureaucrats who are in the position of control. Obviously, this is a serious problem for popular government.

A different but also significant perspective on the political relationship between elected officials (the president, in particular) and bureaucrats and bureaucracies is provided by Woodrow Wilson, a prominent political scientist (and president of Princeton University) before he became President of the United States. In "The Study of Administration" (1887), Wilson outlines the proper relationship between a professional bureaucracy and elected officials.[3] Writing in the earliest stages of the Progressive Era, Wilson makes a stark distinction between "politics" and "administration." According to Wilson, "politics," or the processes by which the goals and ends of government are determined, is the sole responsibility and prerogative of the people and their elected officials. "Administration," or the execution of the means necessary to achieve the political ends, is the responsibility of the bureaucracy. Why is administration the responsibility of the bureaucracy? Because only bureaucrats have the expertise necessary for the efficient and effective execution of the policies chosen to achieve popularly determined political goals. For Wilson, there is an important conceptual and practical distinction (and separation) between politics and administration.

Two points deserve additional emphasis. The politics–administration dichotomy is plainly inconsistent with an executive branch dominated by a spoils system. A spoils system prevents the development of the skill and expertise necessary for the bureaucracy to effectively execute its administrative responsibilities. Also, under a spoils system

---

[3] This article is generally credited with establishing the field of public administration.

in which personal and partisan political alliances determine bureaucratic personnel, there can be no distinction between politics and administration. Second, though both Weber's and Wilson's perspectives are consistent with an executive branch structured in a manner consistent with a civil service system, the Weberian and Wilsonian theories imply dramatically different political relationships between elected officials (primarily the president) and bureaucrats. In Wilson's (1887) characterization of the distinction between politics and administration, politics is the primary determinant of public policy, and so the president is in a position of dominance in relation to the bureaucracy. Weber does not see (and would not agree) with Wilson's politics–administration dichotomy, and so Weber's bureaucrats are in a position not only to execute policy to achieve the goals of their political "superiors," but are also able, by virtue of their skill and expertise advantages, to achieve their own policy goals. Wilson conceptualizes a president–bureaucracy relationship in which the president is dominant, and in Weber's conceptualization of the same relationship, the bureaucracy is dominant.

Current literature on the relationship between the president and the bureaucracy reflect these dramatically conflicting theories. In the academic literature on bureaucratic and regulatory policy making, there are at least four prominent perspectives toward bureaucratic politics. The first perspective, *agency independence*, is based on the presumption that regulatory agencies (and, to a somewhat lesser extent, cabinet-level agencies) have a significant degree of policy-making independence. From this perspective, neither the president nor Congress dominates the policy-making activity of the agencies, and both the president and Congress struggle to guide and influence agency activities. According to this perspective, bureaucrats have their own professional and political goals, and the behavior of the agency reflects the goals of the bureaucrats. Proponents of this perspective argue that the ability of appointed officials to control career bureaucrats is far more limited than generally thought, for several reasons. First, it is difficult to dismiss or discipline career bureaucrats, so some of the conventional tools for addressing personnel problems are unavailable. Second, just as the "stick" is not a particularly useful option for controlling federal bureaucrats, the "carrot" is also of little effect. The types of raises, bonuses, and nonfinancial incentives provided by private corporations to top performers are prohibited within the context of the federal civil service. Since rewards are somewhat more limited, the argument goes, compliance is somewhat more difficult to achieve. Third, appointed officials often serve relatively short tenures, so by the time they are sufficiently knowledgeable about the organization to make an effort to effectively coordinate its activities, they move to another position or agency, or return to the private sector. Finally, if the appointed official does serve a sufficiently long tenure to gain the knowledge and expertise necessary to manage the agency and attempt to move it in the direction of the appointing president's policy goals, the appointee may "go native." Going native is a reference to the habit of political appointees altering their policy orientations so as to coincide with those of the career bureaucrats rather than the appointing president. Time spent in the agency environment, surrounded by career bureaucrats with a different perspective than the president makes it increasingly difficult for political appointees to maintain their allegiance to the president (and independence from the agency). After "going native," even if effective management is possible, the president's policy objectives no longer guide appointees, and so presidential control is quite circumscribed.

One variation on the independent agency perspective is a *principal–agent* model. Principal–agent models of bureaucratic politics are rational choice models of the relationship between a principal, the president, and an agent, a bureaucrat. Remember from our discussion of the "move the median" model of the judicial appointment process that rational choice models are highly stylized.[4] Nevertheless, principal–agent models highlight the implications of two important characteristics of the relationship between presidents and bureaucracies: (1) bureaucratic policy objectives may be different from presidential policy objectives (for reasons discussed above), and (2) the president has significantly less information about the bureaucrat's behavior than the bureaucrat (what is technically referred to as an "informational asymmetry"). Because of this informational asymmetry, bureaucratic behavior may deviate, sometimes significantly, from that preferred by the president. To address this problem, the president has two options: (1) close the gap between the president's policy preferences and those of the bureaucrat through the use of the appointment process; or (2) structure the relationship with the bureaucrat in such as way as to minimize the extent of the informational asymmetry. For different reasons, neither of these options is particularly effective.[5]

A second perspective toward bureaucratic and regulatory policy making is the *congressional dominance theory.* Proponents of this

---

[4] Many details are assumed away so that the model focuses on the most important aspects of the relationship.

[5] Miller (1992) is a thoughtful treatment of the fundamental obstacles to effective management and oversight inherent in principal–agent relationships.

perspective argue that the broad parameters of agency policy making are determined by the internal political dynamics of the House and Senate. Major policy initiatives produced by federal agencies result from changes in the underlying political dynamics of legislators, particularly those who sit on the committee and subcommittee that oversee the activities of the relevant agency.

While not technically a congressional dominance theory, the *iron triangle* perspective also suggests a significant role in bureaucratic policy making for legislators – in this case the members of the committee or subcommittee that oversees the activities of the agency. Iron triangles may develop in those policy arenas in which the preferences of major industry groups, legislators on the relevant committees and subcommittees, and bureaucrats in a relevant agency have interrelated and mutually reinforcing preferences. The traditional example is weapons procurement policy (see Adams 1981). In weapons procurement, the defense industry depends upon the military's need for new and increasingly expensive weaponry. In order to provide adequate domestic security and to achieve U.S. military goals abroad, the Defense Department seeks the very best new (and often expensive) weapons and weapons systems. Members of House and Senate Armed Services Committees (and various subcommittees) are in a position to provide the necessary funds for these new weapons and weapons systems, and they stand to benefit at the ballot box if these armaments are produced in (and thus bring jobs to) their districts and states.

In the iron triangle, each actor has control over some resources that one or more other actors seek. The unfortunate implication of this set of mutually beneficial relationships is the absence of an effective *public* check on the inefficiencies (i.e., purchase of unnecessary or unnecessarily expensive weapons and weapons systems) these political relationships are likely to produce. Some evidence suggests that the worst excesses of iron triangles were mitigated to some extent by the efforts to enhance fiscal responsibility in the 1990s, but given the current political environment, it is not clear that those earlier constraints are still viable.

A third perspective is the *presidential control theory*. Proponents of this perspective argue that presidents are not only in a position to effectively manage the activities of cabinet-level agencies and regulatory agencies, but that significant shifts in the policy-making orientation or activities of these agencies can be traced to political pressures emanating from the White House. While the presidential control theory implies that presidential politics influences decision making in both cabinet agencies and independent regulatory agencies, it does recognize the more significant obstacles to effective presidential control over the policy-making activities of regulatory agencies than the policy-making activities of the cabinet-level departments.

Presidential control is predicated on the president's capacity to do one or all of the following in a bureaucratic context in which his own policy goals and objectives are consistently thwarted by the agency:

1. *Replace the agency head with someone whose energies will be more consistently devoted to achievement of the president's policy objectives.* The president's ability to remove a recalcitrant agency head varies by type of agency. Department secretaries serve at the pleasure of the president; directors of independent agencies do not. Similarly, the president's ability to install a satisfactory replacement depends to some extent on the policy preferences of the senators who must confirm a new appointee. As we saw in the case of the politics of Supreme Court appointments, presidents cannot always depend on getting their ideal candidate.

2. *Restructure the agency.* Presidents may restructure and reorganize federal agencies in an effort to more effectively achieve their own policy goals. Recent evidence suggests that agencies created by executive order "are more amenable to presidential control" than agencies created by Congress (Waterman 2009; also see Howell 2003, Lewis 2008). Still, while reorganizational efforts may generate the structural change necessary to fully realize the president's policy goals, reorganization might also be unsuccessful.

3. *Restrict agency resources.* Although presidents have not had the power to impound appropriated funds (i.e., prohibit the expenditure of agency funds authorized and appropriated by Congress) since the passage of the *Congressional Budget and Impoundment Control Act of 1974*, presidents may effectively limit the resources distributed to an agency by (1) limiting the agency's budgetary request (through OMB's coordination of the president's budget), (2) utilizing the deferral or rescission processes (similar, but not legally equivalent to impoundment), and (if necessary) (3) actively advocating against congressional efforts to augment the baseline agency request in the president's budget. Again, Congress can always pass an appropriation that exceeds the president's request, so the president's ability to use this tool depends upon at least some level of congressional support.

Additional variants of the presidential control perspective include the *administrative presidency* and the unitary presidency. The administrative presidency is a response to legislative frustrations and failures;

traced back to the Nixon presidency, the administrative presidency is an effort to gain significantly greater control over the executive branch through expansive interpretation of the president's appointment and removal prerogatives and the president's budget-making and budget-coordinating authority (see Nathan 1983; Waterman 1989; and Waterman 2009). More specifically, it involves extensive presidential efforts to remove or restrain recalcitrant career bureaucrats, the weighting of personal loyalty far more heavily than policy expertise and experience in appointment decisions, and using all legal means necessary to restrict budgetary expenditures deemed inconsistent with the president's policy objectives (Waterman 2009). As we discussed in Chapters 3 and 4, the theory of the *unitary* presidency presumes an even more dramatic consolidation of executive authority in the person of the president. As Waterman argues, "[i]t posits that the president has sole responsibility for the control and maintenance of the executive branch" (2009: 6). Taken to its theoretical extreme – with the president as the final arbiter, rather than the Supreme Court, of the proper interpretation of "executive" powers – it is difficult to discern any theoretical boundaries to the exercise of presidential authority under the broad umbrella of the unitary presidency.

Scientifically oriented research on the president's use of unilateral policy-making tools such as executive orders to manage federal agencies makes up a vital and growing literature in the study of presidential power and bureaucratic policy making (see Howell 2003; Krause and Cohen 2000; and Warber 2006). Significantly, while Howell (2003) and Warber (2006) both indicate the significance of the president's use of executive orders to manage the federal bureaucracy, they have distinct views on the trend (or lack thereof) in utilization of executive orders for these purposes. While Howell (2003) finds increasing reliance on executive orders during the modern presidency, Warber (2006) uncovers no evidence of this growth in the use of unilateral authority. This is clearly an area for additional research.[6]

A fourth perspective is the *multi-institutional model* of bureaucratic politics. Proponents of the multi-institutional theory of bureaucratic policy making argue that the president is a particularly important actor in the arena of bureaucratic politics but that she is not the only significant actor. Presidents find themselves in a policy-making "game" with other actors (at the very least an agency and Congress),[7] and in

---

[6] Krause (2009) and Rudalevige (2009) provide specific suggestions for future work in this burgeoning research agenda.

[7] These formal games may also include additional agencies, the Supreme Court, or a second chamber of Congress.

this game, the rules identify the nature of the relationship between the actors and the powers that each actor possesses. In our system of government, these relationships and powers are determined by the Constitution and legislative statute. The games are often represented in a manner consistent with the model of the Supreme Court appointment process presented in the previous chapter, though the multi-institutional models of bureaucratic policy making tend to be somewhat more complicated because of the increased number and complexity of the moves of the game. These games are also occasionally presented in two or more spatial dimensions. Examples of multi-institutional models can be found in Hammond and Knott (1996), Huber and Shipan (2002), Ferejohn and Shipan (1990), and Morris (2000).

The primary findings of the multi-institutional perspective focus on the conditional nature of presidential influence. In some circumstances, the president may be able to elicit policy action from the agency that is fully consistent with presidential preferences. In other cases, the Senate may pose an obstacle to the achievement of presidential objectives through its confirmation authority. Even the credible threat of a confirmation fight might prevent the president from removing an agency head that is not managing in a manner fully consistent with presidential preferences. The president also may face a troublesome director at an independent agency, a director the president is not in a position to remove. In a multi-institutional model, to know what the president can achieve in a bureaucratic policy-making scenario, it is not enough to know the president's preferences. One must also know what the agency wants, what Congress wants, and, maybe, what the Court is willing to allow. These models are not simple, nor are the games they depict trivial. And yet they are still gross simplifications of reality. Just as all theories are.

THE EMPIRICAL STATE OF THE LITERATURE – WHY SO MANY THEORIES?

Simply put, each of the theories above is consistent with a body of empirical research. Niskanen (1971) provides a wealth of evidence consistent with a broadly independent bureaucracy, an independence largely founded on the informational advantages that are the focus of principal–agent models. Weingast and Moran (1983) find evidence in support of the congressional dominance model; and the presidential control model is consistent with the results presented in research by Waterman (1989); Wood (1988); and Wood and Waterman (1991 and 1993). The work of Morris (2000) and Huber and Shipan (2002) present considerable empirical support for the multi-institutional model of bureaucratic policy making.

Given the complexity of the nature of bureaucratic politics and the considerable number of actors involved even in the simplest real world examples of bureaucratic policy making, the diversity of theoretical perspectives should come as no surprise. The true *puzzle* is how it has been possible to maintain each of these perspectives in the face of empirical testing. Increasingly, it appears that the prevalence of diverse empirical results consistent with a set of theories is attributable to two primary explanations:

1. The empirical tests themselves could not discriminate between the theoretical predictions of multiple theories. In essence, results that were characterized as consistent with only one theory were actually consistent with at least one other theory as well.
2. The multi-institutional theory has a great deal of explanatory power. As the predictions of multi-institutional theory are inherently sensitive to institutional and political context, it is possible that some institutional settings produce results consistent with congressional dominance theory; some produce results consistent with presidential control; and some produce results consistent with bureaucratic independence. Without an understanding of the contextual sensitivity of the predictions of the multi-institutional theory, one might see results seemingly consistent with another theory and simply misunderstand the true theoretical meaning of the results.

The theoretical power of and empirical support for the multi-institutional model are just beginning to fully manifest themselves. Why has it taken so long? It has taken so long, in part, because the multi-institutional model was developed in reaction to the confusion of theoretical conjectures and empirical results flowing from the agency independence, congressional dominance, and presidential control perspectives. The multi-institutional model offers the opportunity to reconcile what had previously appeared to be irreconcilable arguments and findings.

Finally, two practical obstacles have also hindered a more effective empirical evaluation of the various theories of the president's relationship with the executive branch. First, as we know from our discussion in Chapter 3, the executive branch is made up of a variety of structurally distinct types of agencies, bureaus, and councils. It would be unreasonable to expect each type of organization to have the same relationship with the president. Still, developing full explanations for the actual differences between these relationships has not been easy. Also, important substantive differences exist between the various agencies and bureaus in the executive branch, and understanding the implications of these substantive differences for the president's various relationships with these agencies has taken time. You wouldn't expect the president's relationships with the U.S. Postal Service, the CIA, and the Department of Agriculture to be identical, but just how these relationships are different (and how they are the same) is not immediately obvious.[8] Second, a full empirical evaluation of the implications of the multi-institutional model depends upon the valid and reliable measurement of the policy preferences of the president, the agency, and relevant members of Congress, and (depending upon the complexity of the model) the Supreme Court. As in the case of the formal model of appointment politics, it is important that the preferences be comparable, so they must be measurable in the same policy space. It is possible to conduct some empirical tests without fully comparable preferences, but a complete understanding of the empirical validity of the multi-institutional model depends, finally, on the development of a methodology for measuring these preferences. Some work in this area has been done (see Chang 2003), but it is limited and preliminary.

So we have learned something that should help us understand the puzzle at the beginning of this chapter. How were political scientists able to maintain such disparate explanations for the relationship between the president and the agencies and bureaus in the executive branch for so long? Because, in the absence of a precise system of measuring the preferences (and informational advantages) of each of the relevant actors, a variety of political contexts – imperfectly characterized – produced a variety of empirical results that were apparently consistent with multiple theoretical perspectives. With new theory – the multi-institutional model – and increasingly successful efforts to measure actors' preferences, we are in a position to move forward to a more scientifically rigorous (and substantively rich) understanding of the relationship between the president and the executive branch.

GUIDED RESEARCH EXERCISES

The guided research exercises for this chapter involve an examination of the impact of presidential partisanship and presidential appointments on monetary policy making. Specifically, you will be examining

---

[8] Wilson (1989) provides various useful typologies for understanding the managerial significance of the substantive distinctions between federal agencies.

the extent to which there is a difference between the Fed Funds rate (a common indicator of the ease or tightness of monetary policy, see Morris [2000]) during Republican presidencies and Democratic presidencies. You will also examine the impact of a change in Fed chairmen on monetary policy.

Data sources

For the exercise in this chapter, you will need data on the Fed Funds rate from 1952 to 2008. You will also need information on the partisanship of the president (which you will have already gathered for the analysis in an earlier chapter) and the terms of office for each of the Chairmen of the Board of Governors of the Federal Reserve for the 1952–2008 time period. Data on the Fed Funds rate over time are available from the FRED (Federal Reserve Economic Data) web site at the St. Louis Federal Reserve Bank at http://research.stlouisfed.org/fred2/.[9] Data on the Fed Chairmen is available from the Board of Governors web site at http://www.federalreserve.gov/bios/boardmembership.htm.[10]

EXERCISES

A. Descriptive Exercises

    1. Hypotheses

        a. The Federal Funds rate is greater (monetary policy is tighter) during Republican administrations than during Democratic administrations for the 1952–2008 time period.

        b. A change in Fed chair has no impact on the magnitude of the Fed Funds rate.

    2. Analysis

        a. Collect and organize the variables listed above from the indicated web sites.

        b. Create the following bar graphs (all averages).

            1. Fed Funds rate by party of the president (1952–2008)

            2. Fed Funds rate by Fed Chairman (1952–2008).

    3. Response to results

        a. Describe the graphic results for Fed Funds rate by party.

        b. Describe the graphic results for Fed Funds rate by Fed Chairman.

---

[9] Last accessed on December 18, 2009.
[10] Last accessed on December 18, 2009.

      c. Determine whether your results are consistent or inconsistent with each of your hypotheses.

      d. Explain your conclusions.

B. Inferential Exercises

  1. Analysis

      a. Complete the descriptive exercises above.

      b. Compute the necessary difference of means test statistics for both analyses.

  2. Response to results

      a. Determine whether your results are consistent or inconsistent with each of your hypotheses.

      b. Evaluate the extent to which the descriptive and inferential results suggest a significant relationship between presidential partisanship and the substance of monetary policy and/or a significant relationship between changes in the Fed chairmanship and the substance of monetary policy.

      c. Explain your conclusions.

C. Multivariate Exercise

  1. Hypothesis – After controlling for the identity of the Fed Chairman, the Fed Funds rate is higher during Republican administrations than during Democratic administrations.

  2. Analysis

      a. Create separate bar graphs of the average magnitude of the Fed Funds rate by party of the president for each Fed Chair who served under presidents of both parties.

      b. Calculate a difference of means test for the effect of the party of the president for each Fed Chair who served under presidents of both parties.

  3. Response to results

      a. Determine whether your results are consistent or inconsistent with your hypothesis.

      b. Explain your conclusion.

IMPORTANT TERMS

agency independence
bureaucracy
congressional dominance
foundations of leadership
  – charisma
  – rule of law
  – tradition

iron triangle
multi-institutional model
politics–administration dichotomy
presidential control
principal–agent model

9

The President and Foreign Policy Making

In 1966, Aaron Wildavsky published an isolated article on the differences between presidential power in domestic policy making and foreign policy making in a journal that no longer exists. Wildavsky was
already a prominent political scientist – probably the leading student
of the American budgetary process – and he would become a leading figure in the literature on policy analysis and culturally oriented
theories of politics and president of the American Political Science
Association among other things – when he wrote the article based on
what he called the "two presidencies thesis." In a nutshell, Wildavsky
argued that in the 1950s and the early 1960s the president's policy-
making powers in the foreign policy arena greatly outstripped his
powers in the domestic policy-making arena. In more specific terms,
Wildavsky wrote:

> The President's normal problem with domestic policy is to get con-
> gressional support for the programs he prefers. In foreign affairs, in
> contrast, he can almost always get support for policies that he believes
> will protect the nation – but his problem is to find a viable policy.
> (1966: 7)

More than four decades later, Wildavsky's "two presidencies" thesis
would appear to have been turned on its head. While an embattled
George W. Bush faced increasing criticism of his handling of the Iraq
War and its aftermath in the waning days of his presidency, he was
also able to win passage of the largest financial bailout legislation in
American history. The fight for the bailout legislation was not easy,
and there is no question that the dramatic economic downturn during the latter part of 2007 and 2008 provided a substantial impetus for
a significant response from the federal government, but it is difficult
to see how this turn of events comports with Wildavsky's characterization of the relative extent of presidential power in the foreign and

domestic policy spheres. The early days of the Obama administration also appeared at odds with Wildavsky's "two presidencies"; there is little evidence of a presidential advantage in foreign policy making. For example, the aftermath of the closing of the detention center at Guantanamo Bay proved far more complicated than the administration initially expected. Presidents certainly cannot expect to win on every domestic policy agenda item, but the domestic policy disadvantages presumed by the "two presidencies" thesis were not in evidence during the recent passage of an enormous stimulus package, the historically unprecedented public investment in a range of multinational corporations (including Chrysler and GM), and the overhaul of the nation's health-care system. President Obama's domestic agenda is at the very least incongruous with a president who sees himself as the victim of a domestic policy disadvantage.

So the puzzle of this chapter is why Wildavsky's two presidencies thesis appears to have been turned on its head in the early years of the twenty-first century? To work through this puzzle, we must address the following related questions:

1. Was Wildavsky right about the "presidencies" of the 1950s and early 1960s?
2. If yes, is Wildavsky's thesis still an accurate characterization of the twenty-first-century presidency?
3. If yes again, are the reasons for the distinctiveness of the presidencies a half century ago the same as the reasons for the distinctiveness of the twenty-first-century presidencies?
4. If Wildavsky's characterization of the distinctiveness of the two presidencies was not fully accurate for the earlier period, in what ways was he correct and in what ways was he wrong? What about for the later (twenty-first century) period?

To answer these questions, we must:

1. Develop a clear understanding of Wildavsky's two presidencies thesis and why he viewed the president as significantly more powerful in the realm of foreign policy than in domestic policy
2. Evaluate the extent to which Wildavsky's argument is still valid
3. Consider the empirical evidence for the two presidencies thesis
4. Conduct your own tests of the two presidencies thesis
5. Revisit the puzzle at the beginning of this chapter and decide whether (1) the two presidencies thesis is no longer valid, or (2) the appearances of the recent exercise of presidential authority in the foreign and domestic policy realms are deceiving, or (3) the two

presidencies thesis is still valid, *but* the recent past was an exceptional time that was not consistent with the theory.

WILDAVSKY'S CASE FOR TWO PRESIDENCIES

Wildavsky's argument about the existence of two presidencies is based on his assessment of a set of distinctions between foreign and domestic policy that all privilege the president and the president's position in the arena of foreign policy. For Wildavsky, the advantages available to the president in foreign policy – but not in domestic policy – were sufficiently significant to treat the domestic policy presidency and foreign policy presidency as distinct. What were the crucial differences between the foreign policy presidency and domestic policy presidency in the early 1960s?

First, the early 1960s were certainly one of the high points of the Cold War. Wildavsky is writing in the aftermath of the Cuban Missile Crisis (1962) and the early stages of substantial American involvement in the Vietnam War.[1] By 1966, the Cold War has made the world a very dangerous place – a place in which foreign policy issues and situations, because of the risk involved, were far more likely to garner the president's attention.

At this time, an anticommunist orientation developed that would come to be known as the Cold War "consensus." This consensus was based on broad support for the need to contain communism and a general willingness to use force to effect the necessary containment. The Cold War consensus was a general agreement on the importance of fighting communism on a worldwide basis. There was overwhelming (if not unanimous) support for the bipolar view of the world as a contest between two superpowers (the U.S. and the U.S.S.R) for global supremacy. While this conflict played out in diplomacy and military preparedness, it was so significant that it also manifested in artistic and cultural realms (including, in particular, sports). According to Wildavsky, this consensus facilitated the exercise of presidential power in the foreign policy realm because it supplied a ready and available congressional coalition for presidential efforts to fight communism. As the fight against communism was the primary component of American foreign policy during this time period, this level of congressional support played an important role in the exercise of presidential authority in the foreign policy realm. This same level

---

[1] The Gulf of Tonkin resolution, authorizing the use of U.S. military force in Southeast Asia without a formal declaration of war, was passed in August 1964.

of bipartisan support was not available to the president on many of the important domestic policy issues of the day. For example, civil rights and voting rights issues were highly controversial even within the Democratic Party. Broad social policy initiatives such as Lyndon Johnson's Great Society programs were also quite controversial. In short, foreign policy consensus fostered the aggrandizement of presidential authority in the foreign policy realm; the absence of a similar consensus limited the exercise of presidential power in the domestic policy sphere.

Wildavsky's foreign policy president is also privileged by the need for speed and decisiveness in the execution of foreign policy. Given the prevalence of high stakes security threats during the heyday of the Cold War – the Cuban Missile Crisis is just the most prominent example of a deadly security threat that required a quick and authoritative response – the president was also advantaged by his ability to coordinate an effective response on a time scale that Congress could not match. The speed of response required in this increasingly dangerous world also plays to the strength of the president. When quick action is required, the president is in a far better position than Congress to respond effectively.

Wildavsky also highlights the ways in which presidents are institutionally privileged in the realm of defense and foreign policy. The president exercises the authority of the Commander-in-Chief and also serves as the nation's primary international negotiator through the treaty power. Add to these powers the ability to make international arrangements through executive agreements and direct policy through executive orders, and one can see that the constitutional position of the president is quite strong.

Finally, presidents hold an informational advantage over their rivals. The informational resources available to the president, especially in the realm of foreign and defense policy, greatly exceed those of any political opponent. Certainly, the president's information is never perfect, but it is more detailed and more extensive than that available to any member of Congress (no matter how senior). According to Wildavsky, even as early as 1966, the president's use of information (and its manipulation) to achieve policy goals and objectives was significant (and was only increasing).

TWO PRESIDENCIES OVER TIME

For the time period in which he was writing – the early to mid-1960s – Wildavsky's two presidencies thesis, and the theoretical foundation on which it was established, has largely gone unchallenged. In "'The Two Presidencies': Eight Years Later" (1975), what was probably the earliest rigorous reassessment of the two presidencies thesis, Donald Peppers argues that the relevance of the two presidencies thesis to our understanding of presidential power in the foreign policy arena has waned somewhat from the 1960s. He writes:

> The Wildavsky article ... came at the end of the propresidency swing. Eight years after its original publication, it has lost something .... Wildavsky was certainly correct: the President *is* (emphasis in original) stronger in foreign policy than he is domestically. But ... without the advantage of hindsight over the last eight controversy-riddled years, "The Two Presidencies" seems to overstate the case. (1975: 462)

In the aftermath of Vietnam, the Cold War consensus that played such an important role in Wildavsky's original argument disintegrated, and the Watergate scandal heightened concerns about the broad exercise of presidential power in any policy-making environment. As our understanding of the exercise of presidential power has deepened over the time period since Wildavsky was writing, there was also serious concern over the ways in which Wildavsky might have failed to adequately distinguish between the exercise of presidential power and the exercise of presidential influence. As Peppers correctly notes, "All of these tactics [those Wildavsky associates with presidential policy making in foreign policy], however, are ploys designed to enhance presidential *influence* (emphasis in original); they do not guarantee to a president the *power* to control foreign policy" (1975: 465).

It is also fair to note that Wildavsky's own initial characterization of the two presidencies thesis highlights the context-specific determinants of the distinctiveness of the foreign policy presidency and the domestic policy presidency. Wildavsky highlights, in particular, the role of the Cold War consensus in the facilitation of the extensive exercise of presidential power in foreign policy. If the Cold War consensus was a pillar of the foreign policy presidency, what happens to the foreign policy presidency when the Cold War consensus ends? What happens to the foreign policy presidency when the Cold War itself ends?

Research on the two presidencies thesis has tended to focus on the extent to which Wildavsky's original empirical results could be replicated in later time periods. For the time period from 1948 to 1964, Wildavsky demonstrates that presidential foreign policy initiatives were far more likely to win congressional approval (nearly two-thirds passed) than presidents' domestic policy initiatives (less than half passed).

In general, research on more recent time periods has cast considerable doubt on the continued distinctiveness of the foreign policy and the domestic policy presidencies. By the late 1970s, the results of several studies suggested that the distinctiveness of the two presidencies began to wane almost immediately following the time period of Wildavsky's analysis. Focusing on a comparison of support for the president on key votes on foreign and defense policy legislation and domestic policy legislation, Sigelman (1979) finds no evidence of a two presidencies result for the time period from 1957 to 1978. Focusing on a somewhat longer time period, Zeidenstein (1981) finds a similar result.[2] Subsequent research also casts doubt on the continued relevance of the two presidencies thesis (see Cohen 1991; Edwards 1986). During the 1980s and 1990s, research that did indicate some limited support for two presidencies tended to suggest that the thesis held only for a certain type of president. For example, Fleisher and Bond (1988) only find support for the two presidencies thesis for Republican presidents. By the turn of the century, a general scholarly consensus was developing, and that consensus was accurately reflected in the title of Fleisher et al.'s (2000) article, "The Demise of the Two Presidencies."

But the two presidencies thesis would not go away. More recent research suggests that presidents may still enjoy significant advantages in the legislative policy-making arena when dealing with foreign and defense policy initiatives that are not available to the president when dealing with domestic policy initiatives. Marshall and Pacelle (2005) find evidence of a two presidencies effect when the president issues executive orders. They find that the strength of the president's party in Congress has a significant effect on the number of executive orders the president issues on domestic policy but no effect on the number of executive orders the president issues on foreign policy. And in a recent article on the theoretical foundations of the two presidencies thesis, Canes-Wrone, Howell, and Lewis (2008) argue that the institutional rationale for the variation in presidential power across foreign and defense policy and domestic policy remains even after the end of the Cold War consensus that played such a crucial role in Wildavsky's original argument. If these institutional factors remain important determinants of the president's relative legislative power

---

[2] Zeidenstein did, however, find some limited support for the two presidencies thesis in Senate votes on policy initiatives of Republican presidents. This sort of piecemeal or partial support is not uncommon in this literature (see Fleisher and Bond 1988).

across policy domains, then there may be reason to think that the time period of the two presidencies has not ended.

Canes-Wrone, Howell, and Lewis (2008) focus on three distinct institutional advantages available to the president:

1. The president is far more likely to be the agenda setter on foreign and defense policy legislation than domestic policy legislation.
2. Presidents have access to more information and information of a higher quality than members of Congress on foreign and defense policy issues.
3. Foreign and defense policy issues are frequently quite significant in presidential elections. Aside from economic issues, foreign and defense policy issues tend to be the most important issues in presidential elections. Foreign and defense policy issues are significantly less important in congressional elections.

Presidents are able to use their agenda-setting advantages on foreign and defense policy issues to set the terms of legislative debate in a manner that is simply not possible on domestic policy issues. Because the president has greater institutional control over the terms of debate on foreign policy issues than domestic policy issues, we would expect to see greater legislative success on foreign and defense policy issues than domestic policy issues. Because the president has an information advantage on foreign policy issues, it is much more difficult for members of Congress to confidently oppose and effectively counter presidents' efforts to achieve their own policy initiatives. As the president does not enjoy the same informational advantage on domestic policy issues, the president's legislative effectiveness is likely to be more limited on domestic policy issues. And finally, members of Congress tend to have far few incentives to counter the president on foreign and defense policy issues than domestic policy issues. Now this is a general pattern or tendency and may not hold during a particularly unpopular war or international conflict, but except for these few cases, electoral incentives mitigate against members of Congress investing the time and the resources necessary to defeat the president on foreign and defense policy issues. Note that each of the three institutional advantages highlighted by Canes-Wrone, Howell, and Lewis (2008) were available to the president at the time of Wildavsky's original presentation of the two presidencies thesis.

Canes-Wrone, Howell, and Lewis (2008) also note that if these institutional advantages are the true foundation of the two presidencies, then scholars' preoccupation with standard roll call studies might underestimate the extent to which presidents exercise differential power across the domestic and foreign policy arenas. A focus on the percent of legislative votes won by the president in each policy domain ignores two other ways in which the president's power might manifest in a legislative setting. First, the president's relative institutional advantages in the foreign policy arena might lead to significantly more congressional delegation to executive branch agencies dealing with foreign policy than domestic policy. Second, the content of foreign policy legislation may be significantly closer to the president's preferences than the content of domestic policy. Policy content cannot be assessed with simple roll call votes. If there is no difference in the passage rate of foreign policy legislation supported by the president and domestic policy legislation supported by the president, then it would appear that there is no foreign policy advantage. If, however, the content of the foreign policy legislation which the president successfully supported is significantly closer to the president's preferences than the content of the domestic policy legislation which the president successfully supported, then we do have evidence of two presidencies. Canes-Wrone, Howell, and Lewis (2008) provide evidence on patterns of congressional delegation and the content of legislation that is consistent with a significant presidential advantage in the foreign and defense policy arena. Reports of the death of the two presidencies thesis were, apparently, premature.[3]

TWO PRESIDENCIES FOR A SINGLE POLICY?

Shortly, you will have a chance to take a look at some data bearing on the two presidencies issues for yourself. But one other significant issue related to the two presidencies thesis is the possibility that the line between foreign and defense policy and domestic policy has been blurred since Wildavsky's writing in the 1960s.

Recent work by Elizabeth Freund (2007) suggests that the two presidencies thesis may face a new issue that has largely been ignored – the disintegration of the distinctiveness of foreign policy issues and domestic policy issues. Policy makers are increasingly dealing with issues that are particularly difficult to place

---

[3] Presumption of a presidential advantage in foreign policy making does not, however, imply the absence of legislative constraints on certain aspects of presidential authority in the foreign policy arena. A recent work by Howell and Pevehouse (2007) makes a strong case for the presence of significant legislative constraints on the president's war-making powers – constraints that vary systematically according to the strength of the president's party in Congress, size of the military operation, and strategic significance of the theater of operations.

in standard policy categories. Freund's work focuses on terrorism issues, and she highlights the difficulties associated with placing terrorism issues in either the foreign and defense policy category or the domestic policy category. Significantly, she finds no evidence of two presidencies in the context of more traditional foreign and defense policy and domestic policy issues, but she finds that George W. Bush was far more successful on terrorism issues than standard foreign and defense policy issues or standard domestic policy issues. In essence, she finds evidence of two presidencies, but one presidency is for issues related to terrorism and the other presidency is for all other issues. Given that the institutional advantages that accrue to the president on standard foreign policy issues are particularly significant in the handling of issues related to terrorism (especially the informational advantage), we may need to rethink not the two presidencies thesis, but the policy categories associated with each presidency.

GUIDED RESEARCH EXERCISES

The guided research exercises for this chapter focus on the differences between the success rate of important legislation supported by the president on foreign and defense policy issues and the success rate of important legislation supported by the president on domestic policy issues. While it is clear from the work of Canes-Wrone, Howell, and Lewis (2008) that roll call studies are not perfect tests of the two presidencies thesis, roll call studies do play a very important role in the literature on the two presidencies thesis. Also, Canes-Wrone, Howell, and Lewis (2008) provide an explanation for why the two presidencies might not manifest in different legislative success rates on foreign policy and domestic policy, but they would agree that the manifestation of differential legislative success rates *is* evidence of the existence of two presidencies.

Data sources

The most commonly used roll call votes in the two presidencies literature are the *Congressional Quarterly key votes* (see, for example, Sigelman 1979). The key votes are a list of a small number of particularly important votes taken in the House and the Senate each year. At the end of each calendar year, *CQ Weekly* publishes a list of these votes, a description of the legislation on which the votes were cast, yeas/nays for each chamber, and an indication of the president's position on the legislation (if the president took a position).[4] For the analysis below, you will need to identify those bills on which the president took a position and to divide each of these bills into one of the two categories – foreign and defense policy and domestic policy. If an issue is too difficult to categorize (and Sigelman 1979 provides guidance on the proper categorization of standard issues), then drop that vote from the analysis.

Author's Note: From both a data-gathering and data-organizing standpoint, these are the most involved guided research exercises. This set of guided research exercises is particularly appropriate for group work or as a group project.

EXERCISES

A. Bivariate Exercises

1. Descriptive Exercises
   a. Hypothesis – The rate of presidential success on foreign policy legislation is greater than the rate of presidential success on domestic policy legislation during the 1993–2008 time period (the Clinton and George W. Bush administrations).
   b. Analysis
      (1) Collect and organize the necessary data described above.
      (2) Calculate the average presidential success rate for foreign policy legislation and the average success rate for domestic policy legislation during the 1993–2008 time period.
   c. Response to results
      (1) Determine whether your results are consistent or inconsistent with each of your hypotheses.
      (2) Explain your conclusions.
2. Inferential Exercises
   a. Hypothesis – The rate of presidential success on foreign policy legislation is greater than the rate of presidential success on domestic policy legislation.
   b. Analysis
      (1) Complete the descriptive exercises above.

---

[4] While *CQ Weekly* is still published as a paper periodical, there is also a digital version. Many college and university libraries include this resource among the set of online periodicals, so paper copies may not be readily available. Check with your professor and the campus library staff to determine the most effective way to access this resource.

(2) Compute a difference of means test for the two averages.

c. Response to results

(1) Determine whether your results are consistent or inconsistent with each of your hypotheses.

(2) Explain your conclusions.

B. **Multivariate Exercises**

What if the two presidencies thesis holds only for a single party? We test that possibility below.

1. Descriptive Exercise

a. Hypothesis – The rate of presidential success on foreign policy legislation is greater than the rate of presidential success on domestic policy legislation during the George W. Bush administration. There is no difference during the Clinton administration.

b. Analysis – Conduct the same analysis as above on the data from the George W. Bush years and the Clinton years separately.

c. Response to results

(1) Determine whether your results are consistent or inconsistent with each of your hypotheses.

(2) Explain your conclusions.

2. Inferential Exercise

a. Hypothesis – The rate of presidential success on foreign policy legislation is greater than the rate of presidential success on domestic policy legislation during Republican administrations. There is no difference during Democratic administrations.

b. Analysis

(1) Complete the descriptive exercises above for the separate Bush and Clinton samples.

(2) Compute a difference of means test for the Bush sample and a difference of means test for the Clinton sample.

c. Response to results

(1) Determine whether your results are consistent or inconsistent with each of your hypotheses.

(2) Explain your conclusions.

IMPORTANT TERMS

agenda setter
asymmetric information

Cold War consensus
Cuban Missile Crisis
delegation
domestic policy
foreign and defense policy
"two presidencies" thesis
Vietnam War

10

The President and Economic Policy Making

In the domestic political arena, macroeconomic policy making is often considered the most important substantive policy responsibility of the American president. Public opinion research demonstrates that the American public consistently identifies the economy or management of the economy as one of the top three policy concerns; during time periods in which there is not a prominent foreign policy threat, the economy is often the top policy concern of the American public. In a survey administered by the Pew Research Center for the People and the Press, respondents indicated that the top two policy priorities were the "economy" and "jobs."[1] A late April 2009 poll fielded by CNN produced similar results. When asked "Which of the following is the most important issue facing the country today," 55% of the respondents indicated "the economy" – more than five times the number of respondents that indicated the second choice.[2] Ironically, the second choice was "the federal budget deficit."[3]

Clearly, 2009 was an economically unusual time in American history. As we struggled through the deepest economic downturn since the Great Depression, it is no surprise that the economy topped the list of national policy concerns. What is interesting is that this economic focus is commonplace even during more productive economic eras, and the economy is never far from the public's mind. The economic focus of public opinion is not simply an academic exercise. As we saw

---

[1] "Economy, Jobs Trump All Other Policy Priorities in 2009: Environment, Immigration, and Health Care Slip Down the List." January 22, 2009. http://people-press.org/report/485/economy-top-policy-priority (last accessed on December 19, 2009).

[2] CNN/Opinion Research Corporation Poll. *The Polling Report.* April 2009. http://www.pollingreport.com/prioriti.htm (last accessed on December 19, 2009).

[3] CNN/Opinion Research Corporation Poll. *The Polling Report.* April 2009. http://www.pollingreport.com/prioriti.htm (last accessed on December 19, 2009).

in an earlier chapter on the presidential selection process, the state of the American economy is one of the key (if not *the* key) determinant of presidential election outcomes. Not only do Americans consistently care about the economy, the state of the economy plays an important role in their political decision making – particularly at the voting booth during presidential elections.

Economists and political scientists who study the politics of economic policy making tend to take one of two theoretical perspectives toward the president's role in macroeconomic politics. Some scholars favor the *political business cycle* (PBC) theory of macroeconomic policy making. Originally developed by Nordhaus (1975) and Tufte (1978), PBC theory attributes changes in the quality of the macroeconomy to the president's efforts to manipulate the economy in advance of a presidential election in order to boost his share of the popular vote. The primary alternative to the PBC is the *party differences model*.[4] According to proponents of the party differences model, Republican presidents will choose policies that minimize inflation and federal deficits, and Democratic presidents will choose policies that maximize employment and income growth.

In the context of these two theories of macroeconomic politics, the final term of the George W. Bush administration is strikingly inexplicable. According to the PBC, income growth and employment should have grown over the course of the election year, but instead, unemployment grew and income contracted as the country plunged into a recession. The party differences model does little better in explaining Bush's final term. While inflation was held in check, the federal government bled red ink at a historically high level, not a pattern consistent with traditional Republican policies and politics.

The second Bush administration is not the only presidency in recent history to frustrate the expectations of the PBC and party differences theories. Clinton was almost Republican in his balancing of the federal budget. By overseeing a declining economy that would rebound just after the 1992 election, George H. W. Bush produced something very close to an anti-PBC during the final year of his administration. And Reagan's large budget deficits were in stark contrast to the fiscal conservatism for which Republicans are traditionally known.

In this chapter, we deal with the puzzle of presidential economic policy making that may no longer fit either theory of macroeconomic politics. After a brief description of the primary components of economic policy making and the policy tools available to the president,

---

[4] Hibbs (1987) is the seminal work in this research program.

we discuss the primary theories of macroeconomic policy making in greater detail and the extent to which each of the most recent administrations has produced outcomes consistent with the expectations of both theories. In an effort to understand the most recent cases of macroeconomic policy making, we look at two specific issues in more detail: (1) the possibility that the parties no longer have distinct policy preferences; and (2) the possibility that the president's policy tools are no longer effective. Research exercises related to these two topics follow this discussion.

COMPONENTS OF ECONOMIC POLICY

Economic policy making includes four primary components: fiscal policy, monetary policy, regulatory policy, and trade policy. Regulatory policy focuses on the government's management and oversight of the marketplace. The federal government regulates a wide variety of products (from toys to food to drugs). It also regulates an array of market transactions (such as the trading of stocks, bonds, and other securities). In fact, in the aftermath of the economic recession in 2008 and 2009, the government initiated an overhaul of its regulation of the banking and financial services industry. Regulatory policy, while very important, tends to be treated as microeconomic policy – policy designed to influence the extent and character of private transactions between consumers and firms – rather than macroeconomic policy – policy designed explicitly to affect the broad national economy.[5] Regulatory policy will not be our primary focus in this chapter.

Trade policy, the management and oversight of exports, imports, and the international position of American firms and consumers, is both microeconomic policy and macroeconomic policy. Trade regulations determine the extent to which certain products can be purchased abroad and brought into the country, and they set the fees (tariffs) that must be paid to import these products. In this regard, trade policy has obvious microeconomic implications; it affects the behavior of consumers and firms doing business on an international scale. However, trade policy also has important macroeconomic consequences. For example, tariff policies may have a significant impact on overall economic growth. High tariffs might induce other countries to install high tariffs on American exports. In the long run, economists generally consider these restrictions on free trade as constraints on

---

[5] The effects of the most recent financial regulatory system suggest that overlooking the macroimplications of micro-oriented regimes can be disastrous.

economic growth (for both countries), so tariffs may affect domestic income growth (and, indirectly, employment levels). During the nineteenth century, the tariff was also a significant source of revenue for the federal government, and a very contentious partisan issue (especially between the Whigs and the Democrats). Following the passage of the Sixteenth Amendment that authorized a direct income tax, the role of the tariff in funding the federal government greatly diminished, and trade policy issues no longer cleave easily along party lines. Like regulatory policy, trade policy will not be a focal point of this chapter.

Fiscal policy

Fiscal policy involves the taxing and spending decisions of the government. Governments at all levels make choices about tax policy and public spending, but the federal government is so large that its taxing and spending decisions have particularly important implications for the condition of the national economy. The macroeconomic significance of federal taxing and spending policy was not always as great as it is today. For many years, the federal government was quite small. Since the early years of the twentieth century, federal government expenditures did not exceed 5% of the gross domestic product (GDP), except for the World War I period, until FDR's administration, at which point federal expenditures doubled (relative to GDP). After the dramatic spike in expenditures during World War II (which peaked at nearly 50% of GDP), expenditures rose to approximately 20% of GDP and have ranged from 18% to 23% until fiscal year 2009–2010 when they are projected to reach 30% of GDP.[6] See Figure 10-1 below.

This information is important because it shows that the economic size of the federal government relative to the overall economy was quite small (approximately 5% or less) until the development of the modern presidency and the administrative state. It was just at this time that economists such as John Maynard Keynes began to argue that substantial increases in government spending – a fiscal policy tool – could be used to boost aggregate economic demand and lever the nation out of the deep depression through which it was suffering. In simplest terms, Keynes held that extensive deficit spending could provide a countercyclical bulwark against a dramatic economic contraction. If the private

---

[6] Data from FRED (Federal Reserve Economic Data), http://research.stlouisfed.org/fred2/ (last accessed on December 19, 2009).

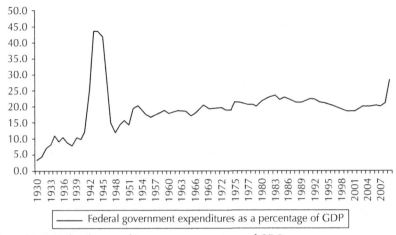

Figure 10-1: Federal expenditures as a percentage of GDP.
*This figure is based on data from the *Budget of the United States, Historical Tables Fiscal Year 2009* available on the GPO web site at http://www.gpoaccess.gov/USbudget/fy09/hist.html (last accessed on December 13, 2009).

sector could not generate sufficient short-term demand, then, Keynes argued, the government should step in to help.[7]

The explicit use of fiscal policy to achieve macroeconomic goals on a national level dates from FDR's administration. Roosevelt's own intellectual relationship with orthodox Keynesian thought was somewhat conflicted, but there is little question that a host of New Deal programs – from income support programs such as Social Security to public works programs such as the enormous Works Project Administration and the Civilian Conservation Corps, to infrastructure programs such as the Tennessee Valley Authority and the Rural Electrification Administration – used deficit spending (especially after his first term in office) to boost aggregate demand. These efforts to jump start the economy were controversial, and evaluations of their success were equally so, but there is little question that they were designed to foster income growth and employment on a national level. By the 1960s, Keynesian economic theory had largely become the orthodoxy in academic circles (see Frendreis and Tatalovich 1994). While the Keynesian perspective has faced significant challenges in academic economic circles, and we will discuss these challenges later in the chapter, Keynesianism provides a theoretical connection between the manipulation of fiscal policy tools such as government

---

[7] Keynes (1936) is the central text on this theory. Mankiw (2006) provides a useful introduction to Keynesian (and post–Keynesian) economics.

borrowing and extensive spending programs and real macroeconomic outcomes such as income growth and increased employment. Keynes provides one set of guidelines for the use of fiscal policy to achieve the types of macroeconomic goals that influence electoral outcomes and provide benefits to partisan groups.

Monetary policy

The federal agency with the primary responsibility for monetary policy is the Federal Reserve (Fed). The Federal Reserve System is composed of a dozen regional reserve banks, the Board of Governors, and the Federal Open Market Committee (FOMC). Besides implementing the nation's monetary policy, the Federal Reserve System also has a variety of regulatory responsibilities in the banking and financial services industry – responsibilities which have grown substantially since the federal bailout of 2008. While these regulatory responsibilities are important in their own right, they are not considered monetary policy and are not our focus.

Our focus is on the primary instruments of monetary policy. The Fed's macroeconomic responsibilities are substantial. It is directed, by statute, to manage the money supply so as to "promote effectively the goals of maximum employment, stable prices, and moderate long-term interest rates" (Federal Reserve Act 2000).[8] There is some evidence that monetary policy may also be used to generate politically desirable macroeconomic outcomes. Monetary policy is the set of rules and procedures that the federal government uses to manage the value and availability of the national currency. In recent years, the Fed has focused its attention on short-term interest rates, specifically an interest rate referred to as the Federal funds (Fed funds) rate. This is a market-determined rate for the overnight lending of banks to each other. While the Fed cannot control this rate, it can set targets for the Fed funds rate. As the Fed funds rate is basically a price for liquidity, it fluctuates according to the laws of supply and demand. Assuming constant demand, an increase in the supply of liquidity (currency) will tend to result in a lower price (or interest rate); a decrease in the supply of liquidity (currency) will tend to result in a higher price (or interest rate).[9]

---

[8] A copy of the amended Federal Reserve Act is available on the Federal Reserve web site at http://www.federalreserve.gov/aboutthefed/fract.htm (last accessed on December 19, 2009).

[9] Any standard macroeconomics text – such as Mankiw (2006) or Froyen (2008) – will provide a more complete description of monetary policy dynamics and the Federal Reserve's primary policy instruments.

The Fed has three primary policy tools for managing the money supply (and, thus, influencing interest rates). First, the Fed is responsible for setting the reserve requirement for commercial banks. The reserve requirement is the percentage of deposits the bank must retain (either in their vaults or on account at a regional Federal Reserve Bank). If the Fed raises the reserve requirement, the supply of money available for lending declines. The standard market response to a decrease in supply is an increase in the cost of liquidity (or the interest rate charged by the bank). The Fed may also raise or lower the *discount rate* – the interest rate at which the Fed makes short-term loans to commercial banks at its *discount window*. As banks are forced to pay more for loans from the Fed, they in turn raise the interest rates on the loans they offer to customers (or other banks) or they make fewer loans (which also results in an increase in interest rates because of the decrease in the supply of liquidity).

While these are important policy tools, the most important monetary policy tool is *open market operations*. The FOMC coordinates the Fed's open market operations. The FOMC is composed of the seven members of the Board of Governors (all appointed by the president and confirmed by the Senate) and the presidents of all twelve of the Reserve Banks (though only five Reserve Bank presidents have voting privileges at any one time). Open market operations are the sale and purchase of government securities in an effort to manage the money supply and influence interest rates. When the Fed purchases government securities from commercial banks, the banks have additional currency to lend and, normally, this would lead to lower interest rates because of the increase in liquidity. When the Fed sells government securities, it is taking money out of circulation (the money that was used to purchase the federal securities). As the supply of money declines, we would expect interest rates to rise.

Interest rates have a significant impact on real economic activity. High interest rates make it difficult to borrow money to invest in business expansion, to purchase a house, to fund a college education, buy a car, and so on. It is the Federal Reserve's stated statutory responsibility to foster long-term economic growth and stable prices (low inflation). Long-term growth is greatly impaired by high interest rates. Unfortunately, the Fed only has a limited impact on the level of interest rates for the types of long-term loans that would be needed to fund business expansion, or buy a house, or fund an education, and the relationship between short-term interest rates and long-term interest rates is not simple. In some cases, a decrease in short-term interest rates may even result in a significant increase in long-term rates. Why would this happen? It might happen because the long-term lenders fear that the decrease in short-term interest rates is fueled by a substantial expansion of the money supply by the Fed, an expansion that might lead to significant inflation. If long-term lenders expect significant inflation over the time period of their loan, they will tend to charge more (in the form of a higher interest rate) for the loan. They charge more to avoid a situation in which the real value of the money they receive in payment for the loan is worth less than the real value of the money they loaned in the first place.

This description of monetary policy and its potential effects is admittedly oversimplified. The relationship between monetary policy and macroeconomic variables such as income growth, unemployment, inflation, and interest rates is quite complex, and economists do not agree about the specific nature of these relationships. We will talk more about these disagreements shortly, but for now, you have at least one rationale for the presence of a relationship between monetary policy and macroeconomic outputs. So let us assume, at least for now, that fiscal and monetary policies do have a relatively predictable impact on macroeconomic outcomes such as interest rates, inflation, employment levels, and income growth. Earlier in this chapter, I briefly mentioned what broad macroeconomic goals presidents might be expected to achieve with the available fiscal and monetary policy tools. Let us take a longer look at the two theories scholars have developed to understand the political economy of presidential economic policy making.

THEORIES OF MACROECONOMIC POLITICS

I mentioned the two most prominent perspectives toward macroeconomic politics – the PBC theory and the partisan differences model – in the introduction to this chapter, but I provided no more than the quickest sketch of these two perspectives. This section includes a more detailed and more comprehensive description and analysis of the PBC theory and the party differences model.

The political business cycle

A PBC is a politically induced pattern of change in income growth and unemployment. Proponents of the PBC perspective (see Nordhaus 1975; Tufte 1978) argue that presidents use economic policy (primarily monetary policy in the Nordhaus version and fiscal policy in the

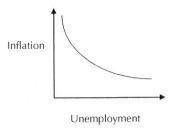

Figure 10-2: Hypothetical Phillips curve.

Tufte version) to boost income growth and employment in the months leading up to an election.[10] If the president's attempt to manipulate the business cycle is successful, then our aggregate vote models lead us to expect the president to win reelection.

The problem with PBCs (generated either by monetary expansion or a significant increase in fiscal spending) is that the desirable qualities of the cycle peak – high income growth and low unemployment – are unsustainable. In the monetary case, a PBC – also occasionally referred to as a political monetary cycle or PMC – depends upon the existence of at least a short-term Phillips curve relationship between inflation and unemployment. A Phillips curve is the depiction of an inverse relationship between inflation and unemployment (see Phillips 1958). See Figure 10-2. In a macroeconomic context in which the Phillips curve accurately captures the relationship between inflation and unemployment, a monetary authority (or a president controlling the monetary authority) can "purchase" a decrease in unemployment – (and, indirectly, a possible increase in income growth) by inflating the currency. The president is basically choosing a position on the Phillips curve that corresponds to higher inflation and lower unemployment (and, probably, higher income growth). As American electorates tend to reward increases in income growth and employment more than they punish increases in inflation, this is an electorally profitable strategy.

However, even in those contexts in which there is a temporary trade-off between inflation and unemployment (a short-run Phillips curve), the decrease in unemployment does not last forever. Once firms and consumers realize that the increase in their income is the result of an inflated currency (and not a change in real income) their investment and purchasing activity will decrease accordingly – which will result in a subsequent increase in unemployment because of the

---

[10] Alt and Chrystal (1983) provide useful descriptions of both PBC perspectives.

drop in demand. What will not return to prestimulus levels is the inflation rate. So, at best, the short-run decrease in unemployment is purchased with a permanent increase in the price level. PBCs are not costless, but the short-term incentives for politicians to induce them are strong, particularly for presidents who can only run for reelection once.[11]

Party differences model

The party differences model offers an alternative to the political dynamics of the PBC.[12] In the context of the PBC, all voters have the same preferences and all politicians are trying to attract the same voters. Thus, the PBC model predicts that all incumbents – regardless of party – will attempt to use fiscal and monetary policy to induce the same macroeconomic cycles. Within the party differences framework, there are two types of voters and two types of politicians.

The two types of voters have distinct macroeconomic preferences. One set of voters – let us refer to them as "Democrats" – have a strong preference for high employment/low unemployment. When trade-offs between employment and inflation must be made,[13] these voters are willing to accept rather more inflation for rather more employment. The second type of voter – the Republican – has a strong preference for stable prices. When trade-offs between employment and inflation must be made, Republicans are willing to accept rather less employment for rather less inflation.

The two types of politicians in the party differences model correspond to the two types of voters. Republican politicians are focused on attracting Republican voters, so they chose macroeconomic policies that tend to result in relatively low inflation. If they must accept somewhat higher unemployment to achieve price stability that is a trade-off they are willing to make because it is a trade-off consistent with the preferences of their voters. The converse is true for Democrats. Democrats traditionally focus on economic policies that boost employment (and, indirectly, income growth). If this increase in employment and income growth comes at the cost of some additional inflation, that is a trade-off Democratic politicians are willing to make because it is a trade-off that is consistent with the preferences of their voters.

---

[11] At least once after the completion of more than half of a full term.
[12] The foundational work on the party differences model is Hibbs (1977) and Hibbs (1987).
[13] Think in terms of the Phillips curve trade-off we discussed earlier.

POTENTIAL OBSTACLES TO THE EFFECTIVE MANIPULATION OF MACROECONOMIC OUTCOMES

Presidents face two primary obstacles in their efforts to generate either PBC or partisan economic outcomes. The first obstacle is the presence of potential conflicts or coordination problems with Congress (in the formation of fiscal policy) and with the Federal Reserve (in the formation and execution of monetary policy). As we know from the previous chapters on the president's relationship with Congress and the president's relationship with other actors in the executive branch, the president's ability to make policy unilaterally, particularly in the domestic policy arena, is quite circumscribed. If the president wishes to use fiscal policy to achieve certain macroeconomic goals (whether those are goals consistent with a traditional PBC or explicitly partisan goals), then he must have some level of congressional support.

Modern presidents do enjoy the fiscal policy advantage of the *president's budget* – a proposed fiscal policy plan which must be submitted to Congress early in the legislative session (as required by the Budget and Accounting Act of 1921). The president's budget is a compilation of agency budgetary requests, organized and integrated by the Office of Management and Budget under the direction of the president. While the president's budget is only a proposal, it is an agenda-setting document that historically sets the parameters of the budget debate. Still, the president's budget nearly always undergoes significant revisions during the legislative process, and depending upon the president's capacity to work effectively with members of Congress – and macroeconomic circumstances more generally – these revisions may be substantial.

In recent years, presidents have also faced significant ratcheting effects in the fiscal policy domain. These ratcheting effects, due to the increasing size of the nondiscretionary portion of the federal budget, have made it very difficult for president's to cut federal spending. Entitlement programs, those which provide goods or services to all who satisfy the participation criteria, have grown substantially over the last three decades. The largest entitlement programs – Social Security, Medicare, and Medicaid – were expected to account for more than forty percent of federal expenditures during FY 2009 (President's Budget for Fiscal Year 2010 (2009). These entitlement programs have proven to be particularly resilient to significant reductions. Debt service is also a constant (and substantial) component of the budget, as are military and defense expenditures. After all of these difficult-to-cut programs and expenditures are accounted for, the domestic discretionary portion of the federal budget is well less than 20% of the total.[14] Because of the relatively small portion of the budget dedicated to discretionary spending, president's intent upon budget cuts and domestic fiscal restraint (e.g., Reagan in the early 1980s) are often frustrated. Even if the president favors fiscal expansion, without sufficient congressional support, meaningful fiscal policy coordination is impossible. Consider the Obama administration's huge fiscal policy stimulus package. Without congressional support, no stimulus package would have been enacted.

Similarly, presidential efforts to achieve macroeconomic goals through the manipulation of monetary policy require support from the Fed. And we must remember that the Fed is an independent agency with an unusual degree of autonomy – largely due to the Fed's unique funding situation (no dependence on an annual congressional appropriation) and the long terms of office for the members of the Board of Governors. There is evidence that the Fed responds to presidential pressures, but it is also clear that the Fed responds to congressional pressures and, in some cases, staunchly maintains its independence (see Morris 2000; Woolley 1984). During the Carter and Reagan administrations, Fed Chairman Paul Volcker was famous for his independence, and as you can see from Figure 10-3, monetary policy, as reflected in the unusually high Fed funds rate, was particularly restrictive during a significant portion of Volcker's tenure from 1979 to the mid-1980s. Neither Fed Chairmen nor the Fed itself are fully independent actors, but presidential influence is only one of a number of factors that determines the character of monetary policy making.

So for both fiscal and monetary policy, the president must be able to garner substantial support among other significant political actors, whether in Congress or at the Fed.

A second significant obstacle to presidential efforts to use fiscal or monetary policy to induce certain macroeconomic outcomes is technical in nature; it may be economically impossible to achieve the desired macroeconomic goals. In the early to mid-1970s, the effectiveness of traditional Keynesian policies came into question as the United States slipped into a period of unprecedented *stagflation*, the coincidence of high inflation and high unemployment. According to the Phillips curve orthodoxy, we should never see high inflation and high unemployment at the same time, and yet that is just what happened during the Carter

---

[14] See The President's Budget for Fiscal year 2010 (2009) for more detailed information on the size of these various components of the annual budget.

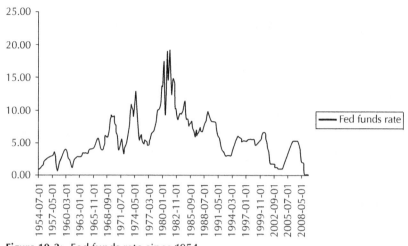

Figure 10-3: Fed funds rate since 1954.
*This figure is based on data from the FRED (Federal Reserve Economic Data) web site hosted by the Federal Reserve Bank of St. Louis. See http://research.stlouisfed.org/fred2/ (last viewed on December 13, 2009).

administration and early Reagan administration. Economists now generally view the Phillips curve trade-off as a short-term phenomenon (if that) and that in the middle term and long term, it is not possible to generate significant improvements in *real* economic variables (such as real income or employment) through the manipulation of the money supply or deficit spending.[15] To the extent there is an economic orthodoxy today, there is relatively little support for the contention that the president (or any other political actor or institution) is in a position to effectively manipulate real, long-term economic variables. This does not mean that the president cannot choose policies that will foster the movement of economic variables over the long-term in either a positive or negative direction. For example, a president may implement an infrastructure investment program that enhances economic competitiveness in the areas served by these infrastructure projects and in so doing, leads to a significant increase in economic activity and the long-term growth of income. By the same token, certain economic policies (e.g., dramatic inflation of the currency) might well lead to a significant long-term contraction in the economy. In short, PBCs and partisan macroeconomic outcomes may be more difficult to produce than the theories of macroeconomic politics would suggest.

[15] Though just when the short-term becomes the middle-term or long-term is a point of considerable controversy among Neo-Keynesian economists and Neoclassical economists.

EMPIRICAL EVIDENCE FOR PBCS AND PARTY DIFFERENCES IN MACROECONOMIC OUTCOMES

The evidence for the existence of PBCs is more limited than the evidence for the existence of party differences in macroeconomic outcomes. In terms of real economic variables such as employment or income growth, there is very little evidence of a PBC in the U.S. (or in other industrialized nations) (see Alesina et al. 1997; Alt and Chrystal 1983; Drazen 2001; Faust and Irons 1999).[16] If we take recent anecdotal evidence into account, the dramatic economic downturn during the most recent presidential election (2008) is very difficult to reconcile with traditional PBC models. A Tufte-style manipulation of the macroeconomy for electoral purposes is apparently quite rare.

The evidence for a PBC in monetary aggregates or short-term interest rates is somewhat stronger, but still not overwhelming. Grier (1989) finds evidence in support of a PBC in Fed policy making; Beck (1987) does not. Abrams and Iossifoy (2006) and Abrams (2008) find evidence of a conditional political monetary cycle (only evident when the Fed Chair and the president are fellow partisans), but Tempelman (2007) discounts even the evidence of a conditional cycle.

The evidence for partisan differences in macroeconomic outcomes is, on the other hand, quite compelling. Hibbs (1977, 1987) presents considerable evidence supporting the contention that unemployment is consistently higher during Republican administrations than during Democratic administrations and that income growth is significantly higher during Democratic administrations than during Republican administrations.[17] Subsequent studies of the relationship between real macroeconomic outcomes (such as employment and income growth) have provided additional support for Hibbs original findings – Democratic presidents tend to generate significantly more employment and income than Republican presidents (see Alesina 1988; Alesina et al. 1993; Alesina and Rosenthal 1989; Bartels 2008; Chappell and Keech 1986). According to Bartels':

> ... the average level of unemployment over the entire post-war era has been almost 30% higher under Republican presidents than under Democrats, while the average rate of real per capita GNP growth has been more than 40% lower. However, despite Republicans' traditional emphasis on curbing inflation, the average inflation rate has

---

[16] See Grier (2008) for a contrasting perspective.

[17] Hibbs (1987) finds little evidence of a significant difference in the rate of inflation during Democratic administrations and Republican administrations.

been virtually identical under Republican and Democratic presidents over this period. (2008: 48)

Bartels' recent analysis is particularly interesting for a couple of reasons. First, he highlights the role of partisan macroeconomic outcomes on the growth in income inequality during the last three decades. He offers substantial evidence that the distinctive character of Democratic and Republican macroeconomic policies has resulted in a significantly higher gap between the income of poor and middle-class families and upper-class families than that which existed in the late 1960s and 1970s.[18] But he also admits that the changing character of the international economy, the U.S. position in the international economy, and the domestic politics of monetary policy making have inhibited the implementation of partisan macroeconomic policies over the past two and a half decades. He writes:

> ... it has become much more difficult in the past quarter-century for presidents to influence the distribution of pre-tax income [through policies designed to curb unemployment or boost real income growth]. The most plausible explanation for this difference is that the increasing impact on the American economy of global trade and credit flows, and the increasing domestic prestige and political independence of the Federal Reserve Board, have reduced the ability of presidents to pursue distinctive partisan macroeconomic policies. (2008: 58)

This would suggest that the Obama administration has its work cut out for it if it plans to provide the types of economic support for poor, working-class, and middle-class families that were common during Democratic administrations of an earlier era.

CONCLUSION

Over the past two decades, American politics have cultivated what has come to be one of the most partisan eras in modern American history. Simultaneously, apparently, the key policy distinction between the political parties during the post–war era – different macroeconomic policy orientations producing different macroeconomic outcomes – has eroded. As scientists, we might reasonably ask the question, "Has this erosion in macroeconomic policy and outcome distinctiveness continued through the most recent time period?" As current as the Bartels' analysis is – and it goes through 2005 in some cases – we now have access to more recent

---

[18] Bartels focuses to an unusual extent on the tax policy component of fiscal policy. Regarding his focus on tax policy, he writes, "[p]artisan differences in economic philosophy and distributional priorities are especially striking in the realm of tax policy" (2008: 54).

data, and the most recent data covers a singular period in macroeconomic policy making. The guided research exercises that follow will provide you with the opportunity to examine the possibility that more recent macroeconomic outcomes are not so different from earlier outcomes – and to address the puzzle with which this chapter began.

GUIDED RESEARCH EXERCISES

The guided research exercises below will lead you through an empirical evaluation of the PBC theory and the party differences model. You will focus on economic data from the last 60 years, so this will be an opportunity for you to examine not only the long-term applicability of these perspectives to the politics of economic policy making, but also the applicability of these perspectives to the political economy from the most recent years. Returning to the puzzle described at the beginning of this chapter, the major research questions to be addressed are the following:

1. Is there evidence of a consistent PBC over the entire postwar (post–World War II) era?
2. To the extent there is some evidence of a PBC over the post–war era, is the evidence stronger during the earlier period (from the Truman administration through the Carter administration) or is the evidence stronger for the later period (from the beginning of the Reagan administration to the present day)?
3. Is there evidence of party differences in macroeconomic outcomes over the entire post–war era?
4. To the extent there is some evidence of party differences in macroeconomic outcomes over the post–war era, is the evidence stronger during the earlier period (from the Truman administration through the Carter administration) or is the evidence stronger for later periods (from the beginning of the Reagan administration to the present day and from the beginning of the Clinton administration to the present day)?

Data sources

For the exercise in this chapter, you will need data on a variety of macroeconomic variables from at least 1948 (the first post–war election, a common starting point for analyses of this type) to 2008. Official election results may be obtained from the Office of the Federal Register at the National Archives at http://www.archives.gov/.[19] There are also a variety

---

[19] Last accessed on December 19, 2009. Note that for most of the necessary economic data, I have provided a base web site, and you are expected to locate the particular

of other sources for this information as well, but authoritative sources are preferred. Data on inflation, income growth, and interest rates are available from the FRED (Federal Reserve Economic Data) web site at the St. Louis Federal Reserve Bank at http://research.stlouisfed.org/fred2/.[20] Unemployment data is available from the Bureau of Labor Statistics' *Current Population Survey* web site at http://www.bls.gov/cps/.[21] The variables you will need for each set of exercises are listed below.

EXERCISES

A. Descriptive Exercises

    1. Hypotheses

        a. Income growth (real GDP growth) is greater during Democratic administrations than during Republican administrations for the 1948–2008 time period.

            (1) Income growth (real GDP growth) is greater during Democratic administrations than during Republican administrations for the 1948–1980 time period.

            (2) Income growth (real GDP growth) is greater during Democratic administrations than during Republican administrations for the 1981–2008 time period.

            (3) Income growth (real GDP growth) is greater during Democratic administrations than during Republican administrations for the 1993–2008 time period.

        b. Unemployment is lower during Democratic administrations than during Republican administrations for the 1948–2008 time period.

            (1) Unemployment is lower during Democratic administrations than during Republican administrations for the 1948–1980 time period.

            (2) Unemployment is lower during Democratic administrations than during Republican administrations for the 1981–2008 time period.

            (3) Unemployment is lower during Democratic administrations than during Republican administrations for the 1993–2008 time period.

        c. Income growth is higher during presidential election years than in other years during the 1948–2008 time period.

variables of interest on their own after reaching the base web site. Specific web site addresses are not provided for each individual variable. Variable-specific web sites are much more likely to change than base web sites, and so only the base web sites are provided in an effort to limit incorrect (outdated) information.

[20] Last accessed on December 19, 2009.
[21] Last accessed on December 19, 2009.

      (1) Income growth is higher during presidential election years than in other years during the 1948–1980 time period.

      (2) Income growth is higher during presidential election years than in other years during the 1981–2008 time period.

   d. Unemployment is lower during presidential election years than in other years during the 1948–2008 time period.

      (1) Unemployment is lower during presidential election years than in other years during the 1948–1980 time period.

      (2) Unemployment is lower during presidential election years than in other years during the 1981–2008 time period.

2. Analysis

   a. Collect and organize the variables listed above from the indicated web sites.

   b. Create the following bar graphs (all averages).

      (1) income growth (annual percentage increase in real GDP) by party of the president (1948–2008)

      (2) income growth by party (1948–1980)

      (3) income growth by party (1981–2008)

      (4) income growth by party (1993–2008)

      (5) annual unemployment rate by party of the president (1948–2008)

      (6) annual unemployment rate by party of the president (1948–1980)

      (7) annual unemployment rate by party of the president (1981–2008)

      (8) annual unemployment rate by party of the president (1993–2008)

      (9) income growth by election year/nonelection year (1948–1980)

      (10) income growth by election year/nonelection year (1981–2008)

      (11) annual unemployment rate by election year/nonelection year (1948–1980)

      (12) annual unemployment rate by election year/nonelection year (1981–2008)

3. Response to results

   a. Describe the graphic results for income growth by party of the president for each time period.

    b. Describe the graphic results for unemployment by party of the president for each time period.

    c. Describe the graphic results for income growth and unemployment by election year/nonelection year for each time period.

    d. Determine whether your results are consistent or inconsistent with each of your hypotheses.

    e. Explain your conclusions.

B. Inferential Exercises

  a. Analysis

    (1) Complete the descriptive exercises above.

    (2) Compute the difference of means test statistic for all analyses.

  b. Response to results

    (1) Determine whether your results are consistent or inconsistent with each of your hypotheses.

    (2) Evaluate the extent to which the descriptive and inferential results suggest a change in the prevalence of PBCs or party differences across time.

    (3) Explain your conclusions.

IMPORTANT TERMS

Board of Governors
discount rate
discount window
Fed funds rate
Federal Open Market Committee
Federal Reserve System
fiscal policy
gross domestic product
Keynesian economic theory
macroeconomic policy
monetary policy
New Deal
open market operations
party differences model
Phillips curve
political business cycle
regulatory policy
reserve requirement
stagflation
trade policy

11

Presidential Greatness

Research on presidential greatness has a long history in the study of the American presidency. Collections of presidential biographies often address the relative success and stature of the presidents. While some scholars focus primarily on the set of presidents they consider great – Landy and Milkis's (2001) *Presidential Greatness* is a prime example – others focus on a subset of presidents that includes the great, the not-so-great, and the failures.[1] In a related literature, researchers construct rankings and ratings, often on multiple dimensions, of all presidents. An excellent example of this type of work is the recent book by Felzenberg (2008), *The Presidents We Deserve*. In this work, Felzenberg ranks each president on a set of six personal or policy-oriented dimensions, including character, vision, competence, economic policy, preserving and extending liberty, and defense policy (broadly understood). Both of these literatures – one based on no more than a few presidents and the other based on the full complement of presidents – revolve around the development of standards of "greatness" and the evaluation of one or more presidents with respect to these standards. Scholars in this vein define "greatness" and rank the presidents accordingly.

Other researchers study the presidential rankings and greatness scores produced by others. In 1948, Arthur Schlesinger Sr. published a ranking of American presidents based on the results of a poll of eminent historians in *Life* magazine. The results of that poll placed Lincoln, Washington, and recently deceased Franklin Roosevelt at the top of the list. Presidents Pierce, Grant, and Harding fell to the bottom of the list. Since then, dozens of surveys have assessed the presidential evaluations of historians and political scientists as well as the

---

[1] James David Barber's (1992) book on presidential character would fall into this category.

general public. In recent polls, whether of experts or average citizens, Franklin Roosevelt, Lincoln and Washington continue to fare quite well.[2] Similarly, recent polls suggest that Pierce, Grant, and Harding continue to rate as "failures." Of the modern presidents, Nixon consistently ranks the lowest. In fact, the consistency of presidential rankings over time – not just those at the very top or those at the very bottom but also in the middle range – is striking (see Cohen 2003). Research on expert and mass public ratings and rankings of presidents attempt to identify the common factors that explain these evaluations. Scholars have suggested a variety of explanations for these presidential ratings – some a little odd[3] – but the general consensus in the literature is that a relatively small number of factors explain the overwhelming preponderance of the variation in expert and mass public evaluations of presidential greatness.

One puzzling aspect of the scientific literature on presidential greatness is the absence of *performance measures.* As you will see in the next section of this Chapter, the most prominent models of presidential greatness focus on explanatory variables that have little to do with a president's performance in office (or at least little to do with a president's *successful* performance in office). I suggest several potential performance measures that might reasonably be related to presidential greatness. Your job will be to address this puzzling gap in the literature by empirically evaluating the effects of these performance measures. The guided research exercises at the end of this chapter will provide directions for that analysis.

EXPLAINING PRESIDENTIAL GREATNESS, TAKE 1

What explains presidential greatness? More specifically, what explains perceptions of presidential greatness? Historians and psychologists dominate the literature on the study of presidential greatness. Not surprisingly, explanations of presidential greatness have tended to focus on either (1) historical eras or (2) personalistic criteria.[4] Arthur

---

[2] Zogby International. 2008. "Roosevelt Holds Top Ranking on Presidential Greatness Scale." See http://www.zogby.com/news/readnews.cfm?ID=1456 (last accessed on December 19, 2009).

[3] At least one scholar suggested that presidential greatness is a function of height (see Sommers 2002). There is some limited empirical support for this position.

[4] There is some disciplinary crossover in this literature. McCann (1992, 1995, 2005), a psychologist, has made significant contributions to the line of research on the relationship between historical eras and presidential evaluations.

Schlesinger Jr. pioneered the historical era approach (see, for example, Schlesinger 1986). In more recent work, McCann (1992, 1995) argues that presidential rankings are a function of electoral support and the nature of the political times during which the presidents serve. Presidents who win large electoral victories during what Schlesinger refers to as "public" eras tend to be ranked very highly. Presidents who win by small margins and/or who serve during "private" eras receive lower rankings (McCann 1995).

The more psychologically oriented strain of research has tended to focus less on the time period (and its social and political characteristics) in which a president served and more on the personal characteristics of the president. In general, the personalistic models outperform the historically based models.[5] The variation in presidential ratings appears to depend upon only a few significant factors, and the literature focused on explaining the results of presidential greatness opinion polls (whether for experts or average citizens) is driven by what is known as the "Simonton model."[6] Over the course of nearly 30 years, Dean Keith Simonton has developed a model of the assessment of presidential greatness that consistently outperforms alternative models. As Cohen argues:

> While some important challenges to Simonton's model exist ... none of the rival formulations statistically outperform his model .... In fact, most of these alternatives appear to be components of his fuller model ... or refinements of points he has [already] made. (2003: 919)

Simonton's work is an excellent example of this aspect of the literature. Simonton developed a model designed to explain the psychological *attachments* to particular presidents and thus, indirectly, the variation in the evaluation of presidents. The Simonton model includes the following variables:

1. tenure in office
2. scandal
3. assassination
4. war hero

---

[5] Simonton (1991 and 1992) directly address the historical models and find significantly greater empirical support for the personalistic model. To my knowledge, supporters of the historical orientation have not been able to clearly demonstrate significant support for era-based variables after controlling for the individual-oriented factors included in the standard Simonton model.

[6] See Cohen (2003) for a more extensive discussion of the significance of the Simonton model to current research on the assessment of presidential greatness.

5. war years
6. intellectual brilliance.

Simonton argues for the primacy of professional background (war hero), personal attributes (such as intelligence) or faults (such as scandal), and other individualistic characteristics (such as time in office and whether or not the president was assassinated) in explaining the variation in presidential evaluations. *Tenure in Office* is simply the number of years (and partial years) of a presidential administration. *Scandal* taps whether or not there was a major scandal during the president's administration. There is a variable indicating whether or not the president was assassinated (*Assassination*) and another variable indicating whether or not the president had a prestigious military career (*War Hero*). Simonton also includes a counter for the number of years spent at war during a presidential administration (*War Years*), and, finally, a measure of presidential intelligence (*Intellectual Brilliance*) is included in the model. With the exception of scandals, all other factors are hypothesized to be positively related to evaluations of presidential greatness (e.g., the number of years at war is positively related to evaluations of presidential greatness).

Tenure in Office and *Assassination* require little explanation. The expectation associated with *Tenure in Office* is that presidents with longer service are significantly more likely to be viewed positively. Presidents have a longer period of time to build a legacy, and presidents with long tenures are in a better position to recover from mistakes than those who have no more than a single term (or less) in office. There is ample evidence to support this contention. Consider Figures 11-1 and 11-2. The first figure illustrates the large gap between the average rank of presidents who served four or fewer years (28th) and the average rank of presidents who served more than four years (14th).[7] The second figure shows the large gap (nearly 200 points) between presidents who served a term or less and those who served more than a term.[8]

As far as the *Assassination* variable is concerned, there is an expectation that these presidents are honored and remembered in a manner that will tend to enhance their historical stature. This is also, in a sense, a control for the artificially abrupt ending of what would have been a longer political career (and thus resulted in a higher score on the *Tenure in Office* variable). Presidents who were assassinated have dramatically higher ranks and scores than other presidents. The

---

[7] For the more statistically minded, this relationship is significant at the .05 level.
[8] This relationship is also significant at the .05 level.

Figure 11-1: Years in office and average rank.[9]
*Data on presidential rank is taken from CSPAN's 2009 Survey of Presidential Greatness (CSPAN 2009). More information can be found at http://www.c-span.org/ PresidentialSurvey/presidential-leadership-survey.aspx (last accessed on December 14, 2009). Data on years in office is available from multiple sources.

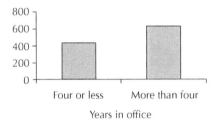

Figure 11-2: Years in office and average score.
*Data on presidential greatness scores is taken from CSPAN's 2009 Survey of Presidential Greatness (CSPAN 2009). More information can be found at http://www.c-span.org/ PresidentialSurvey/presidential-leadership-survey.aspx (last accessed on December 14, 2009). Data on years in office is available from multiple sources.

difference in ranks is illustrated in Figure 11-3; it is dramatic and statistically significant (at the .05 level).

To be considered a *War Hero*, a president must have attained a "national reputation" (Simonton 2001: 298) as a military figure. In contrast to the negative impact of a scandal, war heroes are assumed to receive additional respect for their previous military service in evaluations of presidential greatness. Though the war heroes do tend to rank higher than other presidents – see Figure 11-4 – the effect of war hero status is somewhat less than the effect we see for tenure in office. The war hero effect is also markedly smaller than the effect attributable to assassination.

---

[9] Note that all figures and tables in this chapter on based on the set of presidents through George W. Bush, excluding William Henry Harrison and James Garfield. Harrison and Garfield are excluded because of their extremely short (one month and six months, respectively) tenures.

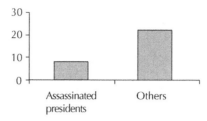

Figure 11-3: Assassinations and average rank.
*Data on presidential rank is taken from CSPAN's 2009 Survey of Presidential Greatness (CSPAN 2009). More information can be found at http://www.c-span.org/Presidential Survey/presidential-leadership-survey.aspx (last accessed on December 14, 2009).

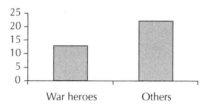

Figure 11-4: War hero status and average rank.
*Data on presidential rank is taken from CSPAN's 2009 Survey of Presidential Greatness (CSPAN 2009). More information can be found at http://www.c-span.org/Presidential Survey/presidential-leadership-survey.aspx (last accessed on December 14, 2009).

Scandal is defined as a "the commission of illegal acts by upper-level officials within the executive branch" (Simonton 2001: 298). Presidents are expected to be punished for dramatic, high-level scandals, and one component of this punishment is diminished historical legacy. Presidents associated with scandal are often located near the bottom of the rankings (e.g., Harding and Nixon) but not always (e.g., Clinton).

The most controversial variable in the Simonton model is *War Years*. Assuming activism in the policy domain most closely associated with the president's constitutional authority enhances presidential stature, Simonton argues – and finds evidence for the assertion – that the number of years the country is at war during a president's administration is *positively* associated with presidential greatness. Significantly, there is no discounting associated with less successful military campaigns, so a year of the Civil War is assumed to have the same effect as a year of the war in Vietnam. Though an admittedly surprising result, previous research suggests considerable support for this relationship (see, most recently, Cohen 2003; Simonton 2001).

Finally, *Intellectual Brilliance* is a broad measure of intellectual capability. Simonton argues that "no individual-difference variable has more practical consequences than does general intelligence" (2006: 511). He goes on to make a detailed and compelling case for the role of intelligence or intellectual capacity in the evaluation of presidents. In short, he clearly documents the associations between (1) intelligence and job performance in a wide array of professional settings, (2) intelligence and leadership, and (3) intelligence and political leadership (Simonton 2006). His own work (and the recent work of others, such as Cohen 2003) has consistently supported the relationship between intelligence and presidential evaluations (see Simonton 1986, 1991, 1992, 2002).

WHAT ABOUT PERFORMANCE?

What if presidential evaluations were based on more than personal characteristics, preadministration professional experience, and the length (and manner of ending) of presidential administrations? What if actual job performance played a crucial role in the presidential evaluations of historians and political scientists as well as average Americans? If that were the case, what sort of performance criteria would be *most* likely to influence evaluations of overall presidential greatness?[10]

Given the president's formal constitutional powers, the most likely criteria revolve around the president's foreign policy powers including the commander-in-chief powers.[11] Unfortunately, effectively capturing the variation in foreign policy success is difficult. Although the Simonton model includes a measure of the number of years the U.S. was at war during each president's administration, the variable does not even attempt to account for the success of the armed conflict. According to the Simonton model, the longer the armed conflict during a presidential administration – regardless of the significance or character of the outcome – the more positive the evaluations of the president. So, Jefferson's five years fighting the Barbary Coast Pirates and Johnson's Vietnam years should result in more positive evaluations – all else equal – than Lincoln's Civil War years or Roosevelt's performance during World War II. If it is performance that matters, then this traditional result is difficult to justify.

[10] The only other effort to clearly assess the impact of policy performance on presidential greatness was Simonton's evaluation of the impact of a dummy variable for "the occurrence of a major financial panic or depression" (1981: 310). He found no relationship between depressions and presidential greatness and, apparently, did not pursue the analysis of this relationship with other (more recent) data.

[11] See Adler (2003) for work in this vein.

Simonton makes a good case for the inclusion of the *War Years* variable in the analysis of presidential greatness, focusing primarily on the public's habit of rallying around the president in times of international conflict and significant security threats. Conventional rally events, however, tend to be relatively brief, and the rally effects themselves are also fleeting (see Kernell 1986). Why we should expect the rally effects to last well beyond the end of a president's administration – in effect, to last permanently in the minds of historians and political scientists (and members of the general public) who are rating presidents decades (or longer) after the ends of their administrations – is unclear.

Regardless of the relationship between war years and presidential greatness, an indicator of the length of time at war is not a measure of foreign policy success. If, on the other hand, we were to score presidents on the basis of their success in achieving war aims, that would obviously tap a significant aspect of foreign policy performance. Conflict scholars in the field of international relations have developed just this type of performance indicator (see Sarkees 2000; Valentino et al. 2006). First, wars are coded by war aim. The options are:

1. complete conquest of targeted state (enemy)
2. regime change (ruler removed or deposed) in targeted state
3. limited territorial conquest of targeted state
4. policy change in targeted state
5. prewar status quo.

Presidential evaluations are based on the extent to which the war aims – however, expansive or limited – were achieved at the end of the conflict. Performance scores include following:

1. total victory (2)
2. partial victory (1)
3. stalemate/no war (0)
4. partial loss (–1)[12]

Since we are focusing on major conflicts, most American presidents are coded "0" because they served during a time at which the U.S. was not participating in a major conflict. Presidents Polk, Lincoln, McKinley, Wilson, FDR, and George H. W. Bush all achieved total victories in the conflicts they fought. Truman's performance in World War II is viewed as a total victory, and his performance in the Korean War is viewed as a stalemate. He might reasonably be given the average of the scores for both wars. Eisenhower's handling of the Korean War

---

[12] No American president has ever suffered a total loss.

is viewed as a stalemate, and Johnson's and Nixon's handling of the Vietnam War are viewed as partial losses. Using this data on military success, we can evaluate whether or not foreign policy performance influences evaluations of presidential greatness. But first, we need to discuss the evaluations themselves in more detail.

Another policy area in which presidents might reasonably be evaluated is economic policy or economic policy outcomes. As we learned in Chapter 5, in the burgeoning literature on presidential elections, variables tapping economic circumstances have a privileged position. In the October 2008 edition of *PS: Political Science and Politics*, nearly all of the models designed to predict the 2008 presidential election included one or more aggregate economic indicators or aggregate public evaluations of economic circumstances. The most common variable in these models – and the most prominent economic indicator in presidential election models more generally – is a measure of income (normally gross domestic product) growth. Generally, it is the change in *real* gross domestic product that is included in the models. In an effort to refine this measure to most closely approximate relative changes in household income over a time period in excess of two centuries, one potential measure of economic performance is the percentage change in the *real per capita* gross domestic product. Details on the source of the data and the by-administration calculations are provided in the guided research section at the end of the chapter.

There is reason to think that performance in office influences evaluations of presidential greatness – in an historical context – just as this performance influences their prospects for reelection (see Abramowitz 2008; Campbell 2008a, 2008b). Economic outcomes play a crucial role in the evaluations of sitting presidents; maybe that same type of evaluative dynamic is at work in the historical evaluation of presidential greatness.

One could argue that presidents are not in control of the American economy; that would seem to be obvious from the daily news from the last year (and from the discussion of the president's role in economic policy making from the last chapter) It is also incorrect to suggest, however, that presidents have little or no influence over economic outcomes – especially the size of the national economy. If the president plays an important role in monetary policy making – influencing an "independent" Federal Reserve's policy actions (see Morris 2000) – then the president's role in fiscal policy is even more significant. The president does play a very important role in the management of the national economy. More importantly for our purposes, there is little question that presidents are held responsible for economic outcomes.

Does this contention necessarily imply that historians (and, to an even lesser extent, the general public) have the information (and incentive) to evaluate the economic performance of all 43 presidents? No, but there are still several reasons to expect a relationship between economic outcomes and presidential evaluations. First, some presidents are famous for dramatic economic growth (e.g., Franklin Roosevelt) while others are infamous for dramatic economic downturns (e.g., Hoover, Carter, and George W. Bush). Second, economic performance is indirectly related to policy activism, which might well be associated with presidential evaluations. Without economic growth, would the Great Society have been possible? Similarly, a contracting economy makes it particularly difficult to initiate important public policy programs. Third, economic growth may be at least partially responsible for the most prominent result in this literature – the relationship between tenure in office and evaluations of presidential greatness. For much of the twentieth century, incumbents faced with a stagnant or contracting economy have failed to win reelection (such as Carter and George H. W. Bush). There is some limited evidence that this effect goes back well into the nineteenth century (see Lynch 1999). Some proportion of the variation in evaluations currently attributable to tenure in office may actually be the result of economic fundamentals.[13] So, there are several plausible rationales for a relationship between economic outcomes and evaluations of presidential greatness. One way to formalize this conjecture is to hypothesize that *growth in per capita real gross domestic product will be positively associated with evaluations of presidential greatness. Ceteris paribus*, presidents who generate more income will receive more positive evaluations. During the guided research exercises, you will have a chance to evaluate this contention.

THE ASSESSMENT OF PRESIDENTIAL GREATNESS

Since the original Schlesinger poll in 1948, an increasingly large number of both professional/elite polls and mass public polls have tapped opinions on presidential greatness.[14] These surveys range over decades in time, they vary in format, and they focus on different target populations. As noted earlier, however, the consistency of the results (both in rankings and in scores) across the various surveys is striking.

---

[13] Cohen (2003) suggests the possibility of this relationship between economic circumstances, tenure in office, and evaluations of presidential greatness.

[14] For example, Schlesinger polled scholars again in 1961, and his son polled scholars in 1996 (see Schlesinger 1962 and Schlesinger 1997). The Sienna Research Institute of Sienna College has periodically surveyed on presidential greatness

Simonton (1986) highlights the consistency of contemporaneous mass and elite rankings and mass and elite rankings over time. Correlations of survey rankings over time – whether elite or mass surveys – tend to range from the low 80s to the upper 90s; and contemporaneous elite and mass survey rankings tend to produce correlations in the high 90s. There have been attempts to dimensionalize presidential greatness. Maranell (1970), for example, argues that there are at least seven distinct dimensions upon which presidential greatness may be evaluated. In a factor analysis of all available scores and rankings in the mid-1980s, Simonton (1986) identified a single primary "greatness" factor and that all scores and rankings easily loaded on this factor.[15] Finally, there is no evidence of respondent bias (i.e., more liberal historians tend to evaluate more liberal presidents more positively) in the presidential rankings (Maranell and Dodder 1970; Murray and Blessing 1983; Simonton 2001). Simonton's authoritative conclusion is simply put: "there is a strong prima facie case that these greatness assessments reveal how U.S. presidents varied in their effectiveness as the nation's highest political leader" (2001: 294).

So that you may compare the consistency of two sets of recent scores (and investigate their differences), I have included the data from the *Wall Street Journal*/Federalist Society (hereafter, *WSJ*) presidential greatness survey and the results from the C-SPAN presidential leadership survey published in early 2009 (the only available scores that include an evaluation of the full George W. Bush administration) in the data table at the end of the chapter. The *WSJ* scores were generated from a survey of 78 historians, political scientists, and legal scholars. Survey respondents were asked to[16] rate every past president (except W. H. Harrison and Garfield) on a scale from 1 to 5, with higher scores indicating higher (better) rankings. The greatness score for each individual president is that president's mean score on this survey scale. For a list of the scores and more information about the survey see http://www.opinionjournal.com/hail/rankings.html.[17] The

---

since 1982. The *Wall Street Journal* has conducted (in collaboration with the Federalist Society) at least two scholarly surveys on presidential greatness, and Zogby International has conducted at least five surveys focusing on assessments of presidential greatness. Single surveys of scholars include the Murray–Blessing survey in 1982 (Murray and Blessing 1983) and the Ridings–McIver survey in 1996 (Ridings and McIver 1997), and single surveys of the mass public include a *Chicago Tribune* survey in 1982 and a C-SPAN survey in 1999–2000).

[15] This factor accounted for 85% of all explained variance and 72% of all variance.

[16] See http://www.c-span.org/PresidentialSurvey/presidential-leadership-survey. aspx for more information. Last accessed on December 19, 2009.

[17] Last accessed on December 19, 2009.

2009 C-SPAN scores were generated from a sample of 65 "presidential historians" – a grouping that included both historians and political scientists (C-SPAN 2009). Survey respondents were asked to rate each past president (through George W. Bush) on a scale from 0 to 100 on 10 different dimensions of greatness including administrative skill, relations with Congress, moral authority, and crisis leadership.

Most of the independent variables in the analysis are coded in a straightforward and sensible manner. *Years in Office* is simply the number of years of an individual president's administration. In an effort to maintain consistency with the Simonton standard, time is recorded to the first decimal place where necessary. *Assassination* is a dummy variable coded 1 for presidents who were assassinated (Lincoln, McKinley, and Kennedy) and 0 otherwise.[18]

Both *Scandal* and *War Hero* are certainly open to interpretation. Nearly every presidential administration must deal with some set of situations which opponents would consider scandals, whether with Franklin Roosevelt's court-packing plan, the XYZ Affair during John Adam's administration, or the Bert Lance affair during the Carter presidency. Simonton has, however, chosen a very restrictive definition of scandal – probably not inappropriately – so the only presidents who are coded 1 on the *Scandal* dummy variable are Grant, Harding, Nixon, Reagan, and Clinton. *War Hero* is coded 1 for Washington, Jackson, W. H. Harrison, Taylor, Grant, T. Roosevelt, and Eisenhower.

The definition of *War Years*, while relatively straightforward, is not uncontroversial. Simonton's definition of *War Years* is simply "the number of years during which the nation was at war" (2001: 298).[19] A more formal operational definition of "war" is not provided, and it is clear from the descriptive statistics provided for this variable, it is not a particularly restrictive definition. The mean that Simonton reports in his (2001) replication study is nearly 1 (0.95), so given the number of administrations, that figure implies 40-plus years of war.[20] That sum

---

[18] Garfield, who was also assassinated, is not in the sample of presidents because of the brevity of his administration.

[19] In response to a question about this measure, Simonton responded (via email) that "a year counted as having a war if U.S. troops were engaged in actual combat against an organized military opponent (i.e., an independent nation-state) with well-defined battle lines demarcating 'enemy territory'. Military actions against informal insurgents did not count (e.g., in the Philippines), but undeclared wars like Vietnam did as well as the Civil War." This would seem to suggest that the aftermath of the war in Iraq and the military conflict in Afghanistan would not count. In fact, this definition poses a fairly serious problem for the proper coding of the war on terrorism, but that is a topic for future work.

[20] Note that this figure is pre–Iraq War.

includes not only Lincoln's Civil War years and Roosevelt's World War II years but also Polk's Mexican War years and Jefferson's five-year conflict with the Barbary Coast pirates. There are certainly reasonable alternatives to this handling of *War Years*, but this is the current standard, and so we will follow it.[21]

Intellectual Brilliance is derived from a factor analysis of over a hundred evaluations of the full sample of presidents (through George W. Bush). The evaluations were based on data generated by coding "personality descriptions" for each president. Note that multiple coders participated in the project and all identifying information was removed from the descriptions in advance of coding. The scores used in this analysis were taken directly from the full table of scores in Simonton (2006). Military success is coded as indicated earlier in the chapter.

Finally, the *Real GDP* measure is based on result generated from the Measuring Worth web site (see www.measuringworth.com). The web site provides a set of useful economic "calculators," one of which calculates per capita real GDP growth for the U.S. from 1790 to 2008 (see Officer and Williamson 2009). As the growth rate estimates are based on changes in end-of-year real per capita GDP figures, the growth rate associated with a particular president's administration was calculated from the end of the year prior to taking office to the end of the final "full" year in office.[22] So, for Lincoln, the growth calculation is based on the difference between real per capita GDP in 1860 (economic production in the year prior to his election) and real per capita GDP in 1864. The growth (or in some cases, decline) in production is then averaged over the number of years of the particular administration. The specific algorithm for calculating annualized real per capita GDP from this data is described in detail on the Measuring Worth web site.[23]

The values and descriptive statistics for all interval-level variables are provided in Table 11-1. Note that there is no trend in presidential evaluations over time, and at least from the standpoint of a visual inspection, there is no evidence of any significant rigidity or stickiness in the shift of evaluations over time. Likewise, the variation in evaluations does not appear to have a temporal component (i.e., the variance in evaluations is not significantly greater in one century than in another).

---

[21] To his credit, Simonton admits that the variable *War Years* might warrant some improvement (see Simonton 1992, and 2001).

[22] Presidents serving a portion of a year get credit for a full year if they serve 183 or more days during that year.

[23] There are various ways to calculate annualized growth estimates, and the Measuring Worth web site provides an excellent and straightforward introduction to the various technical issues (see http://www.measuringworth.com).

Table 11-1: Values and descriptive data for all interval-level variables

President	WSJ scores	C-SPAN scores	Real GDP growth	Years in office	Intellectual brilliance	Years at war
George Washington	4.92	854	4.05	8	0.3	0
John Adams	3.36	545	2.47	4	0.6	0
Thomas Jefferson	4.25	698	−0.46	8	3.1	5
James Madison	3.29	535	0.63	8	0.6	4
James Monroe	3.27	605	1.02	8	−1.4	0
John Quincy Adams	2.93	542	−0.36	4	1.2	0
Andrew Jackson	3.99	606	2.28	8	−0.6	0
Martin Van Buren	2.77	435	−0.41	4	−0.3	0
John Tyler	2.03	372	2.44	3.9	0.2	0
James Polk	3.7	606	2.72	4	−0.6	2
Zachary Taylor	2.4	443	1.06	1.3	−1.2	0
Millard Fillmore	1.91	351	7.51	2.7	−0.7	0
Franklin Pierce	1.58	287	0.64	4	−0.3	0
James Buchanan	1.33	227	1.57	4	−0.8	0
Abraham Lincoln	4.87	902	4.69	4.1	0.8	4
Andrew Johnson	1.65	258	−2.17	3.9	−1.2	0
Ulysses Grant	2.28	490	1.68	8	−1.4	0
Rutherford B. Hayes	2.79	409	5.58	4	−0.1	0
Chester Arthur	2.71	420	−2.14	3.5	0.9	0
Grover Cleveland	3.36	523	−1.05	8	−0.5	0
Benjamin Harrison	2.62	442	3.08	4	−0.7	0

President	WSJ scores	C-SPAN scores	Real GDP growth	Years in office	Intellectual brilliance	Years at war
William McKinley	3.33	599	4.55	4.5	−0.6	1
Theodore Roosevelt	4.22	781	−1.05	7.5	0.9	0
William Howard Taft	3	485	1.21	4	0	0
Woodrow Wilson	3.68	683	0.66	8	1.3	2
Warren Harding	1.58	327	7.62	2.4	−2	0
Calvin Coolidge	2.71	469	1.33	5.6	−1.5	0
Herbert Hoover	2.53	389	−10.13	4	0.5	0
Franklin Roosevelt	4.67	837	9	12.1	0.9	4
Harry Truman	3.95	708	−0.11	7.8	0.2	3
Dwight Eisenhower	3.71	689	0.86	8	−0.7	1
John Kennedy	3.21	701	3.66	2.8	1.8	0
Lyndon Johnson	3.17	641	3.88	5.2	−0.2	4
Richard Nixon	2.22	450	1.69	5.5	0.4	5
Gerald Ford	2.59	509	4.31	2.5	−0.6	1
Jimmy Carter	2.47	474	1.67	4	0	0
Ronald Reagan	3.81	671	2.59	8	0.4	1
George H. W. Bush	2.92	542	0.39	4	−0.3	1
Bill Clinton	2.77	605	2.65	8	1	1
George W. Bush		362	1.61	8	−0.7	7

The quantitative study of presidential greatness goes back at least 60 years to the initial Schlesinger survey. Surprisingly, the role of policy *performance* in the analysis of presidential greatness has been quite limited. Current models of presidential greatness tend to focus on personal characteristics, period effects, or administration-specific factors (such as length of administration or years at war) that are not directly related to performance in office. The inclusion of a variable relating to the occurrence of a scandal during an administration is the only prominent component of the standard model related to performance, and, as I argue earlier, it is more an indicator of malfeasance than a proper indicator of performance.

The guided research exercises provide you with an opportunity to scientifically examine the relationship between presidential performance – in the arenas of economic policy making and foreign and defenses policy making – and evaluations of greatness. Theoretically, there are good reasons to think (and hope) that economic policy performance and foreign policy performance play a role in public and professional evaluations of presidential greatness. Based on the extensive existing literature, it would appear that they do not. The next step is for you to evaluate the significance of these potential relationships.

GUIDED RESEARCH EXERCISES

Data sources

All of the data needed for the exercises below is provided in the text of the chapter and/or in Table 11-1. Additional economic variables may be gathered from the Measuring Worth web site.[24]

EXERCISES

   A. **Bivariate Exercises**
      1. Descriptive Exercises
         a. Hypotheses
            (1) Average annual real economic growth is directly related to presidential greatness for the presidents in our sample.
            (2) Military success is directly related to presidential greatness for the presidents in our sample.
         b. Analysis
            (1) Create a scatter plot of average annual real income growth against scores of presidential greatness.
            (2) Draw (estimate) a regression line for this scatter plot.

---

[24] The web address for the Measuring Worth web site is included in the text of this chapter.

(3) Calculate the average presidential greatness score for the presidents in each category of military success (i.e., calculate the average presidential greatness score for all presidents who scored a "2," calculate the average presidential greatness score for all presidents who scored a "1," etc.)

   c. Response to results

     (1) Describe the slope of the regression line. Is the line flat or steep? Does it slope down or slope up?

     (2) Describe the variation in mean presidential greatness scores across the categories of military success.

     (3) Explain your conclusions.

2. Inferential Exercises

  a. Hypotheses[25]

     (1) Average annual real income growth is directly related to presidential greatness.

     (2) Military success is directly related to presidential greatness.

  b. Analysis

     (1) Complete the descriptive exercises above.

     (2) Compute the standard error for the slope coefficient for the regression line calculated above and report the p-value for the coefficient.

     (3) Compute difference of means tests for presidential greatness for each pair of categories of military success examined above.

  c. Response to results

     (1) Determine whether your results are consistent or inconsistent with each of your hypotheses.

     (2) Explain your conclusions.

B. **Multivariate Exercises**

What if the effect of economic policy performance and/or foreign policy performance on presidential greatness can only be accurately gauged when controlling for other important independent variables. In this exercise, you will investigate this possibility.

1. Inferential exercise

  a. Hypotheses

     (1) Average annual real income growth is directly related to presidential greatness.

---

[25] Note that these hypotheses are more general than the hypotheses listed in the descriptive exercises section. These hypotheses are not limited to a particular time period.

         (2) Military success is directly related to presidential greatness.

    b. Analysis – Estimate a linear regression model of presidential greatness that includes the following variables:

         (1) annualized real income growth

         (2) military success

         (3) years in office

         (4) intellectual brilliance

         (5) scandal

         (6) years at war

         (7) assassination

    c. Response to results

         (1) Determine whether your results are consistent or inconsistent with each of your hypotheses.

         (2) Explain your conclusions.

IMPORTANT TERMS

assassination

historical eras

  • Public eras

  • Private eras

intellectual brilliance

personalistic criteria

scandal

tenure in office

war hero

war years

Bibliography

Abramowitz, Alan I. 2008. "Forecasting the 2008 Presidential Election with the Time-for-Change Model." *PS: Political Science and Politics.* XLI: 691–696.

Abrams, Burton A. 2008. "A Rejoinder to A Commentary on 'Does the Fed Contribute to a Political Business Cycle'." *Public Choice.* 134: 489–490.

Abrams, Burton A. and Plaman Iossifoy 2006. "Does the Fed Contribute to a Political Business Cycle?" *Public Choice.* 129: 249–262.

Adams, Gordon 1981. *The Iron Triangle: The Politics of Defense Contracting.* New York: Council on Economic Priorities.

Adler, David G. 2003. "Presidential Greatness as an Attribute of Warmaking." *Presidential Studies Quarterly.* 29: 466–483.

Adler, E. Scott and Daniel S. Lapinski, eds. 2006. *The Macropolitics of Congress.* Princeton, NJ: Princeton University Press.

Alesina, Alberto 1988. Macroeconomics and Politics. In *National Bureau of Economic Research Macroeconomics Annual 1987.* Edited by Stanley Fischer. Cambridge, MA: MIT Press.

Alesina, Alberto and Howard Rosenthal 1989. "Partisan Cycles in Congressional Elections and the Macroeconomy." *American Political Science Review.* 83: 373–398.

Alesina, Alberto, John Londregan, and Howard Rosenthal 1993. "A Model of the Political Economy of the United States." *American Political Science Review.* 87: 12–33.

Alesina, Alberto, Niccolo Roubini, and Gerald Cohen 1997. *Political Cycles and the Macroeconomy.* Cambridge, MA: MIT Press.

Alt, James E. and Alex Chrystal 1983. *Political Economy.* Berkeley, CA: University of California Press.

APSA Committee on Political Parties 1950. "Toward a More Responsible Two-Party System: A Report of the Committee on Political Parties." *American Political Science Review.* 44: Supplement.

Bailey, Jeremy D. 2007. *Thomas Jefferson and Executive Power.* Cambridge: Cambridge University Press.

Bailey, Michael A. 2007. "Comparable Preference Estimates across Time and Institutions for the Court, Congress and the President." *American Journal of Political Science.* 51: 433–448.

Barber, James David 1992. *Presidential Character: Predicting Performance in the White House.* 4th edition. New York: Prentice Hall.

Barrett, Andrew W. 2004. "Gone Public: The Impact of Going Public on Presidential Legislative Success." *American Politics Research.* 32: 338–370.

Barron, Maggie 2008. "The Real Presidential Legacy." Brennan Center for Justice. http://www.brennancenter.org/blog/category/economic_opportunity.

Bartels, Larry M. 2008. *Unequal Democracy: The Political Economy of the New Gilded Age.* Princeton, NJ: Princeton University Press.

Beck, Nathaniel 1987. "Elections and the Fed: Is There a Political Monetary Cycle?" *American Journal of Political Science.* 31: 194–216.

Berelson, Bernard, Paul F. Lazarsfeld, and William N. McPhee 1954. *Voting.* Chicago, IL: University of Chicago Press.

Binder, Sarah A. 1999. "The Dynamics of Legislative Gridlock, 1947–1996." *American Political Science Review.* 93: 519–533.

Binder, Sarah A. 2003. *Stalemate: Causes and Consequences of Legislative Gridlock.* Washington, DC: Brookings Institution Press.

Binder, Sarah A. 2008. "Taking the Measure of Congress: Response to Chiou and Rothenberg." *Political Analysis.* 16: 213–225.

Bordo, Michael D., Claudia Goldin, and Eugene N. White 1998. *The Defining Moment: The Great Depression and the American Economy in the Twentieth Century.* New York: National Bureau of Economic Research.

Brace, Paul and Melinda Gann Hall 1993. "Integrated Models of Judicial Dissent." *Journal of Politics.* 55: 914–935.

Brace, Paul and Melinda Gann Hall 1997. "The Interplay of Preferences, Case Facts, Context, and Structure in the Politics of Judicial Choice." *Journal of Politics.* 59: 1206–1231.

Budget and Accounting Act. Public Law 67–13. 42 Statute 20. Enacted June 10, 1921.

Calabresi, Steven G. and Christopher S. Yoo 2008. *The Unitary Executive: Presidential Power from Washington to Bush.* New Haven, CT: Yale University Press.

Cameron, Charles 2000. *Veto Bargaining: Presidents and the Politics of Negative Power.* New York: Cambridge University Press.

Campbell, Angus, Philip E. Converse, Warren E. Miller, and Donald E. Stokes 1960. *The American Voter.* New York: Wiley.

Campbell, James E. 2003. *The American Campaign: U.S. Presidential Campaigns and the National Vote.* College Station, TX: Texas A&M University Press.

Campbell, James E. 2008a. "The Trial-Heat Forecast of the 2008 Presidential Vote: Performance and Value Considerations in an Open-Seat Election." *PS: Political Science and Politics.*" XLI: 697–701.

Campbell, James E. 2008b. "Editor's Introduction: Forecasting the 2008 National Elections." *PS: Political Science and Politics.* October: 679–681.

Campbell, James, Lynne L. Cherry, and Kenneth A. Wink 1992. "The Convention Bump." *American Politics Quarterly.* 20: 287–307.

Canes-Wrone, Brandice 2001. "The President's Legislative Influence from Public Appeals." *American Journal of Political Science.* 45: 313–329

Canes-Wrone, Brandice 2006. *Who Leads Whom? Presidents, Policy, and the Public.* Chicago, IL: University of Chicago Press.

Canes-Wrone, Brandice and Scott de Marchi 2002. "Presidential Approval and Legislative Success." *Journal of Politics.* 64: 491–509.

Canes-Wrone, Brandice, Michael C. Herron, and Kenneth W. Shotts 2001. "Leadership and Pandering: A Theory of Executive Policymaking." *American Journal of Political Science.* 45: 532–550

Canes-Wrone, Brandice, William G. Howell, and David E. Lewis 2008. "Toward a Broader Understanding of Presidential Power: A Reevaluation of the Two Presidencies Thesis." *Journal of Politics.* 70: 1–16.

Carmines, Edward G. and James A. Stimson 1989. *Issue Evolution: Race and the Transformation of American Politics.* Princeton, NJ: Princeton University Press.

Carpenter, Daniel P. 2001. *The Forging of Bureaucratic Autonomy: Reputations, Networks, and Policy Innovation in Executive Agencies, 1862–1928.* Princeton, NJ: Princeton University Press.

Chang, Kelly H. 2003. *Appointing Central Bankers: The Politics of Monetary Policy in the United States and the European Monetary Union.* New York: Cambridge University Press.

Chappell, Henry J. and William R. Keech 1986. "Party Differences in Macroeconomic Policies and Outcomes." *American Economic Review: Papers and Proceedings.* 76: 71–74.

Chiou, Fang-Yi and Lawrence S. Rothenberg 2008a. "Comparing Legislators and Legislatures: The Dynamics of Legislative Gridlock Reconsidered." *Political Analysis.* 16: 197–212.

Chiou, Fang-Yi and Lawrence S. Rothenberg 2008b. "The Search for Comparability: Response to Binder." *Political Analysis.* 16: 226–233.

Clark, William Roberts 2003. *Capitalism, Not Globalism: Capital Mobility, Central Bank Independence, and the Political Control of the Economy.* Ann Arbor, MI: University of Michigan Press.

Cohen, Jeffrey E 1991. "Historical Reassessment of Wildavsky's 'Two Presidencies' Thesis." *Social Science Quarterly.* 63: 549–555.

Cohen, Jeffrey E. 2003. "The Polls: Presidential Greatness as Seen in the Mass Public – an Extension and Application of the Simonton Model." *Presidential Studies Quarterly.* 33: 913–924.

Conley, Richard 2003. *The Presidency, Congress, and Divided Government: A Postwar Assessment.* College Station, TX: Texas A&M University Press.

Converse, Philip E. 1964. The Nature of Belief Systems in Mass Publics. In *Ideology and Discontent.* Edited by David E. Apter. New York: Free Press.

Cooper, Phillip J. 2002. *By Order of the President: The Use and Abuse of Executive Direct Action.* Lawrence, KS: University Press of Kansas.

Cronin, Thomas E. 1979. "Presidential Power Revised and Reappraised." *Western Political Quarterly.* 32: 381–395.

Cronin, Thomas E. 1989. *Inventing the American Presidency.* Lawrence, KS: University Press of Kansas.

CSPAN 2009. *2009 Historians Presidential Leadership Survey.* http://www.c-span.org/PresidentialSurvey/presidential-leadership-survey.aspx

Cuzán, Alfred G. and Charles M. Bundrick 2008. "Forecasting the 2008 Presidential Election: A Challenge for the Fiscal Model." *PS: Political Science and Politics*. XLI: 717–722.

Dailey, William O., Edward A. Hinck, and Shelly S. Hinck 2007. *Politeness in Presidential Debates: Shaping Political Face in Campaign Debaters from 1960 to 2004*. Lanham, MD: Rowman & Littlefield Publishers.

Danelski, David 1964. *A Supreme Court Justice is Appointed*. New York: Random House.

Dickinson, Matthew J. 2008. The Politics of Persuasion: A Bargaining Model of Presidential Power. In *Presidential Leadership: The Vortex of Power*. Edited by Bert A. Rockman and Richard W. Waterman. New York: Oxford University Press.

Downs, Anthony 1957. *An Economic Theory of Democracy*. New York: Harper.

Drazen, Allan 2001. "The Political Business Cycle after 25 Years." *NBER Macroeconomics Annual 2000*. Cambridge, MA: MIT Press.

Druckman, J. N. 2003. "The Power of Television Images: The First Kennedy-Nixon Debate Revisited." *Journal of Politics*. 65: 559–571.

Edwards III, George C. 1986. "The Two Presidencies: A Reevaluation." *American Politics Quarterly*. 14: 247–263.

Edwards III, George C. and Andrew Barrett 2000. "Presidential Agenda Setting in Congress." In *Polarized Politics: Congress and the President in a Partisan Era*. Edited by Jon R. Bond and Richard Fleisher. Washington, DC: CQ Press.

Edwards III, George C., Andrew Barrett, and Jeffrey Peake 1997. "The Legislative Impact of Divided Government." *American Journal of Political Science*. 41: 545–563.

Ellis, Joseph J. 2007. *American Creation*. New York: Knopf.

Enelow, James M. and Melvin J. Hinich 1984. *The Spatial Theory of Voting: An Introduction*. Cambridge: Cambridge University Press.

Enelow, James M. and Melvin J. Hinich 1990. *Advances in the Spatial Theory of Voting*. Cambridge: Cambridge University Press.

Epstein, Lee and Jack Knight 1998. *The Choices Justices Make*. Washington, DC: CQ Press.

Epstein, Lee and Jeffrey A. Segal 2005. *Advice and Consent: The Politics of Judicial Appointments*. Oxford: Oxford University Press.

Erikson, Robert S. 1989. "Economic Conditions and the Presidential Vote." *American Political Science Review*. 83: 567–573.

Fair, Ray C. 1978. "The Effect of Economic Events on Votes for President." *The Review of Economics and Statistics*. May: 159–173.

Fair, Ray C. 2002. *Predicting Presidential Elections and Other Things*. Palo Alto, CA: Stanford University Press.

Faust, J. and J. Irons 1999. "Money, Politics, and the Post-War Business Cycle." *Journal of Monetary Economics*. 43: 61–89.

Federal Reserve Act. 2000. 114 Statute 3028. As amended December 27, 2000.

Felzenberg, Alvin S. 2008. *The Leaders We Deserved (And a Few We Didn't): Rethinking the Presidential Rating Game*. New York: Basic Books.

Ferejohn, John and Charles R. Shipan 1990. "Congressional Influence on Bureaucracy." *Journal of Law, Economics, and Organization.* 6: 1–21.

Feyerabend, Paul 1993. *Against Method.* 3rd edition. London: Verso.

Fisher, Louis 2004. *Presidential War Power.* Lawrence, KS: University Press of Kansas.

Fisher, Louis 2007. *Constitutional Conflicts Between Congress and the President.* 5th edition. Lawrence, KS: University Press of Kansas.

Fleisher, Richard and Jon R. Bond 1988. "Are There Two Presidencies?" *Journal of Politics.* 50: 747–767.

Fleisher, Richard, Jon R. Bond, Glen S. Krutz, and Stephen Hanna 2000. "The Demise of the Two Presidencies." *American Politics Quarterly.* 28: 3–25.

Fleisher, Richard, Jon R. Bond, and B. Dan Wood 2008. Which Presidents Are Uncommonly Successful in Congress. In *Presidential Leadership: The Vortex of Power.* Edited by Bert A. Rockman and Richard W. Waterman. New York: Oxford University Press.

Frendreis, John P. and Raymond Tatalovich 1994. *The Modern Presidency and Economic Policy.* Itasca, IL: F.E. Peacock Publishers.

Freund, Elizabeth 2007. *Sovereigns or Servants: Presidential Relations with Congress in Domestic and Foreign Policy.* Dissertation. University of Maryland, College Park.

Friendenberg, Robert V., ed. 1997. *Rhetorical Studies on National Political Debates-1996.* Westport, CT: Praeger.

Froyen, Richard T. 2008. *Macroeconomics.* 9th edition. New York: Prentice Hall.

Geer, John 1988. "The Effects of Presidential Debates on the Electoral Preferences for Candidates." *American Politics Quarterly.* 16: 486–501

Gerber, Alan S. and Donald P. Green 2000. "The Effects of Canvassing, Direct Mail, and Telephone Contact on Voter Turnout: A Field Experiment." *American Political Science Review.* 94: 653–663.

Gerber, Alan S. and Donald P. Green 2001. "Do Phone Calls Increase Voter Turnout? A Field Experiment." *Public Opinion Quarterly.* 65: 75–85.

Gerber, Alan S., Donald P. Green, and Christopher W. Larimer 2008. "Social Pressure and Voter Turnout: Evidence from a Large-Scale Field Experiment." *American Political Science Review.* 102: 33–48.

Gilmour, John B. 1995. *Strategic Disagreement: Stalemate in American Politics.* Chicago, IL: University of Chicago Press.

Gilmour. John B. 2002. "Institutional and Individual Influences on the President's Veto." *Journal of Politics.* 64: 198–218.

Green, Donald P. and Alan S. Gerber 2005. "Recent Advances in the Science of Voter Mobilization." *The Annals of the American Academy of Political and Social Science.* 601(1): 142–154.

Green, Donald P., Alan S. Gerber, and David W. Nickerson 2003. "Getting Out the Vote in Local Elections: Results from Six Door-to-Door Canvassing Experiments." *Journal of Politics.* 65: 1083–1096.

Green, Donald P., Bradley Palmquist, and Eric Shickler. 2002. *Partisan Hearts and Minds: Political Parties and the Social Identities of Voters.* New Haven, CT: Yale University Press.

Greider, William 1989. *Secrets of the Temple: How the Federal Reserve Runs the Country.* New York: Simon and Schuster.

Grier, Kevin 1989. "On the Existence of a Political Monetary Cycle." *American Journal of Political Science.* 33: 376–389.

Grier, Kevin 2008. "U.S. Presidential Elections and Real GDP Growth, 1961–2004." *Public Choice.* 135: 337–352.

Hallinan, Joseph T. 2009. *Why We Make Mistakes: How We Look Without Seeing, Forget Things in Seconds, and Are All Pretty Sure We Are Way Above Average.* New York: Broadway.

Halstead, T. J. 2007. *Presidential Signing Statements: Constitutional and Institutional Implications.* Washington, DC: Congressional Research Service.

Hamilton, Alexander and James Madison 2007. *The Pacificus-Helvidius Debates of 1793–1794.* Indianapolis, IN: Liberty Fund.

Hamilton, Alexander, John Jay, and James Madison 2001. *The Federalist (Gideon Edition).* Edited by George W. Carey and James McClellan. Indianapolis, IN: Liberty Fund.

Hammond, Thomas H. and Jack H. Knott 1996. "Who Controls the Bureaucracy? Presidential Power, Congressional Dominance, Legal Constraints, and Bureaucratic Autonomy in a Model of Multi-institutional Policymaking." *Journal of Law, Economics, and Organization.* 12: 119–166.

Hart, Roderick P. 1987. *The Sound of Leadership: Presidential Communication in the Modern Age.* Chicago, IL: University of Chicago Press.

Herrnson, Paul and Irwin L. Morris 2007. "Presidential Campaigning in the 2002 Congressional Elections." *Legislative Studies Quarterly.* XXXII: 629–648.

Hibbs, Douglas A. 1977. "Political Parties and Macroeconomic Policy." *American Political Science Review.* 71: 1467–1478.

Hibbs, Douglas A. 1987. *The American Political Economy: Macroeconomics and Electoral Politics.* Cambridge, MA: Harvard University Press.

Hillygus, D. Sunshine and Simon Jackman 2003. "Voter Decision Making in Election 2000: Campaign Effects, Partisan Activation, and the Clinton Legacy." *American Journal of Political Science.* 47: 583–596.

Hillygus, D. Sunshine and Todd G. Shields 2008. *The Persuadable Voter: Wedge Issues in Presidential Campaigns.* Princeton, NJ: Princeton University Press.

Hinckley, Barbara 1994. *Less than Meets the Eye: Foreign Policymaking and the Myth of the Assertive Congress.* Chicago, IL: University of Chicago Press.

Hinich, Melvin J. and Michael Munger 1997. *Analytical Politics.* New York: Cambridge University Press.

Holbrook, Thomas M. 1994. "The Behavioral Consequences of Vice-Presidential Debates: Does the Undercard Have any Punch?" *American Politics Quarterly.* 22: 469–482.

Holbrook, Thomas M. 1996. *Do Campaigns Matter?* Thousand Oaks, CA: Sage.

Holbrook, Thomas M. 1999. "Political Learning from Presidential Debates." *Political Behavior.* 21: 67–89.

Holbrook, Thomas M. 2008. "Incumbency, National Conditions, and the 2008 Presidential Election." *PS: Political Science and Politics*. XLI: 709–712.

Howe, Daniel Walker 2007. *What Hath God Wrought: The Transformation of America, 1815–1848*. Oxford: Oxford University Press.

Howell, William G. 2003. *Power Without Persuasion: The Politics of Direct Presidential Action*. Princeton, NJ: Princeton University Press.

Howell, William G. and Jon C. Pevehouse 2007. *While Dangers Gather: Congressional Checks on Presidential War Powers*. Princeton, NJ: Princeton University Press.

Huber, John D. and Charles R. Shipan 2002. *Deliberate Discretion? The Institutional Foundations of Bureaucratic Autonomy*. New York: Cambridge University Press.

Hume, David 1995 (1748). *An Inquiry Concerning Human Understanding*. New York: Prentice Hall.

Jones, Edward E. and Victor A. Harris 1967. "The Attribution of Attitudes." *Journal of Experimental Social Psychology*. 3: 1–24.

Jordan, Stuart V. and David M. Primo 2008. "The Bad News About 'Going Public.'" Paper presented at the Annual Meeting of the American Political Science Association.

Kelley, Christopher 2006. "The Significance of the Presidential Signing Statement." In *Executing the Constitution: Putting the President Back into the Constitution*. Edited by Christopher S. Kelley. Albany, NY: State University of New York Press.

Kellstedt, Paul M. and Guy D. Whitten 2008. *The Fundamentals of Political Science Research*. Cambridge: Cambridge University Press.

Keohane, Robert O. 2009. "Political Science as a Vocation." *PS: Political Science & Politics*. XLII: 359–364.

Kernell, Samuel 1976. "The Truman Doctrine Speech: A Case Study of the Dynamics of Presidential Opinion Leadership." *Social Science History*. 1: 20–44.

Kernell, Samuel 2007 (1986). *Going Public: New Strategies of Presidential Leadership*. 4th edition. Washington, DC: CQ Press.

Ketcham, Ralph 1986. *The Anti-Federalist Papers and the Constitutional Convention Debates*. New York: Signet.

Key, Jr., V. O. 1966. *The Responsible Electorate: Rationality in Presidential Voting, 1936–1960*. Cambridge, MA: Belknap Press.

Keynes, John Maynard 1936. *The General Theory of Employment, Interest and Money*. New York: Harcourt, Brace & Company.

King, Gary 1993. "Small-n Issues in Presidency Research, and How to Resolve the Problem." In *The Methodology of Presidential Research*. Edited by George Edwards III, John H. Kessel, and Bert A. Rockman. Pittsburgh, PA: University of Pittsburgh Press.

King, Gary, Robert O. Keohane, and Sidney Verba 1994. *Designing Social Inquiry*. Princeton, NJ: Princeton University Press.

Krasno, Jonathan S. and Donald P. Green 2008. "Do Televised Presidential Ads Increase Voter Turnout? Evidence from a Natural Experiment." *Journal of Politics*. 70: 245–261.

Kraus, Sidney 1996. "Winners of the First 1960 Televised Presidential Debate Between Kennedy and Nixon." *Journal of Communication*. 46: 78–96.

Krause, George A. 2009. "Organizational Complexity and Coordination Dilemmas in U.S. Executive Politics." *Presidential Studies Quarterly*. 39: 74–88.

Krause, George A. and David B. Cohen 2000. "Opportunity, Constraints, and the Development of the Institutional Presidency: The Case of Executive Order Issuance, 1939–1996." *Journal of Politics*. 62: 88–114.

Krehbiel, Keith 2007. "Supreme Court Appointments as a Move-the-Median Game." *American Journal of Political Science*. 51: 231–240.

Krutz, Glen S. and Jeffrey S. Peake 2009. *Treaty Politics and the Rise of Executive Agreements: International Commitments in a System of Shared Powers*. Ann Arbor, MI: University of Michigan Press.

Kuhn, Thomas S. 1996. *The Structure of Scientific Revolutions*. 3rd edition. Chicago, IL: University of Chicago Press.

Lakatos, Imre 1970. Falsification and the Methodology of Scientific Research Programmes. In *Criticism and the Growth of Knowledge, Volume 4: Proceedings of the International Colloquium in the Philosophy of Science, London, 1965*. Cambridge: Cambridge University Press.

Landy, Marc and Sidney M. Milkis 2001. *Presidential Greatness*. Lawrence, KS: University Press of Kansas.

Lanoue, David J. and Peter R. Schrott 1991. *The Joint Press Conference: The History, Impact, and Prospects of Televised Presidential Debates*. Westport, CT and London: Greenwood Press.

Lazarsfeld, Paul F., Bernard Berelson, and Hazel Gaudet 1944. *The People's Choice: How the Voter Makes Up His Mind in a Presidential Campaign*. New York: Duell, Sloan and Pearce.

Leloup, Lance T. and Steven A. Shull 1979. "Congress versus the Executive: The 'Two Presidencies' Reconsidered." *Social Science Quarterly*. 59: 704–719.

Lessig, Lawrence and Cass Sunstein 1994. "The President and the Administration." *Columbia Law Review*. 94: 106–108.

Lewis, David E. 2008. *Politicizing Administration: Policy and Patronage in Presidential Appointments*. Princeton, NJ: Princeton University Press.

Lewis-Beck, Michael S. and Charles Tien 2008. "The Job of President and the Jobs Model Forecast: Obama for '08?" *PS: Political Science and Politics*. October: 687–690.

Lindsay, James M. and Wayne P. Steger 1993. "The 'Two Presidencies' in Future Research: Moving Beyond Roll-Call Analysis." *Congress & the Presidency*. 20: 103–117.

Lynch, G. Patrick 1999. "Presidential Elections and the Economy, 1872–1996: The Times They are a' Changing or the Song Remains the Same." *Political Research Quarterly*. 52: 825–844.

Mankiw, N. Gregory 2006. *Macroeconomics*. New York: Worth Publishers.

Maranell, Gary M. 1970. "The Evaluation of Presidents: An Extension of the Schlesinger Polls." *Journal of American History*. 57: 104–113.

Maranell, Gary M. and R. Dodder 1970. "Political Orientations and the Evaluation of Presidential Prestige: A Study of American Historians." *Social Science Quarterly*. 51: 415–421.

Marshall, B.W. and R. L. Pacelle 2005. "Revisiting the Two Presidencies: The Strategic Use of Executive Orders." *American Politics Research*. 33: 81–105.

Mayer, Kenneth 1999. "Executive Orders and Presidential Power." *Journal of Politics*. 61: 445–466.

Mayer, Kenneth 2001. *With the Stroke of the Pen: Executive Orders and Presidential Power*. Princeton, NJ: Princeton University Press.

Mayhew, David R.1994.*Congress: The Electoral Connection.*. New Haven, CT: Yale University Press.

Mayhew, David R. 1991. *Divided We Govern: Party Control, Lawmaking, and Investigations, 1946–1990*. New Haven, CT: Yale University Press.

Mayhew, David R. 2005. *Divided We Govern: Party Control, Lawmaking, and Investigations, 1946–2002*. 2nd edition. New Haven, CT: Yale University Press.

McCann, Stewart J. H. 1992. "Alternative Formulas to Predict the Greatness of U.S. Presidents: Personological, Situational, and Zeitgeist Factors." *Journal of Personality and Social Psychology*. 62:469–479.

McCann, Stewart J. H. 1995. "Presidential Candidate Age and Schlesinger's Cycles of American History (1789–1992): When Younger is Better." *Political Psychology*. 16: 749–755.

McCann, Stewart J. H. 2005. "Simple Method for Predicting American Presidential Greatness from Victory Margin in Popular Vote (1825–1996)." *Journal of Social Psychology*. 145: 287–298.

McCarty, Nolan and Adam Meirowitz 2007. *Political Game Theory: An Introduction*. New York: Cambridge University Press.

McDonald, Forrest 1995. *The American Presidency: An Intellectual History*. Lawrence, KS: University Press of Kansas.

McGuire, Kevin and James A. Stimson 2004. "The Least Dangerous Branch Revisited: New Evidence on Supreme Court Responsiveness to Public Preferences." *Journal of Politics*. 66: 1018–1035.

Meernik, James 1993. "Presidential Support in Congress: Conflict and Consensus on Foreign and Defense Policy." *Journal of Politics*. 55: 569–587.

Middleton, Joel A. and Donald P. Green 2008. "Do Community-Based Mobilization Campaigns Work Even in Battleground States? Evaluating the Effectiveness of Move On's 2004 Outreach Campaign." *Quarterly Journal of Political Science*. 3: 63–82.

Miller, Gary J. 1992. *Managerial Dilemmas: The Political Economy of Hierarchy*. New York: Cambridge University Press.

Mills, C. Wright 1959. *The Sociological Imagination*. Oxford: Oxford University Press.

Moraski, Byron J. and Charles R. Shipan 1999. "The Politics of Supreme Court Nominations: A Theory of Institutional Constraint and Choices." *American Journal of Political Science*. 43: 1069–1095.

Morris, Irwin L. 2000. *Congress, the President, and the Federal Reserve: The Politics of American Monetary Policymaking*. Ann Arbor, MI: University of Michigan Press.

Morris, Irwin L. and Michael C. Munger 1998. "First Branch, or Root? The Congress, the President, and the Federal Reserve." *Public Choice*. 96: 363–380.

Morrow, James D. 1994. *Game Theory for Political Scientists*. Princeton, NJ: Princeton University Press.

Murray, Robert K. and Tim H. Blessing 1983. "The Presidential Performance Study: A Progress Report." *Journal of American History*. 70: 535–555.

Nathan, Richard P. 1983. *The Administrative Presidency*. New York: John Wiley & Sons.

Neustadt, Richard E. 1960. *Presidential Power: The Politics of Leadership*. New York: John Wiley & Sons.

Neustadt, Richard E. 1990. *Presidential Power and the Modern Presidents*. New York: Free Press.

Niskanen, Jr., William A. 1971. *Bureaucracy and Representative Government*. Chicago, IL: Aldine-Atherton.

Nordhaus, William 1975. "The Political Business Cycle." *Review of Economic Studies*. 42: 169–190.

Norpoth, Helmut 2008. "On the Razor's Edge: The Forecast of the Primary Model." *PS: Political Science and Politics*. XLI: 683–686.

Officer, Lawrence H. and Samuel H. Williamson 2009. "Annualized Growth Rate of Various Historical Economic Series." *MeasuringWorth*. http://www.measuringworth.com/growth/.

Osborne, Martin J. 2004. *An Introduction to Game Theory*. Oxford: Oxford University Press.

Panagopoulos, Costas and Donald P. Green 2008. "Field Experiments Testing the Impact of Radio Advertisements on Electoral Competition." *American Journal of Political Science*. 52: 156–168.

Parsons, Talcott 1951. *Toward a General Theory of Action*. Cambridge, MA: Harvard University Press.

Patterson, Jr., Bradley H. 2000. *The White House Staff*. Washington, DC: Brookings Institution.

Peppers, Donald 1975. The Two Presidencies'; Eight Years Later. In *Perspectives on the Presidency*. Edited by Aaron Wildavsky. Boston, MA: Little, Brown.

Phillips, Alban W. 1958. "The Relationship between Unemployment and the Rate of Change of Money Wages in the United Kingdom, 1861–1957." *Economica*. 25: 283–299.

Popper, Karl 1953. The Problem of Induction. In *Popper Selections*. Edited by David Miller. Princeton, NJ: Princeton University Press.

Powell, Richard J. 1999. "Going Public' Revisited: Presidential Speechmaking and the Bargaining Setting in Congress." *Congress & the Presidency*. 26: 153–170.

President's Budget for Fiscal Year 2010, The. 2009. Office of Management and Budget. Washington, DC: Government Printing Office.

Ragsdale, Lyn 1998. *Vital Statistics on the Presidency*. Washington, DC: CQ Press.

Riccards, Michael Various years. *The Ferocious Engine of Democracy*. Multiple volumes. Madison Books.

Ridings, William J. 2001. *Rating the Presidents: A Ranking of U.S. Leaders, from the Great and Honorable to the Dishonest and Incompetent*. Revised edition. Charleston, SC: Citadel Press.

Ridings, William J. and Stuart B. McIver 1997. *Rating the Presidents: A Ranking of U.S. Leaders, from the Great and Honorable to the Dishonest and Incompetent.* Charleston, SC: Citadel Press.

Rockof, Hugh 1998. Ideological Change and the Growth of the Federal Bureaucracy. In *The Defining Moment: The Great Depression and the American Economy in the 20th Century.* Edited by Michael D. Borda, Claudia Goldin, and Eugene N. White. Chicago, IL: University of Chicago Press.

Rohde, David and Dennis Simon 1985. "Presidential Vetoes and Congressional Response: A Study of Institutional Conflict." *American Journal of Political Science.* 29: 397–427.

Rohde, David and Kenneth Shepsle 2007. "Advising and Consenting in the 60-Vote Senate: Strategic Appointments to the Supreme Court." *Journal of Politics.* 69: 664–677.

Rudalevige, Andrew 2005. *The New Imperial Presidency: Renewing Presidential Power after Watergate.* Ann Arbor, MI: University of Michigan Press.

Rudalevige, Andrew 2009. "The Administrative Presidency and Bureaucratic Control: Implementing a Research Agenda." *Presidential Studies Quarterly.* 39: 10–24.

Sarkees, Meredith Reid 2000. "The Correlates of War Data on War: An Update to 1997." *Conflict Management and Peace Science.* 18: 123–144.

Schlesinger, Arthur M. 1948. "Historians Rate the U.S. Presidents." *Life.* 25: 65–66, 68, 73–74.

Schlesinger, Arthur M. 1962. "Our Presidents: A Rating by 75 Historians." *New York Times Magazine.* July: 12–13, 40–41, 43.

Schlesinger, Arthur M. 1973. *The Imperial Presidency.* New York: Houghton Mifflin.

Schlesinger, Arthur M. 1986. *The Cycles of American History.* Boston, MA: Houghton Mifflin.

Schlesinger, Jr., Arthur M. 1997. "Ranking the Presidents: From Washington to Clinton." *Political Science* Quarterly. 112: 179–190.

Schrott, Peter R. and David J. Lanoue 2008. "Debates Are for Losers." *PS: Political Science and Politics.* XLI: 513–518.

Segal, Jeffrey A. and Albert D. Cover 1989. "Ideological Values and the Votes of Supreme Court Justices." *American Political Science Review.* 83: 557–565.

Segal, Jeffrey A. and Harold Spaeth 2002. *The Supreme Court and the Attitudinal Model Revisited.* New York: Cambridge University Press.

Segal, Jeffrey A., Charles M. Cameron, and Albert D. Cover 1992. "A Spatial Model of Roll Call Voting: Senators, Constituents, Presidents, and Interest Groups in Supreme Court Confirmations." *American Journal of Political Science.* 36: 96–121.

Segal, Jeffrey, Richard Timpone, and Robert M. Howard 2000. "Buyer Beware? Presidential Success through Supreme Court Appointments." *Political Research Quarterly.* 53: 557–573.

Shaw, Daron 1999. "The Effect of TV Ads and Candidate Appearances on Statewide Presidential Vote." *American Political Science Review.* 93: 345–361.

Shaw, Daron 2006. *The Race to 270*. Chicago, IL: University of Chicago Press.

Shields, Todd G. and Chi Huang 1995. "Presidential Vetoes: An Event Count Model." *Political Research Quarterly*. 48: 559–572.

Shields, Todd G. and Chi Huang 1997. "Executive Vetoes: Testing Presidency-vs. President-Centered Perspectives of Presidential Behavior." *American Politics Quarterly*. 25: 431–457.

Shipan, Charles R. and John Ferejohn 1990. "Congressional Influence on Bureaucracy." *Journal of Law, Economics, and Organization*. 6: 1–20.

Sigelman, Lee 1979. "A Reassessment of the Two Presidencies Thesis." *Journal of Politics*. 41: 1195–1205.

Simonton, Dean Keith 1981. "Presidential Greatness and Performance: Can We Predict Leadership in the White House." *Journal of Personality*. 49: 306–322.

Simonton, Dean Keith 1986. "Presidential Greatness: The Historical Consensus and Its Psychological Consensus." *Political Psychology*. 7:259–283.

Simonton, Dean Keith 1991. "Predicting Presidential Greatness: An Alternative to the Kenney and Rice Contextual Index." *Presidential Studies Quarterly*. 21: 301–305.

Simonton, Dean Keith 1992. "Presidential Greatness and Personality: A Response to McCann (1992)." *Journal of Personality and Social Psychology*. 63: 676–679.

Simonton, Dean Keith 2001. "Predicting Presidential Performance in the United States: Equation Replication on Recent Survey Results." *Journal of Social Psychology*. 141: 293–307.

Simonton, Dean Keith 2002. "Intelligence and Presidential Greatness: Equation Replication Using Updated IQ Estimates." *Advances in Psychology Research*. 13: 143–153.

Simonton, Dean Keith 2006. "Presidential IQ, Openness, Intellectual Brilliance, and Leadership: Estimates and Correlations for 42 U.S. Chief Executives." *Political Psychology*. 27: 511–526.

Skowronek, Stephen 1982. *Building a New American State: The Expansion of National Administrative Capacities, 1877–1920*. New York: Cambridge University Press.

Skowronek, Stephen 1997. *The Politics Presidents Make: Leadership from John Adams to Bill Clinton*. Cambridge, MA: Belknap Press of Harvard University Press.

Skowronek, Stephen 2008. *Presidential Leadership in Political Time: Reprise and Reappraisal*. Lawrence, KS: University Press of Kansas.

Sommers, Paul M. 2002. "Is Presidential Greatness Related to Height?" *College Mathematics Journal*. 33: 14–16.

Squire, Peverill 1988. "Why the 1936 Literary Digest Poll Failed." *Public Opinion Quarterly*. 52: 125–133.

Stimson, James A. 2004. *Tides of Consent: How Public Opinion Shapes American Politics*. New York: Cambridge University Press.

Tempelman, Jerry H. 2007. "A Commentary on 'Does the Fed Contribute to a Political Business Cycle?'" *Public Choice*. 132: 433–436.

Thach, Jr., Charles C. 2007. *Creation of the Presidency, 1775–1789: Study in Constitutional History*. Chicago, IL: University of Chicago Press.

Tufte, Edward R. 1978. *Political Control of the Economy*. Princeton, NJ: Princeton University Press.

U.S. Constitution. Various articles.

Valentino, Benjamin, Paul K. Huth, and Sarah E. Croco 2006. "Covenants Without the Sword: International Law and the Protection of Civilians in Times of War." *World Politics*. 58: 339–377.

Vavreck, Lynn 2009. *The Message Matters: The Economy and Presidential Campaigns*. Princeton, NJ: Princeton University Press.

Warber, Adam L. 2006. *Executive Orders and the Modern Presidency: Legislative from the Oval Office*. Boulder, CO: Lynne Rienner Publishers.

Waterman, Richard W. 1989. *Presidential Influence and the Administrative State*. Knoxville, TN: University of Tennessee Press.

Waterman, Richard W. 2009. "The Administrative Presidency, Unilateral Power, and the Unitary Executive Theory." *Presidential Studies Quarterly*. 39: 5–9.

Weber, Max 1978 (1922). *Economy and Society*. Berkeley, CA: University of California Press.

Weingast, Barry R. and Mark J. Moran 1983. "Bureaucratic Discretion or Congressional Control? Regulatory Policymaking by the Federal Trade Commission." *Journal of Political Economy*. 91: 765–800.

White, Leonard D. 1954. *The Jacksonians: A Study in Administrative History 1829–1861*. New York: Macmillan.

White, Leonard D. 1959. *The Federalists: A Study in Administrative History*. New York: Macmillan.

Whittington, Keith E. 2007. *Political Foundations of Judicial Supremacy: The Presidency, the Supreme Court, and Constitutional Leadership in U.S. History*. Princeton, NJ: Princeton University Press.

Whittington, Keith E. and Dan Carpenter 2003. "Executive Power in American Institutional Development." *Perspectives on Politics*. I: 495–513.

Wildavsky, Aaron 1966. "The Two Presidencies." *Trans-Action*. 4: 7–14.

Wildavsky, Aaron B. 1979. *Speaking Truth to Power: The Art and Craft of Policy Analysis*. New York: Little Brown & Company.

Wilson, James Q. 1989. *Bureaucracy: What Government Agencies Do and Why They Do It*. New York: Basic Books.

Wilson, Woodrow 1887. "The Study of Administration." *Political Science Quarterly*. 2: 197–222.

Windt, Jr., Theodore O. 1994. The 1960 Kennedy-Nixon Presidential Debates. In *Rhetorical Studies of National Political Debates: 1960–1992*. 2nd edition. Edited by Robert V. Friedenberg. Westport, CT: Praeger.

Wlezien, Christopher and Robert Erikson 2001. "Campaign Effects in Theory and Practice." *American Politics Research*. 29: 419–436.

Wood, B. Dan and Richard W. Waterman 1991. "The Dynamics of Political Control of the Bureaucracy." *American Political Science Review*. 85: 801–828.

Wood, B. Dan and Richard W. Waterman 1993. "The Dynamics of Political-Bureaucratic Adaptation." *American Journal of Political Science*. 37: 497–528.

Wood, B. Dan 1988. "Bureaucrats, Principals, and Responsiveness in Clean Air Enforcements." *American Political Science Review*. 82: 215–234.

Wood, Gordon 1998. *The Creation of the American Republic, 1776–1787.* Chapel Hill, NC: University of North Carolina Press.

Woolley, John T. 1984. *Monetary Politics: The Federal Reserve and the Politics of Monetary Policy.* New York: Cambridge University Press.

Woolley, John T. 1991. "Institutions, the Election Cycle and the Presidential Veto." *American Journal of Political Science.* 35: 279–304.

Yalof, David Alistair 2007. "Conservative Supreme Court Will be Bush Legacy." *UCONN,* http://www.uconnmagazine.uconn.edu/fwin2007/feature4.html.

Yates, Jeff 2002. *Popular Justice: Presidential Prestige and Executive Success at the Supreme Court.* Albany, NY: SUNY Press.

Zaller, John R. 1992. *The Nature and Origins of Mass Opinion.* Cambridge: Cambridge University Press.

Zeidenstein, Harvey G. 1981. "The Two Presidencies Thesis Is Alive and Well and Has Been Living in the U.S. Senate Since 1973." *Presidential Studies Quarterly.* 11: 511–512.

Index

Made in the USA
Middletown, DE
24 September 2019